Little Church in the Wilderness

Richard L. Smith

© Copyright 2017, Richard L. Smith

All Rights Reserved

No part of this book may be reproduced, stored in a retrieval system, or transmitted by any means, electronic, mechanical, photocopying, recording, or otherwise, without written permission from the author.

ISBN: 978-1-970024-79-1

Other Books by Richard L. Smith

Time Lacuna	2003 Authorhouse	ISBN 1-4107-8383-0
Out of China:	2005 Xulon	ISBN 1-59781-502-0
New Eden:	2009 iUniverse	ISBN 978-1-4401-0781-
Powerless	2011 iUniverse	ISBN 978-4620-5365
Sedna 2016	2016 Accurance	ISBN 978-1-943767-88-

This novel is dedicated to the many wonderful and dedicated priests who have inspired and guided me through life.

Table of Contents

Chapter 1: The Calling 1
Chapter 2: The Journey 13
Chapter 3: Minnesota 31
Chapter 4: Whitefish 57
Chapter 5: Priest and Healer 77
Chapter 6: The Blizzard 89
Chapter 7: Leech Lake 95
Chapter 8: The Dedication 109
Chapter 9: The Clinic 117
Chapter 10: Confronting Evil 125
Chapter 11: A Crisis of Faith 135
Chapter 12: The Tinker 153
Chapter 13: Tecumseh 169
Chapter 14: Family Matters 183
Chapter 15: Homeward Bound 201
Chapter 16: The Epidemic 223
Chapter 17: Reassignment 233
Chapter 18: End Days 247

Preface

Little Church in the Wilderness is an inspirational story, a product of my imagination inspired by the desire to write a novel about a priest gifted with the ability to heal both body and soul. My main character, Father Todd Bose, is an amalgam of all the wonderful priests I have known these many years, yet in many respects for me he is a real person.

Upper Minnesota in the 1870s was a wilderness sparsely populated by a few logging towns and Indian villages accessible only by Mississippi River steamboats. A small contingent of Irish Catholic farmers migrated to Minnesota after the Civil War and tried to scratch a living out of the skimpy soil and harsh winters in the country near the Canadian border. It was life at the edge of survival, yet what they missed most was access to the Sacraments, so they petitioned the local bishop in St. Paul to send a priest to form a parish and build a church. Lacking a priest to assign, the bishop asked his longtime friend, the bishop of Baltimore, to send a missionary to Minnesota. The Baltimore bishop selected a newly ordained priest, Father Todd Edward Bose, as missionary to the struggling Catholic settlement. Father Bose was young, energetic, gifted, and entirely devoted to his priestly vocation. As an orderly in a hospital during the Civil War, he learned how to treat wounds and cure sicknesses and demonstrated a special talent for doctoring. Nevertheless, he remained unaware that God had blessed him with special graces as a healer. He accepted his missionary assignment, settled in Whitefish, built a church, and over a lifetime served his parishioners as priest and doctor. Challenged by life in the wilderness, he unselfishly ministered to the souls and health of the residents and Indians in upper Minnesota. His unique talent as a priest and healer became well known throughout upper Minnesota, whereupon Indians and white folks alike sought his help. Contrary to many recognized cases, Father Bose remained reluctant to claim that his cures were miraculous and refused to take personal credit for them, insisting that those healings were a result of his doctoring skills and God's grace working through him. Although fictional, Father Bose

Richard L. Smith

represents the tradition of service, dedication, and love so characteristic of many of our priests.

All the characters depicted in this story as well as descriptions of places that existed over 100 years ago are fictional and any resemblance to real people or places is merely coincidental.

Chapter 1
The Calling

Spring, 1872

Father Bose awoke to an insistent knocking on his bedroom door. He strained to read his alarm clock in the false dawn gloom that filtered through the only window in his room. The hands read 5.45, earlier than his normal 6:15 time to get up and prepare for the 7:00 a.m. Mass in St. Catherine's Catholic Church.

"What is it?" he groused.

The persistent knocking continued.

He climbed out of bed, put on his robe, and opened the door. Martha, the rectory housekeeper, stood in the doorway holding a small candle in her plump hand. A sweet smile graced her rotund face. "Father, sorry to wake you so early, but a messenger from the bishop's office is here to deliver an important letter personally to you."

A message arriving at this early hour usually meant that a parishioner was dying and requested the Last Rights, but a messenger from the chancery at this hour was most unusual. Todd hurriedly dressed and, trailed by their shadows, followed Martha down the dimly lit hallway to the rectory dining room. The room was warm, heated by a Franklin stove burning brightly with a fresh load of coal. The messenger was sitting at the kitchen table grasping a cup of steaming coffee. He gulped down the remainder of coffee in his cup, then stood up and with a nod handed a sealed envelope to Todd. He then excused himself to return to the chancery. Todd opened the envelope and read a short note from Gwen Bowler, the secretary to Bishop Allen of the Baltimore Diocese.

Bishop Allen would like to meet with you this morning on an important matter. I've scheduled an appointment for you at 10 a.m. in the chancery.

The chancery was on the northwest side of Baltimore, at least a 45-minute ride by buggy across town. He would have to rush through the seven o'clock Mass, and then after a quick breakfast, drive the parish buggy to the chancery. Todd took a seat at the kitchen table next to the sexton, John Bourn. The pastor of St. Catherine's, Father Ed Timbale, entered the kitchen, and took his seat at the head of the table. The elderly priest had finished celebrating the six o'clock Mass and was ready for Martha to serve his breakfast. Todd would have to wait for breakfast until after he said Mass. He showed Father Timbale the bishop's message.

"What could the bishop possibly want with me, a mere assistant pastor?" Todd mused. "He hasn't contacted me since my ordination last year, and I've only been here at St. Catherine's for a few months, not time enough to make an impression, good or bad."

Father Timbale nodded but did not offer an answer.

Last week, ten months after arriving at St Catherine's, Father Bose celebrated his thirtieth birthday, not that any parishioner knew either the date or the year of his birth. After his ordination, his assignment to St. Catherine's hadn't been Todd's first choice. He had hoped for a parish outside Baltimore, perhaps in a small farming community like the one where he grew up, but his wish went unanswered. He pondered why God had led him to become a priest in a big city rather than doctor in a small town, which had been his childhood dream.

*****

Todd Bose was born in 1841 to Matilda and John Bose on his father's farm in northwestern Pennsylvania. As a young boy, he learned to work long hours caring for the farm animals, milking cows, harvesting their 100-acre farm, and with his two younger brothers helping his father run their small dairy farm. Hard work honed him into a muscular, well-built young man believing in a good work ethic and dedicated to his studies at the one-room schoolhouse two miles from his house. His only day of rest was Sunday, and after the one-hour wagon ride to St. John's, the local Catholic Church in Spartansburg, Todd assisted Father Taylor at Mass. When he entered high school in Corry, he was a strapping six-footer with stock of wavy blond hair and light-brown skin. His pleasant personality and good looks attracted many admirers, including several young women. He was not only a straight "A" student, but he also excelled in high school sports, especially in rugby.

Matilda Bose gained a reputation as the local healer; the folks would come with minor ailments or ask for help in treating their farm animals. There was no veterinary in the county, and the nearest physician was at the hospital in Titusville, twenty miles away. Neighbors and their children would often show up at the farm asking Matilda to treat their minor ailments or help with their animals. As a young boy Todd imitated his mother's talent for doctoring, and as a teenager Todd's reputation for healing spread. Folks would call on Matilda or Todd to treat minor ailments or come to their farm to treat their animals. Matilda taught Todd how to remove splinters, treat cuts and burns, and splinter broken bones. She maintained a cabinet of home remedies for a variety of disorders from fevers to stomach aches. Todd delivered animals and treated any infirmity with as much talent as his mother displayed. John Bose claimed his son's healing talent was a special gift from God and encouraged Todd to go into veterinary medicine. Nevertheless, encouraged by his mother and friends, Todd decided instead to become a physician.

He applied to Rutgers College in New Jersey and based on his high school scholastic records and recommendations from the local high school principal and the doctor in Titusville where he assisted as an orderly in the summertime, Rutgers admitted him with a full scholarship. Todd decided to become a general practitioner, a "country doctor" as he called it, and entered the premedical program in the fall of 1859. In his freshman year he joined the Rutgers rugby team, and each summer he returned as an orderly at the Titusville hospital learning to treat illnesses, suture wounds, and patch broken bones. His aptitude and doctoring skills amazed the chief resident. He quickly learned his trade, and the doctor sent glowing reports about Todd's potential as a doctor to the Rutgers dean. However, an incident on the rugby field in the fall of his senior year caused him to reexamine his career plans.

The Rutgers rugby team was playing Princeton, and in final minutes with Rutgers leading by a goal, Princeton's best player Jimmy

Taylor rushed with the ball in his arms toward the end zone to score the winning point. Todd tackled him so hard that the boy's head hit the ground and the football went flying. Todd staggered to his feet but Jimmy remained spread eagle on the field, not moving a muscle. The boy's teammates gathered around him as the coach, his assistant, and the team trainer ran onto the field. The trainer worked on the boy for several minutes, but Jimmy did not respond. The coach slowly shook his head as if to say the injury was beyond serious and called for a stretcher. Todd felt responsible; he hadn't needed to hit Jimmy that hard. This was his fault. He pushed through the stunned crowd of onlookers and stood over the limp body. The Princeton players tried to push Todd away, but he pushed back and then knelt beside Jimmy. Placing one hand on the boy's head, he prayed silently. He prayed harder and more fervently than he had ever prayed before.

"Dear God, please don't let this poor boy die at my hands."

He felt a tingling warm sensation extend from his shoulder down his right arm to his hand, where the warmth intensified. Todd was tempted to remove his hand but he didn't. The warmth then began to flow from his hand into the boy's forehead. After a few seconds Jimmy groaned, and then opened one eye. Recognizing his opponent, he hissed, "Get off me you big oaf!"

Surprised at the boy's vehement response, Todd fell backwards and, slowly getting to his feet, backed out of the crowd.

"Are you all right?" he heard the coach ask Jimmy in utter amazement.

"Of course I'm all right. Why are all of you standing around me? Did we score?"

Todd retreated to the bench and sat down as the trainer and his helper led the still woozy Jimmy off the field. The game ended and the Princeton coach, after congratulating the Rutgers coach for their win, looked for Todd among the celebrating Rutgers players. Finding him sitting alone on the bench, he stood over him and asked, "What did you do when you knelt beside Jimmy? The boy wasn't breathing and had no pulse. I thought he was dead."

"I just asked God not to take him," Todd answered.

The coach looked perplexed but leaned over, grabbed Todd's hand, and began to shake it. "You are an extraordinary young man, Todd Bose. God heard your prayer and gave Jimmy back to us. With no pulse and not breathing, I thought Jimmy was dead. Yet now by your prayer and succor he lives. God must have a special plan for you."

For the next few weeks, Todd pondered this extraordinary incident. He couldn't get the coach's words out of his mind, especially the part about God having a special plan for him. During summer break at his farm, he decided to consult with their parish priest, Father Taylor. He had a special admiration for Father Taylor, the kindly Irish pastor of St. John's church in Spartansburg who had trained him as an altar server and tutored him when he had difficulty with high school algebra. Todd explained the football incident to the elderly priest and asked, "Was it a miracle, Father, like some people at school keep saying?"

Father Taylor smiled and said, "I don't know if you can call it a miracle, son. Possibly the boy was knocked out and came around when you knelt beside him. No matter, I think God heard your prayer answered your petition. Todd, I've watched you grow into a fine young man this past decade and have noted your devotion as an altar server and in prayer. God looks favorably on you and the Princeton coach's comment was insightful. God does have a special plan for you. You have an exceptional relationship with Jesus and He has given you extraordinary talents including the talent as healer. I know that you are considering becoming a doctor, but please consider entering the seminary."

"But Father, I have always wanted to be a medical doctor. Even when I was a child, I took care of sick animals and doctored my friends. I'm told that I have a talent as a general practitioner and I have done well in my studies at Rutgers and enjoyed my hospital internships. What you suggest is a complete change of career plans and I think my mother and father would be terribly disappointed in such a choice."

"Don't worry about your mom or dad. In the end, John will accept your change of plans, and if he hesitates, I will speak with him. This may seem like a big career change, but it isn't. Instead of doctoring people's bodies, you will heal their souls and, given your innate talents, perhaps you will do both. Todd, please think about what I have suggested; it comes from my heart."

Todd pondered the priest's advice and, despite his father's initial disapproval, after graduation from Rutgers he decided not to enter medical school but applied for admission to the seminary in Baltimore. Bishop Allen interviewed Todd and reviewed his brilliant academic record. On Father Taylor's recommendation, the bishop accepted Todd's petition to enter the seminary. To honor his father's wishes and Father Taylor's advice that he should test his calling, he postponed entering the seminary and worked for a year on the farm while studying and praying with Father Taylor. With his calling burning even more fervently in his heart, he entered the seminary in the fall of 1863.

The Civil War raged that year and several of his former high school and Rutgers classmates joined the Union Army, as did both of his brothers who never returned from that horrible war. Wounded soldiers poured into the Baltimore hospitals and although exempted from military service, Bishop Allen asked Todd to take a few months off from his seminary studies and spend that time treating wounded soldiers at St. Michael's Hospital in Baltimore. For most of 1864 and part of 1865, Todd cleaned and sutured wounds, set broken bones, treated diseases, amputated limbs, and prayed with dying soldiers. When the war ended in the spring of 1865, Todd returned to the seminary.

After six more years of study and discernment, in the spring of 1871 Bishop Allen ordained Todd Edward Bose "a priest forever according to the order of Melchisedech," and assigned him to the small Baltimore parish of St. Catherine's. Father Timbale, the pastor of St. Catherine's, recently celebrated his eighty-fourth year having served as its pastor for fifty-five years. Declining in health, he asked Bishop Allen for a vibrant young priest to assist him. While in the seminary Todd's vitality, dedication to his studies, and prayerfulness made a lasting impression on the bishop, who thought this vibrant young priest was just what Father Timbale and St. Catherine's needed.

Obedient to the bishop's wishes, Father Bose buried himself in his duties as Fr. Timbale's assistant. He impressed the congregation when for the first time he climbed into the pulpit and in a strong clear voice delivered a homily on the Sermon on the Mount. Aware that all in the congregation were dirt-poor, he focused on the line where Jesus proclaimed, "Blessed are the poor, for theirs is the kingdom of heaven." His sermon contrasted against those delivered by Father Timbale, whose stale sermons and gravely voice had put many a parishioner to sleep each Sunday. His warm manner and good looks made him a favorite with parishioners, especially with the young women.

Now only a year into his assignment the bishop had summoned him, but for what possible purpose? Todd returned to his room, dressed in his cassock, and then went into the church sanctuary to prepare for Mass. After the service, Todd found Dan the rector and asked him to hitch their horse to the buggy. He then joined Fr. Timbale in the rectory for his after-Mass breakfast.

Father Timbale was reading the Office of the Hours, a prayer every priest said daily, and looked up as Todd sat down at the table.

"And what does Bishop Allen want with you so early in the morning?"

"His secretary said he wants to see me this morning, but she didn't say why," Todd answered.

Father Timbale put down his prayer book and looked intently at Todd. "It is most unusual for the bishop to request the presence of my assistant without consulting me first. Why do you think this is?"

Todd sensed that Fr. Timbale felt slighted by the bishop's summons to Todd, so he busied himself with his breakfast and didn't offer a response. Martha broke the uncomfortable silence when she entered the room with a plate of scrambled eggs and hot muffins.

"So, Father Bose, Bishop Allen wants to see you this morning. What is this all about?"

Father Timbale stiffened and glared at his housekeeper rebuking her, "This is Fr. Bose's business, Martha, and obviously none of our own."

Todd quickly finished his breakfast and looked at his pocket watch. It was 8:45. He went out to the stable where Dan had just finished hitching the mare to the buggy.

"Be careful with Jenny today," he warned. "She's been acting a bit skittish lately."

Todd thanked Dan and climbed onto the buggy, took the reins in his hands, and gently urged the mare out onto the street.

Downtown Baltimore, crowded and congested this April morning, made for slow going. Wagons loaded with lumber, bricks, clothing, and household goods made their way down the dusty and crowded main street toward the harbor where stevedores waited to load the ships. Wagons parked alongside store fronts waited to unload their freight and partially blocked the street. Todd weaved his buggy along the street to avoid these obstacles. As he drove past the fire station, suddenly the door opened and a smoke-belching fire wagon pulled by two stout horses burst out onto the street. The wagon bells clanged as the fireman driver whipped his horses into a frenzy. Startled, Jenny bolted and charged out of control down the street after the wagon. Todd pulled on the reins and tried to slow the frightened horse, but she would have none of it. A half block past the fire station, she ran headlong into a parked wagon, smashing the buggy against a lamppost. Unhurt, Father Todd climbed off the buggy and examined Jenny, who had calmed down but was still trembling. Jenny seemed all right, but not so the buggy. The left wheel was askew and, on close examination, a carriage bolt that held the axle to the carriage had torn loose. A livery stable was down the street, so Todd hitched Jenny to the lamppost and walked to the stable where a worker was busy shoeing a horse.

"Can you fix my buggy? Todd asked. The man looked up and noticed the black cassock and hat.

"Sure, Father. Where is it?" Todd took him back to the buggy and the man examined the broken undercarriage. "Father, it's fixable. Bring the buggy back to the stable." Todd gingerly led Jenny down the street as the broken wheel jostled from side to side. Once inside the stables, the man took off the broken wheel and began fixing the undercarriage.

Todd glanced at his pocket watch. It was 9:25, and he was still a half hour's drive from the chancery. The mechanic repaired the wheel and after a fifteen-minute delay, Todd resumed his journey. At 10:20, he entered the bishop's office and stood in front of the secretary's desk. Gwen gave him a cold stare.

"Father, you're fifteen minutes late," she said curtly. "Bishop Allen doesn't tolerate late arrivals. Take a seat and he will be with you shortly."

Todd grimaced but decided to save his excuse for the bishop and found a seat. Twenty minutes later Gwen ushered him into the office. Bishop Allen was busy signing papers and without looking up motioned Todd to take a seat in front of his desk.

Without looking up he said, "A little late are we?"

Todd shifted uneasily in his chair. "Please accept my apology. The buggy broke down in town and I had to have it fixed."

The bishop grunted and resumed signing his papers. A minute later, he looked up.

"So, tell me, Father, how's it going at St. Catherine's?"

"It is a good parish with many wonderful people that I am just getting to know. For me it has been a welcomed assignment," Todd answered.

"And how is Father Timbale? I assume he is well."

"Yes, he is well, but feeling his age."

The bishop nodded, and then looked long and hard at Todd.

"Father Todd, I called you here today to ask you to take a challenging assignment. I am aware of your wish to serve in a rural parish, and the new assignment I have in mind for you is about as rural as it can get."

The bishop paused to let his words sink in. Todd smiled nervously.

"My longtime friends, Father Quinn and Bishop Byrne in St. Paul, have asked me to send a missionary to upper Minnesota. They want someone young and energetic, a priest who could start a parish in a small village north of Grand Rapids, which is not far from the Canadian border. The name of this village is Whitefish, and the Catholic families in that small community have petitioned their local bishop for a priest to be their pastor and build a church. Father Quinn, the pastor of St. Paul's Cathedral, has made his life's work bringing Catholic families out of the squalor and poverty of the large eastern cities to homestead in the northwestern wilderness of Minnesota. Four years ago, he encouraged twenty-four pioneer families from Boston to emigrate to Whitefish and now they have petitioned Bishop Byrne of St. Paul for a missionary priest to serve them. I wrote Father Quinn that I had someone in mind, and YOU are that someone."

Todd pondered the bishop's words: *"Missionary, pioneers, build a church?" Was this what God was asking of me?*

"So, what do you think? Are you up to this challenge?"

Todd smiled and looked the bishop in the eye. "I will gladly accept any assignment and go wherever you send me."

"Good then." He took out a handkerchief and blew his nose. "This will not be an easy assignment, Father Bose. Father Quinn said that Whitefish is a small community mostly of German dirt farmers, and before those Boston families immigrated, almost all the residents were Lutheran. President Lincoln signed the Homestead Act ten years ago which gives each pioneer 160 acres of bottomland to ranch or farm. Bishop Byrne provided each family with two horses, a wagon, some farm animals, and $150 to help settle them. They are dirt-poor and barely able to scratch a living out of the Minnesota soil. Father Quinn told Bishop Byrne that his people miss the sacraments and long for a priest to form their own parish. They have little money with which to build a church, but Father Quinn promised me that they are good hardworking individuals, resilient and determined."

"Will I report to Bishop Byrne or to you?"

"You will remain as a missionary priest attached to the Baltimore diocese. We will continue to pay your $15 a month salary and provide $10 a month living allowance. You will report to me, but you need to stay in touch with Bishop Byrne for it's his diocese. We will both look forward to your monthly progress reports from Whitefish."

Still a bit bewildered, Todd nodded his agreement.

"When am I to leave for Minnesota?"

"Immediately. Please report to the St. Paul Cathedral chancery when you arrive in St. Paul. Father Quinn will be expecting you."

The bishop handed Todd an envelope and told him to open it. Inside was a letter of introduction to Bishop Byrne and Father Quinn, a ticket on the B&O Railroad to Chicago, another ticket from Chicago to St. Paul on the St. Paul and Pacific RR, and $100 cash. The train reservation was for next Monday, three days away. "Report to Bishop Byrne and then meet with Father Quinn. He will arrange for you to take a Mississippi steamboat to Grand Rapids where you will meet a parishioner named Mike Dunn a week from this coming Monday. Mike will take you on horseback to Whitefish. Do you have any questions?"

"No," Todd said, "but I do have a request. I haven't seen my mother and father for over two years, and it may be some time before I can again visit them. They live in northwest Pennsylvania and I could stop on my way to Chicago in Pittsburg to visit them. I would like to spend a few days with them. Would this be possible?"

Bishop thought for a minute and then answered. "Father Quinn and Bishop Byrne are expecting you next week, but it is important that you first visit your folks. I will contact them and explain your delay. You can get off the train in Pittsburg and continue on to St. Paul after you spend a few days with your family."

Todd thanked Bishop Allen, who stood, shook Todd's hand, and then handed him a six-inch wood crucifix tied to a rawhide necklace.

"This crucifix has an imbedded relic of St. Paul, said to be part of the cross he was crucified on. Pope Pius X blessed it and gave it to me. The rawhide necklace is to remind you that your mission will be that of a pioneer. Northern Minnesota is mostly untamed wilderness, but you will find your parishioners come from sturdy stuff. May this crucifix and God's special grace go with you."

Todd knelt as the bishop gave him a special blessing,

Todd had no idea where Grand Rapids was and didn't know anything about Minnesota, but he decided to visit the chancery library before he returned home. After spending some time in the library poring over maps of Minnesota and studying its brief history, Todd hurried back to St. Catherine's with the news of his new assignment, which dismayed Father Timbale.

The old priest sat down. "Father Todd, I appreciated your help here at St. Catherine's and I need you here. You have made a difference at St. Catherine's and I am saddened the bishop has seen it best to reassign you. Where is your new assignment?"

"Whitefish … in upper Minnesota."

"Minnesota? That is not part of our diocese. Why in the world is the bishop sending you to Minnesota?"

"It is a missionary assignment. Father John Quinn in St. Paul is a friend of Bishop Allen and asked him for a priest to form a parish in Whitefish. It will be a difficult assignment and one that requires a young, energetic priest willing to work in a pioneer setting. That is why he picked me."

"I see," Fr. Timbale said. "I will ask the bishop for another assistant, but I doubt that he has anyone that he can send. When do you leave?"

"My train leaves Monday morning at 9:00 a.m.," Todd answered. "Not much time for good-byes."

"Monday? That's the day after tomorrow. You will have barely enough time to pack and say good-bye to the congregation. I will announce your new assignment at Sunday Mass, and you can give your final sermon to St. Catherine's parishioners."

Todd nodded in agreement. "I'm sorry to leave you and St. Catherine's. One's first assignment is always a memorable one, and you and the parish have been patient and kind to me. I will always remember your thoughtfulness. Wish me luck."

Father Timbale looked like someone had punched him in the stomach. "God go with you Father. You will need my prayers, not luck."

Chapter 2
The Journey

Monday, April 12, 1872

The cold drizzle on that April morning dampened both the streets and Todd's mood as Dan urged the buggy forward through the busy Baltimore streets that led to the train station. Todd struggled with rising emotions of anticipation and trepidation. He was on a mission that would try his body and soul. He knew the Holy Ghost would guide and protect him, yet he was giving up his comfortable urban life to serve people he had never met in a wilderness filled with unknown dangers and few comforts. The book about Minnesota that he borrowed from the diocese library described the northern part of the territory as uncivilized woodlands inhabited by Indians and wild animals, a setting of harsh winters and hot, mosquito-infested summers. Furthermore, the book said the upper part of the state contained some unmapped backwoods where dangerous bears, wolves, mountain lions, and wolverines roamed.

What would his new parishioners in Whitefish be like? Would they accept and trust a young and inexperienced priest as their pastor? He had never formed a parish or built a church, and his management skills had never been tested. Was he up to this task? Where would he live and what would he eat? So many unanswered questions, yet he reminded himself that this mission was God's will and He would provide. As the carriage bounced along the cobblestone street, a short prayer calmed the butterflies fluttering in his stomach. The buggy eventually pulled into the station crowded with wagons, buggies, and horses. A passenger train belched black smoke and hissed clouds of acrid steam as it waited on a sidetrack. Todd climbed down from the buggy, adjusted his shoulder bag, and grasped his satchel. Todd hadn't brought much with him; only a few underclothes, socks, nightclothes, an extra cassock and Roman collar, a stole (the sign of his priestly office), and an alb and a silk chasuble to wear while saying Mass. He also packed an extra pair of boots, a Mass kit, his Office prayer book, a bound journal, and a Bible. He wore a heavy wool overcoat over his cassock, a wool scarf, and fedora hat. Next week Father Timbale would ship the rest of his clothes and personal items by train and riverboat to Grand Rapids, the nearest town to Whitefish.

He looked up at Dan and smiled. "Good-bye, Dan. Thank you for the ride and your friendship these past months."

The sexton stoically sat in the buggy with the reins loosely held in one hand and the buggy whip in the other. Without looking at Todd, he put down the whip and handed him a folded map. "Here is a map of Minnesota. I visited St. Paul sometime back and bought this map as a souvenir. You will have more use for it than I ever will, so please take it."

Todd took the map as Dan cracked the whip and the buggy lurched forward. Dan glanced back at the forlorn figure standing alone in the street and said, "Good luck to you, Father. You will certainly need it." Then he was gone and with him Todd's last ties to St. Catherine's and Baltimore.

Todd made his way inside the station and found the ticket window where he confirmed his prepaid reservations. The clerk punched his ticket to Chicago.

"I see you have a weeklong stopover in Pittsburg," he commented. "Be sure not to miss your connection to Chicago because reservations for the following week are all filled."

Todd had planned this stopover as possibly the last time he could visit his parents in Spartansville. The realization saddened him as he climbed on the train and found an empty seat in the passenger car next to the observation car. He stowed his satchel and backpack in the overhead rack, and then sat down and began praying the Office of the Hours, a prayer recited daily by every priest.

At 9:00 a.m. the engineer blew the steam whistle three times, and the train puffed out of the station. As the train gathered speed, Todd disrupted his prayer and looked out the window at the outskirts of Baltimore as it faded in the distance. Two hours later and after several train stops, he finished praying the Office and returned to watching the countryside slide by. They passed one small farm after another, each reminding him of his home in Spartansville. Eventually the small farms gave way to the hilly country of West Virginia, now clothed by a deciduous forest leafing out from its winter slumber. A small boy sitting in the seat across the aisle had been watching him, and when Todd put his prayer book away, the boy slid into the empty seat beside him.

"Are you a man of the cloth?" the boy asked, taking note of his cassock and Roman collar.

"If you mean a minister, no I am not a minister. I am a priest."

The boy looked puzzled. "Isn't a priest the same as a minister?"

"Yes basically we are the same, ordained to minister to souls. I do so in the Catholic Church, and ministers do so in Protestant churches."

The boy's eyes grew large. "You minister to souls? Do I have one?"

"You surely do," Todd said, a bit surprised at the question. "What is your name?"

"Jimmy. What's yours?"

"I'm Father Todd. Jimmy, don't you pray and go to church?"

"Na, I don't know how to pray and never been in one of those churches. My dad says religion is all a bunch of hooey."

Todd looked past Jimmy at the seat across the aisle. A gentleman in a three-piece business suit sat alone reading a book. "Is that your father over there?" Todd asked as he nodded toward the man across the aisle.

"Yea, that's my dad."

"And he never taught you to pray or took you to a church?"

"Nope, I've never been inside one of them. What do you do in church?"

"We pray and worship God."

"Why do you do that?"

"Because God created you and me and loves each one of us. Just as you show respect and love for your parents when you visit with them, we do the same with God."

Jimmy looked pensive. "My mom died when I was born and my dad is raising me. I think she used to go to church." Then he smiled and said, "I'm going back to the observation car and stand on the back platform. Want to come with me?"

"No thank you," Todd said. The boy slid out of the seat and went to the back of the car.

Todd returned to watching the countryside slip away between puffs of thick black smoke from the engine's smokestack. A few minutes later, Jimmy came back down the aisle holding his hand over his right eye and crying as he fell into the seat with his dad.

"Something's in my eye," he sobbed.

The man pulled Jimmy's hand away from his eye and, taking a handkerchief from his pocket, began dabbing the boy's eye." Jimmy's sobs grew into muffled screams.

"Hold still," his father demanded. "You caught a cinder in your eye and I can't get it out with you squirming around like an injured worm."

"It hurts," Jimmy whined.

Todd got up from his seat and leaned into the bench where Jimmy's dad struggled to hold the boy's head motionless on his lap while he dabbed the eye with his handkerchief.

"Can I help?" Todd offered.

The man looked up and recognized Todd's Roman collar. "Father, my name is Bill, Bill Farthing. The boy caught a cinder in his eye, and unless he stays still, I can't get it out. Could you try to remove it as I hold the boy's head still?"

While caring for the Union soldiers in the Baltimore Hospital, Todd had removed bullets, sutured countless wounds, set broken bones, amputated limbs, and removed charred bits of rifle batting from soldiers' eyes. He knew how to remove objects without scratching the eyeball.

"Hold his head still and I'll have a look," Todd said. He knelt beside the boy and pried his eyelid back. A cinder about the size of a pinhead had burned itself into the boy's inside eyelid, and a few red spider veins crisscrossed his irritated eyeball.

"This cinder must come out before it scratches the eyeball and cornea," Todd warned. "Keep the boy's head as still as possible while I try to remove it."

Bill looked apprehensive. "Father, with all due respect, do you know what you are doing?"

"Yes, I do. I worked in the Baltimore Hospital and know how to treat eye wounds."

Bill clamped Jimmy's' head between his legs. Todd took a clean handkerchief from his pocket and gently tried to remove the cinder firmly embedded in the boy's eyelid. Todd looked toward the boy's father. "This will need a better instrument than a handkerchief. I will find the conductor and see if there is a doctor on board who has his medical kit with him. Do not to let Jimmy rub his eye."

Todd found the conductor in the next car, and they went together from car to car asking if there was a doctor on board, but no one came forward. Unsuccessful in their search, Todd and the conductor returned to the boy and his father. "We couldn't find a doctor, but if you wish I'll try again to remove the cinder," Todd offered. Bill readily agreed.

Todd opened his satchel, took out a small pair of tweezers from his medical kit, and the conductor disinfected them with a bottle of whiskey he carried in his pocket. Todd then forced the boy's eyelid open so he could get a clear look at the area underneath the lid. The cinder remained firmly impeded in Jimmy's eyelid, and by now the entire eye had turned red with a network of spiderlike blood vessels that crisscrossed the iris. Before probing with his tweezers, Todd wanted to flush the boy's eye out with water. He removed a small vial of blessed water from his Mass kit and used it to purge the boy's eye. A few drops of lemon added to the distilled holy water inhibited bacterial growth and he reasoned the slightly acidic water would not only help flush the cinder out but also would help prevent infection. Jimmy flinched when a few drops of the water hit his eye.

"It stings," he sobbed.

"Just for a little while," Todd said gently as he flushed the eye a second time.

"Why don't you pray for God to take the cinder away?" Jimmy said between sobs.

"Don't talk nonsense," Bill rebuked his young son.

Todd was taken aback by the boy's wish and more so by his father's response.

He flashed a miffed look at Bill. "A prayer couldn't hurt and it certainly is not nonsense."

Admonished, the man looked down and cleared his throat.

Todd blessed the boy and then held his hand over the damaged eye and prayed, "Dear God, please let me safely remove the cinder from Jimmy's eye."

He held the tweezers in one hand, folded the boy's eyelid back with the other, and searched the eyelid and the surrounding tissue for the cinder, yet there was no sign of it.

"Thank God," Todd said. "The water must have flushed the cinder out." He examined the eyeball and the cornea for scratches, but none was visible, nor was there any sign of the hot cinder that had burned the eyelid. The red spider veins that had previously covered the boy's iris were also disappearing. Another exam a few minutes later showed an unblemished eye and the iris and cornea were clear.

Todd looked at Bill. "Jimmy is a lucky boy," he said. "Thanks to washing the eye with distilled holy water, the cinder is gone and it doesn't look like there was any permanent damage to his eyelid or cornea."

Bill extended his hand. "Father, your doctoring prevented serious damage to my son's vision. I thank you from the bottom of my heart."

Jimmy looked first at his dad and then back at Todd. "It wasn't the water. The minute you placed you hand over my eye and prayed my whole eye became warm and stopped hurting. It doesn't hurt now either."

"More nonsense," Bill said as he hugged the boy. "It was the water."

The conductor had remained standing in the aisle and hovering over the operation without saying a word, but now he spoke up. "No, it was more than the water. I have seen children get cinders in their eyes many times before, yet I have never seen anyone come away without some serious damage to their eyesight. Look, the boy's eye isn't even red. No, I think the boy is right. We have witnessed a miraculous healing."

Mr. Farthing looked lost in thought. Clearly he wasn't ready to admit to a miracle at the hands of this young priest, but neither could he explain why Jimmy's eye showed no signs of damage. The eye wasn't even red, as one might have expected. All he could do was to hug his son and thank Todd. "It was the water," he repeated as he hugged Jimmy to his breast.

Todd returned to his seat to ponder the event. Was it the flushing with holy water or something more profound? The minute he placed his hand over the boy's eye he felt a warming sensation centered in his hand. He remembered the incident on the football field some years back, when his hand experienced that same warm glow when he placed it on the player's head. *A most unusual experience*, he thought.

As the train lumbered on, undulating back and forth on uneven tracks, the conductor came through announcing the next stop would be Harpers Ferry.

Mr. Farthing began gathering his luggage from the overhead bin. "This is our stop. My sister will meet us here and drive us home," he said to Todd. "I'm not sure what happened today. When the conductor called this a miracle, my first thought was that such a pronouncement was hokum. I was certain the water had flushed the cinder out of Jimmy's eye. After thinking about it, I must admit that Jimmy's sudden healing defies explanation. The water may have flushed the cinder out, but I cannot explain how the spider veins on his iris faded so quickly and how it is the cinder left no burn mark on his eyelid. Jimmy convinced himself that you performed a miracle, and he wants to learn more about your Catholic faith. I need to talk to someone about this. Could you recommend a priest in Harpers Ferry whom I might contact?"

"A seminarian who graduated with me is Father Bergen. He is the assistant pastor at St. Andrew's Church in the Ferry. Although recently ordained, he is an older priest who served as a Union officer during the Civil War, and after the war he decided to become a priest. He has experienced much in his long life. I suggest you call him and make an appointment."

"I'll do so. Thank you, Father Bose. I'm not sure if this was what Jimmy calls a miracle or just natural happenstance, but Jimmy and I are very grateful to you."

"I am also a bit baffled," Todd admitted. "God go with you, and write to me at Whitefish, Minnesota. I will be the pastor there and I want to hear about your meeting with Father Bergen."

Mr. Farthing nodded. Jimmy hugged Todd as their train pulled into the Harpers Ferry station. The brakes squealed and the train lurched to a stop as Mr. Farthing and Jimmy disappeared down the aisle. Todd watched out the window as a well-dressed woman hurried down the platform, kissed Bill, and then hugged Jimmy.

"There's always a reason for everything, and often the unexplained is just God's way of testing our faith," Todd mumbled and returned to reading his Office.

****

The train made its way to Pittsburg, where Todd got off and found a hotel. The next morning, he rented a horse-and-buggy for the 80-mile trip to Spartansville and later that afternoon arrived at his father's farmhouse.

Matilda and John Bose were eating supper in the kitchen when Todd opened the kitchen door. Neither of them had any idea that he was coming, for his arrival preceded the letter announcing his travel plans. Elated to see their son but concerned about his unexpected visit, they asked what brought him home. He explained that he was on his way to northern Minnesota to accept his new assignment as a missionary in a small village. They were proud of their priest-son and delighted with his assignment at Saint Catherine's. Nevertheless, the news of a new assignment greatly disturbed them. John pondered why, after only ten months at Saint Catherine's, Bishop Allen would assign him to a backwoods mission in Minnesota of all places.

Matilda looked perplexed and asked, "Son, did you do something in Baltimore to cause Bishop Allen to banish you to this frozen Minnesota wasteland?"

"No, Mom, nothing like that. Bishop Allen is a good friend of Bishop Byrne in St. Paul. His friend asked him to send a missionary to Whitefish to serve a group of emigrants from Boston. The priest he selected had to be someone young and vigorous and a person who knows about farming and farm folk. Since Bishop Allen knew I was raised on a farm and remembered that I had asked to serve in a rural parish, he asked if I would accept this assignment, and I did."

"How long can you stay?" Matilda asked.

"Just a few days," Todd explained. "I must catch a train from Pittsburg to Chicago on Monday, then another train to St. Paul. Finally, I will catch a riverboat that will take me up the Mississippi to Grand Rapids and then by horseback to Whitefish Lake."

"Where is Whitefish Lake?" Matilda asked.

Todd unfolded the Minnesota map that Dan gave him on the kitchen table and circled Grand Rapids with a pencil. "Grand Rapids is 120 miles northeast of St. Paul, perhaps twice that by way of a Mississippi River boat. There are few roads in northern Minnesota, and the only way to get around is by riverboat."

Todd leaned over the map and pointed to a small, unmarked lake in a valley between two parallel rows of mountains. "I think this is Whitefish Lake," he said.

"According to this map, as the crow flies this valley is about 40 miles north of Grand Rapids. There are no roads in the area and one must travel to Whitefish on horseback. 'Wilderness' is how Bishop Allen described northern Minnesota."

"Tell us about your missionary assignment," John asked.

Todd explained about his meeting with Bishop Allen and his new assignment.

"And that's all you know?" Matilda said.

"Mom, Dad, there isn't much more that I can tell you. I am to build a church in the wilderness."

John got his *Farmers' Almanac* from the sitting room and brought it into the kitchen. He found the chapter on Minnesota and read, "Says here that upper Minnesota north of the Mesabi Mountains is just about the coldest place in the US east of the Mississippi, colder even than Maine, and that's damn cold. The growing season in those parts is only mid-June to mid-September. There are no towns between Grand Rapids and Canada, but the few farms in the area grow potatoes, squash, and corn in the meager soil. Not a good place to farm I'd say."

"Dad, I don't know why these folks chose northern Minnesota. I suspect it had something to do with Lincoln's Homestead Act that gave 160 acres of bottomland to anyone who was willing to settle on it. That was ten years ago and I suppose most of the best farmland like that in Kansas and southern Minnesota has already been claimed. Northern Minnesota might have been the only place left to homestead."

"Looks like a frozen wilderness to me," John mumbled. "So, your assignment is to build a church in the wilderness. What do you know about building a church for heaven's sake?"

"Dad, remember when I helped you and your neighbors raise our barn? How about the time I helped you build the bunkhouse for our workers, and helped you build the shed? I built a lot of stuff around here over the years. You taught me how to use a hammer and saw."

John sighed and commented. "I just have a hard time picturing a priest wielding a hammer and saw,"

"I don't think Canon Law forbids that," Todd said, laughing. "Besides, I imagine the folks in Whitefish will be the ones who will build the church."

John rummaged around in his storage trunk in the attic, extracted a rolled-up parchment, and spread it out on the kitchen table. The parchment was a detailed architectural drawing of a church.

"Your grandfather built St. John's church in Spartansburg, and these are his architectural drawings."

"I didn't know granddad built St. John's," Todd said in amazement. "You never told me that."

"Well, he designed it and the parishioners built it. He was a self-taught architect. The whole town pitched in and helped build the church from these plans almost seventy years ago. Take these plans with you to Minnesota. Perhaps they will be helpful when you build your church."

The plans were for a small church, perhaps large enough to seat 100 persons. Todd had never thought of St. John's as small. Now as he looked over these plans, he realized that it would be just the right size for Whitefish, and it thrilled him that his grandfather had designed it.

Todd helped John around the farm for the next few days and, on Sunday, they made the trip into town to attend Mass at St. John's. Delighted to see Todd, Father Taylor invited him into the rectory after Mass for coffee.

"Todd, tell me about St. Catherine's," Father Taylor asked.

"I was only there for ten months before Bishop Allen called me in and gave me a new assignment."

"And what would that assignment be?"

"I am on my way to a small village in upper Minnesota where I am to form a parish and build a church."

"That is a far place from Baltimore and Bishop Allen's diocese. How is it that he is sending you so far away?"

"Bishop Allen is a close friend of Bishop Byrne in St. Paul who asked him to send a missionary to serve a community of Catholic immigrants from Boston. I am that missionary."

Father Taylor took Todd's hand and smiled. "Todd, I have known you since you were an altar boy. Even then, I sensed something special and remarkable about you. Your ordination thrilled me and made me proud of you. I heard rumors about you performing a healing at the college and that you healed many folks while serving at the Baltimore hospital. Even as a child, you helped heal animals and even some children. Some folks claim you performed miraculous healings, but I don't think this is the case. You have a natural talent for doctoring, but if these cures are truly miracles then God is working through you to perform his work. You are a tool in God's hands, just as the Apostle Paul was a tool for God to work his wonders. Remember that Jesus sent his apostles out commanding them to heal the sick and spread the Gospel. This then may be your mission."

"Father, I do not know why God chose me for this mission. I feel inadequate and not up to the task."

"Your assignment in Minnesota has some greater significance that is not now clear, but it will gradually become so. Cooperate with Him, follow your intuition, and eventually He will reveal all to you."

Todd thanked Father Taylor who gave him his blessing and asked him to write.

"I will do so, Father," Todd promised.

On the ride back to the farm, Todd remained silent until John asked him what Father Taylor had to say.

"He gave me some advice and his blessing and said my mission has some special meaning."

"What special meaning?" John asked.

"Right now, I don't know. Father Taylor assures me that eventually I will know."

John and Matilda did not inquire further.

*****

Early the following Monday morning Todd hugged his parents, not knowing when he would next see them again, waved good-bye, and then made his way to Pittsburg where he caught the train for Chicago later that afternoon. All that night the train lurched and swayed across Pennsylvania and on into Ohio where after a long stop in Wheeling, they continued across Ohio to Columbus where he changed trains to Chicago. On Tuesday afternoon, the train slowed as it pulled into the Chicago train terminal yard, which was also the terminus for the B&O line. Todd marveled at this busy yard, several times the size of the freight yard in Baltimore. Their single-track split into two, and then split repeatedly as the train moved slowly toward the main terminal. They passed small locomotives pushing individual freight cars up a shallow incline then let each car independently roll down the hill onto a predetermined siding where it slammed into a waiting line of freight cars. Yard workers consulting clipboards swarmed about the yard throwing switches to direct each car onto a predetermined siding. Lines of boxcars, tankers, gondolas, and flatcars loaded with lumber made up trains of various lengths. Clouds of steam erupted from a roundhouse at one end of the yard where workers prepared each engine for its cross-country journey. As their train neared the passenger terminal, it passed by several passenger cars waiting in long lines for their turn to hook onto one of those locomotives. All this activity moved with precision like gears in a fine watch.

Todd's train crept into the main terminal that extended for the better part of a city block and finally lurched to a stop. He gathered his backpack and valise and disembarked into a crowd of other passengers, each person rushing this way and that way to their separate destinations. A sign pointed to the lobby, but as he made his way against the main passenger flow, the constant jostling almost caused him to lose his valise. He made his way inside the main lobby and searched in vain for the St. Paul and Pacific RR counter. He went over to a six-sided kiosk marked with a sign that read "Information" and asked the agent for directions to the St. Paul and Pacific RR counter. The agent smiled and asked to see Todd's ticket. After examining the ticket, he pointed to the other side of the lobby where there was a long counter marked with a "Northern Pacific" sign. Several lines of passengers stood at the counter awaiting their turn.

"But I was looking for the St. Paul and Pacific RR counter," Todd protested, pointing to the printed ticket jacket cover.

"They used to be the St. Paul and Pacific RR until the Northern Pacific Railroad bought them last month," the agent explained. "I guess they have yet to change their preprinted ticket jackets. Nevertheless, it is now Northern Pacific that you want."

Todd thanked the man and joined the line of people standing in front of the ticket counter. After a long wait, he handed his ticket to the ticket agent. She looked at it and announced, "The last train to St. Paul left ten minutes ago at 3:00 p.m. You will have to wait for the next train scheduled to leave tomorrow morning at 8:00 a.m. on track six."

Todd looked at his watch. It read 3:10 p.m.; his train wouldn't leave for another seventeen-plus hours, so he had to figure out where to spend the night. The rows of wood benches that graced the lobby reminded him of the benches in St. Catherine's church, but none looked comfortable enough to spend the night.

"Do you know of a nearby hotel where I might get a room for a reasonable price?' he asked the agent.

"You might try the hotel down the street. I understand you can rent a room for the night for seventy-five cents."

Todd shouldered his knapsack, grabbed his valise, and headed down the street to the hotel.

The Wharton Hotel looked a bit seedy and in bad need of a coat of fresh paint. Two men sat near the entrance sharing sips from a bottle covered by a paper bag. Todd glanced at them and then entered the hotel lobby and rang the small bell on the counter. A man wearing a green visor appeared from the inner office door. Noticing Todd's Roman collar, he asked, "What can I do for you Father?"

"Do you have a clean, inexpensive room for the night?"

The clerk nervously cleared his throat and offered advice. "Father, you might find a hotel closer to the lake that would be … well, more comfortable."

Desperately tired, Todd didn't want to find a "more comfortable" hotel. Besides, this hotel was only a block away from the train station. "I'm sure I can be comfortable here."

The clerk nodded and then pushed the register across the counter. Todd signed his name and town and passed the register back to the clerk.

"Our hotel is not much to write home about, but the rooms and beds are clean and our rooms are less expensive than the Royal Hotel three blocks down the street."

The clerk read Todd's signature. "Father Bose from Baltimore," the clerk repeated. "Where are you headed?"

"St. Paul," Todd said. "You say your rooms and beds are clean? That is good enough for me, and right now I need to take a nap."

Todd looked at the sign over the counter that read,
"Rooms $1.25/night."

This was more than the seventy-five cents the ticket agent said, but he didn't want to haggle and handed the money to the clerk. "Do you know of a place where I can get a meal?"

The man turned around to the pegboard behind him, chose a key marked #22, and handed it to Todd.

"There's a Chinese restaurant just down the street."

Todd took the key and climbed the stairs leading to room number twenty-two at the end of a long hallway. His room was drab, dimly lit by a single window. A lone wood chair sat next to a small table holding a kerosene lamp, a few sheets of writing paper, and a pencil. A two-drawer dresser and single bed provided the only other furniture. Todd pushed the window curtains aside and glanced out expecting to see something of the city below, but solid brick wall ten feet away blocked any hope of a view.

He deposited his backpack and valise in the room, took off his shoes, and lay down on the bed. In a few minutes he was fast asleep. It was 9:00 p.m. before he awoke. Refreshed and hungry, he hurried downstairs and into the city street. He searched for the Chinese restaurant and saw a restaurant sign named "Hop Sing" a block down the street from the hotel. Inside the Hop Sing restaurant, it was drab and poorly lit and contained eight tables, with only one unoccupied. Todd sat down at the empty table under a large painting of a dragon and examined the soiled menu. It was unreadable, every item written in Chinese characters. After a few minutes, a waiter came over to the table and asked, "What you order?"

Todd didn't know what to order, so he randomly pointed to a menu item and said, "I'll have that."

"No, too much," the waiter said pensively.

Todd looked over to the table next to his and noticed both customers eagerly eating from bowls of rice laced with chunks of fish. I'll have what they are having," he said.

"Too much," the waiter repeated.

"It will be all right. I'll just eat as much as I can."

The waiter looked confused. "Too much," he repeated, this time more forcefully.

"Just bring me a bowl of rice with fish like those customers are eating, and I will also have a beer."

The waiter shrugged his shoulders and disappeared into the kitchen. Seconds later a flood of shouting in Chinese erupted from the kitchen. Considering the volume of raised voices, it sounded more like an argument than a discussion. Five minutes later the waiter reappeared with a steaming bowl of rice and fish and set it in front of Todd with a pair of chopsticks and a glass of foamy, warm beer. Todd took the chopsticks and raised a bite to his mouth. Wow! Whatever was in this dish was hot, very hot indeed. Todd's mouth burned. He reached for the beer and took a long soothing swig. The waiter stood a few tables away watching Todd and an inscrutable smile graced his face.

"The waiter must have meant 'too hot' not 'too much,' Todd surmised. He was hungry, so ignoring the fire in his mouth he ate the entire bowl of rice, putting out the inferno with sips of lukewarm beer.

Returning to his hotel room, he undressed and climbed into bed. The hotel seemed unusually noisy for this time of night, but Todd thought it would quiet down as the other guests settled in for the night, but it didn't. People laughed and chatted in the hallways and came and went all nightlong, opening and slamming doors without regard for others who wanted to sleep. Despite the clamor, he eventually fell asleep only to be awakened by loud noises coming from the room next door. The paper-thin walls did little to muffle the sounds his neighbors were making. Their laughter and the rhythmic thumping and squeaking of bedsprings gained in cadence until after a muffled shriek, the noise suddenly stopped. More doors opened and closed and after a short period of quiet, the clamor next door resumed. Todd realized that he had booked a room in a hotel that rented rooms by the hour. *No wonder the clerk suggested I'd be more comfortable in another hotel,* he thought. Business continued unabated well into the wee hours of the morning.

At the first hint of daylight, Todd dressed, checked out of the hotel, and returned to the train station. His train was due to leave two hours later at 8:00 a.m., so he looked around for somewhere to eat breakfast. He couldn't find a restaurant in the train station, but a cart at one end of the lobby was selling hot muffins and coffee. He purchased a muffin and a cup of steaming coffee and sat down to eat and wait for the call to board his 8:00 a.m. train. The "all aboard" call came at 7:45. He climbed aboard the train waiting on track six and found a seat on the car at the front of the train. At exactly 8:00 a.m., the train whistle blew twice and the train chugged out of the station and headed toward St. Paul. The train stopped at every small station along the way and waited for some time at Madison to allow the engineers to load more coal and water. Tired from a lack of sleep the previous evening, Todd laid his head on a pillow and closed his eyes. Soon the rhythmic clickety-clack of the train wheels and gentle swaying of the car lulled him into a fitful sleep. He awoke with a start when the conductor came through the car announcing that the next stop would be Eau Claire, a three-hour train ride from St. Paul. He looked out the window and noticed that the sun was low in the western sky. Somehow, he had snoozed all the way across Wisconsin, from Madison to Eau Claire, 250 miles. An hour after the stop at Eau Claire, the conductor announced the next station was Manomonie, and then two hours after that he came through to announce St. Paul. The train pulled into the St. Paul station and shuddered to a stop. Todd gathered his valise and backpack, and then climbed onto the platform. He was supposed to meet at the chancery the next day, April 22, with Father Quinn and Bishop Byrne. It was evening, so his next task was to find a room for the night. The city of St. Paul was not nearly as big as Baltimore or Chicago, yet the train station was busier and larger than Todd expected. He found a taxi buggy waiting outside the station and instructed the horseman to take him to a hotel closest to the St. Paul Cathedral and diocesan chancery. He checked into the hotel and although well rested from his long sleep on the train, that night he slept soundly.

Chapter 3
Minnesota

Todd woke with a start to a bright shaft of sunshine streaming in from the only window in his room. He looked at his pocket watch. It read 8:20 a.m. He left his possessions in his room and told the clerk he would be staying through Friday night. Today he was supposed to meet with Bishop Byrne and Father Quinn, but did not have a specific time. The hotel clerk told him St. Paul's Cathedral was up the hill from the hotel and wouldn't be hard to find.

"Just look for the twin bell towers," he suggested.

The street outside was congested with people, horses, and wagons. He was hungry but breakfast could wait, and perhaps because he was fasting, he could ask to say Mass at the cathedral. He walked up the hill and from the summit and on an even higher hill, he could see the Cathedral towers gleaming in the morning sun. The gothic-style church dominated the entire top of the hill, its twin towers each topped with a huge cross looked over the entire city. *The two-story brick building next to the church must be chancery,* he thought. Todd climbed the chancery stairs, entered the building, and approached the desk at the center of the lobby. An elderly woman greeted him as he stepped forward.

"Good day, Father. How may I help you?"

Todd smiled and said, "I'm Father Todd Bose from Baltimore. I am supposed to meet with the Bishop today."

The woman frowned. "What time is your appointment?"

"I wasn't given a specific time. I just arrived in town last night and my instructions are to meet with Bishop Byrne today. If it isn't convenient to meet with the bishop this morning, would you be so kind to schedule a time for me later today and I will return then. I am staying at the Palace Hotel."

"I would be glad to do so except that Bishop Byrne left this morning and will be out of the office today and tomorrow. He is across the river in Minneapolis and isn't expected to return until Saturday afternoon."

Todd was taken aback.

"Oh my, this is a problem because I am supposed to see the bishop on my arrival from Baltimore. You see, I am the new missionary from Baltimore and the pastor for the community of Whitefish. The weekly steamboat leaves for Grand Rapids tomorrow morning, and on Monday I am to meet a Mr. Mike Dunn who will take me to Whitefish."

She smiled. "Father Bose, you must be the missionary that Father John Quinn, our cathedral pastor, was expecting. My name is Mrs. Penrose. Father Quinn is responsible for helping immigrants from the East Coast to settle in Minnesota. Father is deeply involved in this project, especially since the government offered homesteading land in Northern Minnesota. Whitefish is his most recent project. I am sure that Father Quinn will want to see you."

Todd relaxed a bit.

"Wait here and I will see if Father is available." Mrs. Penrose got up and walked down the narrow wood-paneled hallway.

A minute later, she came back and asked Todd to follow her down the hall to an office door marked "Father John Quinn, Pastor." She knocked gently. From inside the room a loud clear voice thundered, "Come in."

Todd stood in the doorway as Mrs. Penrose went back down the hallway. Dwarfed by a huge oak desk, the portly white-haired priest dressed in a black cassock and Roman collar looked over his glasses perched at the end of his nose, smiled warmly, and waved Todd inside. "Please, please come in, Father Bose, and have a seat. I've been expecting you."

Father Quinn stood and extended his plump, warm hand over the desk as Todd approached. Todd shook it and sat down.

"And how was your trip from Baltimore?" Father Quinn asked. His smile increased until it almost extended from ear to ear.

"Uneventful, but long and exhausting," Todd answered.

"Can I assume Bishop Allen is in good health back in Baltimore?"

"Oh yes, he is doing very well thank you," Todd said.

"What has Bishop Allen told you about Whitefish?

"I regret that he didn't say very much, except that Whitefish is in the backwoods of Northern Minnesota and the Catholic residents there are Irish pioneers from Boston who have petitioned Bishop Byrne for a resident priest."

"That about sums it up," Father Quinn said as he stood up and walked over to a large map of Minnesota hanging on the wall. He beckoned Todd to join him and traced the contours of the Mississippi River as it snaked from St. Paul to Grand Rapids. He pointed to an east-west range of mountains north of Grand Rapids and marked on the map as the Mesabi Range. Two lakes sat nestled in a narrow valley north of the range. Father had penciled in *Whitefish Lake* beside the larger of the two lakes.

He pointed to his pencil mark and said, "The town lies on the western side of this lake which the locals have named Whitefish. "Are you a fisherman, Father Bose?"

"I have done some fishing in the streams and lakes around my folks' Pennsylvania farm, mostly for trout and bass," Todd answered.

Father Quinn nodded. "Whitefish are native to the Northwest, a species like trout, but they have a lot of bones. The Indians like to smoke them. I suspect this is how the lake got its name."

The area surrounding Whitefish was unmarked except by dozens of small lakes and a few meandering rivers. No roads, towns, or even other villages marked the map within several inches of the spot marked "Whitefish." The only nearby community marked on the map was the town of Grand Rapids. The Canadian border ran across the top of the map and lay a few inches to the north.

Father Quinn cleared his throat. "When I began this immigration project, Whitefish was a community of about forty-five folks, mostly Lutheran families of German extraction. After President Lincoln signed the Homestead Act ten years ago, Bishop Byrne and I began to sponsor families, mostly from the slums of large eastern cities, to homestead in Minnesota. It wasn't long before all the good bottom land in lower Minnesota was homesteaded. Four years ago we sponsored eighteen Catholic families, thirty-three parishioners in all, to migrate from Boston and homestead near Whitefish Lake where there was available land. We provided a few animals, tools, wagons, seed, and farm implements. Nevertheless, it has been difficult for these pioneers the past four years. Each family staked out 160 acres of farmland, cleared and tilled the land, and finally built log cabins and barns. The winters up there are harsh, perhaps the coldest south of Canada. The growing season is short with five months of winter and with only a few summer months to plant and harvest crops. The soil is rich but filled with large rocks deposited by a melting glacier."

Father Quinn looked at Todd who looked a bit bewildered and smiled. "Oh, most folks don't know this, but a glacier once covered all of Northern Minnesota. The same glacier that filled the Great Lakes."

He returned to his desk and invited Todd to have a seat before he continued.

"The newly arrived families had to clear trees and move boulders before they could plant farms. Even four years later, these folks are barely subsisting, yet they are made from sterner stuff than average city folk. You, Father Bose, will be their priest, and they will be your people."

There followed an awkward minute of silence as Todd tried to internalize the remoteness of Whitefish, marked by Father Quinn's pencil.

"How do I get to Whitefish? I didn't see any roads marked on the map."

"You'll take a riverboat to Grand Rapids and from there travel to Whitefish, a couple of days journey on horseback."

Father Quinn handed Todd a folder. Inside was a ticket on the weekly steamboat *Itaska* to Grand Rapids, scheduled to embark from the St. Paul docks at 8:00 a.m. Saturday morning. Todd examined the ticket and looked perplexed.

"Father, I was told to see Bishop Byrne before I left for Whitefish. Now it appears I am scheduled to leave before he returns from Minneapolis."

"I understand your concern. Of course, the Bishop Byrne would like to meet you before you go, but it is not necessary. Your administrator is still Bishop Allen in Baltimore and I am sure you will keep Bishop Byrne and myself informed about how you and your parish are doing. Whitefish parish is in Bishop Byrne's diocese, so he and I will look forward to your monthly reports. Next summer, or perhaps the following fall, both of us intend to visit Whitefish to consecrate the church that your parishioners intend to build, providing that it has been built by then. Keep us informed and we will keep you in our prayers. Have you said Mass yet this morning?"

"No, I was hoping to do so in the cathedral."

"Follow me to the side altar in the cathedral. I said Mass earlier this morning, but I will be happy to serve yours."

Father Quinn led Todd into St. Paul's Cathedral by a side door leading to the sacristy, where Todd vested for Mass. They then entered the empty small side chapel to the right of the main altar where a midmorning Mass was already in progress.

After Mass, Father Quinn asked, "Would you like to join me for brunch?"

"Yes, I would," Todd answered. "I am starving."

Todd followed Father Quinn into the chancery dining room and their housekeeper served them a brunch of ham, eggs, and pancakes.

"I wanted to spend a few minutes alone with you, get to know you better, and tell you a bit about the people in Whitefish before I sent you off," Father Quinn offered between sips of coffee.

Todd smiled as he caressed the crucifix hanging from his neck.

Father Quinn had noticed the crucifix when they met, but up to now he hadn't tried to satisfy his curiosity about it. "Tell me about the crucifix," he asked.

"It was a gift from Bishop Allen," Todd offered. "It contains a relic of St. Paul blessed by Pope Pius IX."

"A very fitting gift indeed for your mission," Father Quinn commented. "St. Paul was the early Church's greatest missionary, and although his mission at times seemed impossible and hopeless, with the help of the Holy Ghost he succeeded in founding many churches and converted hundreds of Gentiles and Jews to Christianity. Yet St. Paul suffered throughout his missionary work. He was threatened, beaten, and imprisoned many times. One time the townsfolk almost threw him off a cliff. All the same, he persevered until his martyrdom. I suspect you will experience your own trials and tribulations, perhaps not as severe as St. Paul's, but severe nevertheless. Keep praying for St. Paul's intersession and he will watch over you."

"I will be sure to do so," Todd promised.

"Life hasn't been easy for the Whitefish immigrants. Life wasn't easy for them in Boston either, but there is no comparison between life in Boston and that in Whitefish. These migrants lack experience as farmers, have little money, and the winters in upper Minnesota are harsh and the land unforgiving. I don't know if there is a colder place in the Midwest USA or a harder place to farm. They are barely subsisting, and just how you are going to find the money to build a church is anyone's guess."

"Somehow God will provide," Todd said.

Father Quinn smiled and took another sip of coffee.

"Mike Dunn who you will meet Monday in Grand Rapids is the person whom you can depend on to help you build this church. I met him last year in Grand Rapids when he petitioned Bishop Allan in the name of the Catholic community to establish a parish in Whitefish. He is a family man and one of integrity and principle, and a master of many trades. He is a leader in the Whitefish community. Place your trust in him as I have."

They finished brunch and returned to Father Quinn's office where he added, "One other bit of business before you depart." He handed him another envelope and said. "Please open it."

Inside was a letter of introduction addressed to the people in Whitefish, a formal document signed by Bishop Byrne forming St. Patrick's parish, and ten $20 greenbacks.

Todd read the letter and the document, counted the money, and placed everything back into the envelope. "Father Quinn, thank you for the cash. I'm sure we will need it in Whitefish. I am curious about selecting Saint Patrick as the parish patron."

"St. Patrick is the patron saint of Ireland, and your new parishioners are from the old sod and know all about the history of this missionary to Ireland. This selection seemed appropriate considering that Patrick's mission was to go form a church in a foreign uncivilized land. Your mission and his have much in common."

Todd thanked Father Quinn. They shook hands and Father Quinn bade him good-bye. Since it was only midday, he decided to walk around town before returning to his hotel.

The afternoon was warm and inviting with cotton ball clouds drifting across the sky. St. Paul's Cathedral occupied a small hill that rose east of the bluffs above the Mississippi river. Todd hiked the few blocks to the lip of the bluff that overlooked the mighty river below. He marveled at the size of the Mississippi, at this point almost a half-mile wide. Barges pushed by tugs traveled up and down the wide river transporting logs, lumber, quarry rocks, and other materials to and from the wharfs that extended a considerable distance down the east side of the river. Across the river the unimposing village of Minneapolis occupied the west side of the Mississippi, sporting a short string of docks and an extensive sawmill and lumberyard marked by gray smoke pouring from a cone-shaped black incinerator. Another lumberyard on Todd's side of the river sat next to the dockyard where dockworkers busily offloaded lumber from wagons and stacked it on a barge tied to the wharf. Docked at the northern end of the wharfs was a small paddle wheel three-deck steamboat. Painted white with red trim and sporting red paddle wheels complete with red splash covers on each side, the steamboat gleamed in the afternoon sun. Two tall fluted black smokestacks protruded from the top deck that housed the wheelhouse in front of a row of staterooms. The middle deck also contained a row of staterooms and several large windows that Todd assumed overlooked a lounge and dining room. Neatly coiled ropes and red painted hatches covered the wood fore deck shared with a large crane. A larger paddleboat was docked some distance further downriver, yet he was too far away to read the names painted on either vessel. Since smoke drifted from the smokestacks and stevedores were busy loading the smaller boat, he assumed that this must be the riverboat *Itaska*.

At the confluence of the Mississippi and a smaller river directly below him, a military compound surrounded by a high stone wall rested on a rise a few yards above the river. *This must be Fort Snelling*, or so he thought. Curious to visit the fort and explore the St. Paul wharfs, he walked down the dusty road leading from the bluff to the river and the fort's open front gate. Unchallenged by a sentry, he walked inside. A dozen wood barracks in need of a coat of paint were arranged in a semicircle around a large parade ground. A US flag with thirty-six stars waved proudly from a tall flag post in the center of the parade ground. A squad of blue coats marched in formation to the singsong cadence of their leader as they rounded the parade ground. A log building with a covered porch dominated the south end of the compound. The large sign hanging over the porch announced *Ft. Snelling Headquarters.* Todd mounted the headquarters steps and stopped at a desk near the entrance. A young private sat at the desk arranging a pile of papers.

He looked up at Todd, noticed the Roman collar, and asked, "Can I help you, Father?"

"I don't have an appointment, but wonder if it would be possible to see the commandant of this fort?"

"You must mean Captain Jeremy Johnson, our post commandant. I will check if he can see you."

The private got up and knocked on the office door behind his desk, and then entered. A few seconds later, he emerged and ushered Todd into the room.

The captain sat behind a large Beachwood desk but stood up and extended his left hand when Todd entered the office. An empty right arm jacket sleeve hung by his side. The balding officer stood over 6 feet high, straight as an arrow, and sported a well-waxed handlebar mustache that extended three inches beyond each corner of his mouth.

"Welcome to Ft. Snelling, Father. I am Captain Jeremy Johnson. How can I be of assistance?"

Todd shook the officer's hand and introduced himself. "I am Father Bose from Baltimore and am traveling to Whitefish. I was hoping you could tell me a little bit about the country north of Grand Rapids."

Captain Johnson looked surprised. "Whitefish you say?"

"Yes, Whitefish."

"I know a bit about Whitefish. It's in the middle of nowhere, north of the town of Grand Rapids. I've been commandant here at Ft.

Snelling since the war ended, yet in all that time I've only been to Whitefish once. There's not much to tell."

Todd pulled out his Minnesota map, unfolded it on the captain's desk, and pointed to a pencil mark and the name Whitefish penciled in northeast of the settlement of Grand Rapids. "This according to Father Quinn is where Whitefish is located."

"Yes, that looks about right," the captain commented. "Calling Grand Rapids a town is a bit of an exaggeration," he said with some obvious distaste. "It is more like a logging camp than a town. What's your business in Whitefish?"

"Bishop Allen of the Baltimore Diocese assigned me as a missionary to Bishop Byrne in St. Paul who has asked me to form a parish and build a church for the eighteen Catholic families living in Whitefish."

"Form a parish and build a church you say. You look like a strong young man, but that's a tall order for a priest."

"The Irish-Catholic immigrants of Whitefish petitioned Bishop Byrne for a priest. I am that priest."

"This must be another of Father Quinn's damn projects," Captain Johnson said sarcastically.

"Yes, Whitefish is his project. Do you know Father Quinn?"

"Yes, but I'd be better-off if I didn't. Father Quinn has been a thorn in my side since he started his immigrant projects. He gets city folks all riled up about free land in Minnesota and then entices them to move here. They come from big eastern cities with stars in their eyes and unprepared for agriculture or the wilderness. They have no idea of what it takes to homestead and grow crops in these parts, and they don't know much about dirt farming either. The first year in Whitefish, they nearly starved and froze to death. I had to go up there with a company of troops to rescue them in the dead of winter. Then in their second year, they got in trouble with the Ojibwa Indians, trespassing on their tribal lands and shooting their deer and elk. This required a trip to Leech Lake to free four immigrants whom the Indians captured for trespassing. If you ask me, Father Quinn and his immigrants are nothing but a big pain in the neck."

The captain's apparent anger grew as he went on.

"They don't respect the treaties we made with the Indians. All this has caused the Army and me big trouble. I keep telling Father Quinn and his flatlanders the Indians have all the Minnesota land west of the Mississippi, especially around Leech Lake, and his people must respect the treaties that our government has made with them. However, they don't listen. They fish and hunt on Indian land and have desecrated sacred Indian burial grounds. With another of Fr. Quinn's projects three years ago it almost came to a shooting war and only through diplomacy and a hatful of compromises was I able to free some captured immigrants from Leech Lake. I imagine someday I'll have to go again to Whitefish on another rescue mission, and I won't be happy when I come."

Father Bose tried to change the subject. "I see that you lost your arm. In the war I suppose."

"Yes, at Gettysburg. I lost it because of damn gangrene caused by what only amounted to a scratch that I got when some damned Reb tried to spear me with his saber. Shot the cuss dead, but I lost my arm because of poor doctoring."

"I spent a year treating soldiers in a Baltimore hospital," Todd explained. "I've seen more cases of gangrene and amputated more limbs than I care to remember. I am sorry for your loss."

Captain Johnson managed a slight smile and then stood up and shook his hand. "There's not much more that I can help you with. Take my warning and stay away from the Indians and their lands. They are mean cusses who would sooner stake you out for the ants to eat than shoot you. In my way of thinking, the only good Indian is a dead Indian. I wish you luck in your mission, Father, and I expect we will meet again someday."

Todd left the fort shocked by the captain's outspoken contempt for the Indians and disappointed that he couldn't offer much information about Whitefish or the upper Minnesota countryside. He hiked along the wagon trail leading to the docks upriver from the fort and surveyed the waterfront. Several warehouses and a tavern named "Pig's Eye" sat beside the road that paralleled the wharfs. *A strange name for a tavern*, he thought. It was mid-afternoon but as he passed by, bawdy piano music and laughter drifted out the doublewide half-doors. A red lamp flickered from an upstairs window. Two scantily clad women sat on the front porch and beckoned him inside with smiles and waves. He ignored the women and hastened his pace aware that for a traveling missionary priest, this was an establishment he should avoid. He walked alongside the wharf toward the paddle wheel riverboat docked at the far end, where workers were busily preparing the boat for departure. Four stevedores unloaded freight from two wagons parked on the road alongside the wharf and several deck hands wrestled cargo into the hold. A wisp of smoke drifted from the two tall smokestacks and as he came closer, he could read the name painted on the boat prow, *Itaska*. He climbed up the gangplank and asked a deckhand where he might find the captain. The man directed him to the captain's cabin located on the top deck next to the wheelhouse. He knocked on the door.

"Come in," a gravel voice commanded. The captain was standing beside his desk examining Mississippi river charts spread on a table before him. A short burly man with penetrating deep blue eyes, a large tousled black beard, and as bald as a cannonball held out his hand and said, "Da name's Captain Pinot, and who might ye be?"

Father Bose grasped the large calloused hand, introduced himself, and then explained that he had passage on the *Itaska* scheduled to sail to Grand Rapids in the morning.

"What business 'ave ye in Grand Rapids?" the captain asked. "Tis nary but a bawdy lumber camp wi'd a general store, a whorehouse, a saloon, a livery stable, and lumber mill, but no church. I doubt dem folks up dere will be very welcoming to a priest."

"Grand Rapids is not my destination. I am meeting a parishioner on Monday who will take me on horseback to Whitefish where I am to establish a parish and build a church."

"Build a church ya say. Damn, your business is your business, but I sure hope you's prepared fer a big disappointment. Most of dem folks who go to upper Minnesota ta farm only finds frustration in dem woods. It's a harsh life up dere, an' nary one for the likes of a young priest. Der's no colder place in da States dan upper Minnesota in da winter. Can't see how dem folks can grow anything. And talk 'bout isolated. It's so cold in Grand Rapids dat wid all dat ice on der river da *Itaska* don't go past Brainerd in da winter months."

The captain stared at Father Bose, hardly believing what he saw. After an uncomfortable pause he added, "But wa'da I know 'bout farming," he said. "I'm just an old sea-salt riverboat captain who couldn't dig in da dirt or hunt if and my damn life depended on it."

Todd didn't comment but instead turned his attention to the detailed river map on the table. The river details didn't interest him, but this was the best map he had yet seen of the surrounding countryside.

"Tell me about the river and the countryside around Grand Rapids," Todd prodded.

"I don't know much about da countryside, but I does know 'bout dis Mississippi River headwaters. I knows it like the back o' my hand. Der river betwixt Brainerd and Grand Rapids is called da headwaters country, der place where der ol' Miss starts her long journey to New Orleans. The trouble be dat da damn river 'bout here keeps changing its mind. Ornery cuss, the headwaters is. Ya can't count on what ya think ya knows. Sandbars appears and disappears overnight, and on each passage new channels opens, and der old ones finds anodder route. Der rapids above dat town is da northern most of navigable waters. I been over every mile of dis river, from da Gulf ta Grand Rapids and back, but no stretch is harder to navigate den der headwaters. One hundred and seventy miles by river and 'bout two and a half-day's cruising from here to the headwaters. Could make it to Grand Rapids in less than a day en a half if I ran at night, but I don't run at night 'cause some big log cumin' down da river could sink us or we could get hung up on a sandbar, so I ties her up in Brainerd at night. The *Itaska* makes da trip once a week ta load lumber from der mill an' deliver supplies to the folks up der. The *Itaska* serves all der small settlements along der river and Brainerd be der only town of any size between here and da Rapids. Other than some smelly lumberjacks headed upriver ta some small mills north of Brainerd, you's be da only passenger headed all the way to Grand Rapids. We'll 'ave several passengers on board tomorrow morning that be headed ta Brainerd."

It was getting late and Todd was beginning to feel tired. It was time to thank the captain for his information, such as it was, and head back to the hotel. When he got back from the long walk he was exhausted, too tired to even eat dinner. He asked the desk clerk to arrange for a buggy in the morning and went up to his room and collapsed on his bed. He slept all that night, and woke Saturday morning when he heard doors opening and closing. He dressed and looked outside. The predawn sky was just beginning to brighten He gathered his belongings, went downstairs, and checked out. After asking the desk clerk to call a taxi, he ducked into the small hotel restaurant for breakfast while he waited for the buggy.

The *Itaska* was getting up steam when he arrived at the docks just as the sun rose. A stevedore showed him to his cabin, the stateroom next to the captain's on the top deck Todd watched from the second deck as four lumberjacks, a young man and his wife with two small children came aboard. The last passenger to board was a tall man dressed in Indian garb. At eight o'clock the *Itaska* slipped its moorings, sounded its whistle, and the paddle wheels began churning the green water. Heavy black smoke poured from the two smokestacks as the riverboat labored upstream and raised a wake that lapped against the shoreline and rocked boats anchored in the river. Upriver the *Itaska* chased rafts of geese to take flight, yet the ducks and coots in the boat's path only scooted across the river to get out of the way.

This Saturday morning the Mississippi was as smooth as glass and Todd watched as rings formed betraying fish as they surfaced to eat insects. Near the shoreline, wisps of fog lifted from the river and, stirred by light winds, dissipated into the cool morning air. Both the eastern and western shores were thick with pine, birch, and spruce forests with few signs of human habitation except when on occasion the forest parted to display a lone shack surrounded by plowed fields and an adjoining dock. For miles, they passed nothing as substantial as a town or village on either side of the river.

As Todd enjoyed watching the river, he noticed a man dressed in a long coat standing alone on the prow. Wishing to talk with a fellow passenger, he walked up to the stranger and said hello. Startled, the man spun around to face him. He was a head taller than Todd was and built with an athlete's physique. His coat momentarily parted to reveal the man's clothes: a beaded chest vest and leather skirt. His garb and chiseled brown face confirmed Todd's initial assumption that he was an American Indian. Todd stifled the impulse to raise his hand and say "How" but instead extended an open hand. The man refused to take it, but instead returned Todd's greeting with a grunt and not even a hint of a smile. Todd withdrew his empty hand and introduced himself. The man turned away and declared, "You Blackrobe."

Todd nodded, "Yes, I am a priest."

The man's expression remained unchanged but he relaxed a bit.

"I know Blackrobes. They come to my village many moons ago and pour water on tribe foreheads. I know this is white man's magic so I keep away and don't talk to Blackrobes. You want to pour water on my forehead?"

"No, I have no intention of pouring water on your head. I just wanted to talk with you. What is your name?"

"White skins call me Running Bear, but my name in Anishinabe is Tecumseh. Where you go?"

"I'm going to Grand Rapids and then on to Whitefish. Do you know of Whitefish?"

Running Bear turned to face Todd and his forehead furrowed. "I know. White skins from there try to hunt our land. We chase them off."

He abruptly turned away and resumed watching the river. Todd understood that he did not wish to talk, so he went to the lounge for a cup of coffee and a biscuit, then back to his stateroom to say the "Office of the Hours" that all priests pray each day.

At 1:00 p.m., the ship's bell sounded and the captain invited Todd and the other seven passengers to join him in the main lounge for lunch served with venison stew and black bread. A large bowl of peanuts sat on the table and all during lunch a small boy shelled and ate peanuts. That afternoon the boy complained to his parents of a stomachache that grew progressively worse. Todd, Running Bear, and the captain were in the lounge when the boy's mother and father brought the boy inside and asked if anyone could help him.

"What is wrong?" Todd asked the boy.

Doubled over in pain, he couldn't speak.

Running Bear grunted and said, "The boy eat many peanuts. I see bad stomach before. He will die."

The boy's mother and father were horrified at this pronouncement. Todd reassured them that he had treated such stomachaches before, and the boy would not die.

"Get me a glass of warm water and some table salt," Todd directed the captain, who obliged.

Todd then poured a heaping tablespoon of salt into the glass, stirred it, and then gave it to the boy's father and instructed him to make the boy drink it.

"What good will this do?" the boy's father protested. "It will probably make him even sicker."

"No, it will cure him," Todd argued. He could see the father was skeptical and was not about to give the boy warm saltwater.

"Watch this demonstration," Todd said.

He took a mouthful of peanuts and chewed them into a spitball and then spit the ball into a shallow dish and poured the warm saltwater over the spitball. Immediately the peanut ball slowly began to disintegrate. The boy's father then forced his son to drink the glass of warm saltwater. Running Bear watched in bewilderment, but said nothing. Fifteen minutes later after a visit to the head the boy was again smiling and none the worse for the experience.

The boy's father extended his hand to Todd. "My name is Seth Meriwether, and this is my wife June. The boy's name is Tom. I am called the tinker in these parts. I sell pots and pans, utensils, and various tools. Where are you going?"

"I get off in Grand Rapids, but I'm headed to Whitefish."

"Whitefish you say. I visit there once or twice a year to sell my wares. Why are you going to Whitefish?"

"Bishop Byrne has asked me to establish a parish and build a church for the good folks of Whitefish."

"That's a tall order. Those Whitefish folks don't have much money to build a church and barely have enough cash to buy a few of my pots and pans or tools. It's hardly worth my trip up there."

Later that evening they pulled into the small settlement of Brainerd, where Captain Pinot tied the *Itaska* up for the night announcing, "Don't make much sense ta navigate der upper parts of dis river in da dark. Most likely we'd end hung up on a sandbar or put a log through da hull."

The passengers including Running Bear disembarked, and Todd and the four lumberjacks remained as the only passengers intending to continue upriver. As Todd ate dinner that night with the captain, he asked if he would have time to visit the town in the morning. Captain Pinot warned him the *Itaska* would be leaving before 9:00 a.m., and he should immediately return to the boat as soon as he heard the whistle. Early Sunday morning as the sun rose, Todd dressed and went into the small town. A whitewashed church at the end of the main street immediately caught his attention. The sign outside announced, *St. Martin's Lutheran Church. Sunday Services at 9:00 a.m.* Todd went inside where the minister was preparing for the morning service. Surprised to see a Catholic priest enter his church, the minister asked his name and what business he had in town. Todd told him that he was traveling to Grand Rapids on the *Itaska*, and it didn't seem right not to visit the only church in town on Sunday.

The minister looked surprised, but he recovered and warmly shook Todd's hand, saying, "I am Deacon Everett. Our church is Lutheran, Father, but you're most welcome to stay and attend our Sunday service at nine."

Todd said the *Itaska* was leaving at nine that morning, but he stayed until he heard the boat whistle sound. He hurried back to the riverboat and after they were underway, Captain Pinot invited him into the wheelhouse. Navigation along this part of the Mississippi headwaters was tricky. The captain said charts were almost useless, as sandbars and depth soundings kept changing. He navigated by spying the river ahead with a small telescope and judging depth by the ripples and river flow. He weaved a zigzag course upriver, navigating around sandbars and avoiding logs and other debris. Three hours after leaving Brainerd, the *Itaska* pulled into a lumber camp and discharged the lumberjacks, and then that evening docked at Grand Rapids. Todd went to the captain's cabin and thanked him for a safe passage.

Captain Pinot shook his hand and handed him a satchel. "Would ya be so kind ta gives dis ta the hotel clerk in town? It's da weekly mail delivery fer Grand Rapids."

Todd took the satchel and made his way down the muddy main street toward a large brown two-story log building in the middle of town named the Grand Hotel. The rustic Hotel, Restaurant and Bathhouse complete with a large covered porch, was one of six buildings that lined the muddy street. A sign hanging over the porch announced, "*Rooms for Rent by the Hour, Night, or Week.*" Next to the hotel sat the General Mercantile, and next to it a barbershop. Across the street were the Rapids Saloon and the J. Yearling Livery Stable. A Community Center completed the commercial part of the town of Grand Rapids. At the west end several houses, a few no more than hastily constructed shanties, lined both sides of the street. A loose plank sidewalk ran between the main downtown buildings. Todd climbed onto the porch, entered the Grand Hotel lobby, and rang the desk bell. An elderly man with a generous white beard appeared from a backroom.

"What can I do for you?" he asked.

"Do you have a room for the night?" Todd inquired.

The clerk turned around to a 4 x 5 board festooned with a dozen hooks, each numbered from one to twelve. A key hung from each hook except for the empty hook intended for number four.

"Pick any room you want. You will be our second guest tonight."

Todd chose room number two and handed the clerk the mail satchel.

"Captain Pinot asked me to give you the mail."

"Thank you," the clerk said as he dumped two dozen letters onto the counter.

The clerk then pushed the register his way. "Father, if you will please sign the register."

After Todd did so, the clerk turned the register around to read the name.

"Father Todd Bose, from Baltimore," he read aloud. "And if I might be so bold to ask, what is your business in Grand Rapids?"

"I have no business in Grand Rapids other than to meet Mr. Mike Dunn from Whitefish. He will be here tomorrow morning to take me to the town of Whitefish Lake."

"Whitefish ain't much you could call a town, hardly even a village. Anyway, Mike is already here. He checked in this morning but is not in his room right now."

"Do you know where I might find him?"

"You might try the saloon across the street."

Todd took his backpack and valise upstairs and opened the door to room number two. It was small with a double bed, dresser, and a table and chair. An oil lamp rested on the table. The room smelled musty. He sat on the bed and it sagged under his weight. He placed his backpack and valise on the bed and went over to the single window that looked out onto the street and opened it. A second-floor porch extended over the entire front of the hotel with a set of stairs at the far end leading to the street below. Going downstairs, he walked across the muddy street and pushed open the double half doors of the saloon aside. Three patrons sat at the bar and five others sat around a table playing poker. Three women dressed in fancy clothes and covered in garish makeup sat at another table and smiled at him when he entered. Todd asked the barkeep if he knew where he could find Mike Dunn. The barkeep nodded to one fellow sitting alone at the far end of the bar. The man was large, almost too big for the bar stool on which he sat. He wore coveralls held up by red suspenders, a red and black wool shirt, and mud-caked boots. A few wisps of black hair escaped from beneath his well-worn cowboy hat held in place by large ears. A wiry black beard accentuated by a handlebar mustache completed the persona of a dirt farmer. He seemed absorbed in his mug of beer, and didn't notice Todd until he took the stool next to him.

"You must be Mike Dunn," Todd surmised.

The man looked up from his beer, smiled, and said, "And you must be Father Bose."

Mike extended his large calloused hand. "Glad to make your acquaintance, Father."

Todd accepted Mike's hand. He shook Todd's as if he were working a pump handle.

"Wasn't 'specting you 'till tomorrow or later tonight," Mike said. "The *Itaska* must have docked early. Now that I've made your acquaintance, can I buy you a beer?" He paused thinking better of his offer, and then added, "Or would it be improper to offer a beer to a priest?"

The afternoon was hot and Todd was thirsty. "No, it would not be wrong to offer me a beer on such a hot evening. Thank you."

"Hey, barkeep ... a cold beer for the good padre," Mike shouted.

"We don't have good beer up in Whitefish, and the homebrew that the saloon has usually serves it warm," Mike lamented as the barkeep placed a foamy mug in front of Todd, "so every time I'm in town I make sure to sip one or two cold ones."

Todd took a swig of beer chilled in a root cellar, wiped the foam from his lip, looked long and hard into Mike's deep-set, moist eyes and then asked, "Tell me about Whitefish."

"So what would you like to know?" Mike asked between sips of beer.

"Just about everything. All that Father Quinn offered about the town was that it is in the wilderness and the new townsfolk have had a hard life, but are good Catholics made from sterner stuff than the average immigrant."

"Yea, well that 'bout sums it up. Hard life indeed! The first year I farmed up there the crops failed, and without the generosity of the Whitefish Lutherans, us former Bostonians would have starved. Then the second winter was colder yet, the harshest winter these parts had seen in several years. We nearly froze to death. It was so cold the mercury thermometers froze at minus 40. Whitefish is far from ideal farmland. The rocky soil is difficult to clear and farm, and last year an early frost ruined much of the crop before anyone could harvest it. With the last frost in early June and first frost in late September, the growing season is short, only four months long. Had it not been for the Army rescue mission from Ft. Stillwell, the whole community would not have made it through that winter."

Todd smiled. "Yes, I met Captain Johnson and he told me about bringing you food that winter."

"Well, the Army saved us but Captain Johnson didn't seem at all happy about doing it. I presume you met with Fr. Quinn in St. Paul. How's he doing?"

"He's well and busy as pastor of St. Paul's Cathedral, but he didn't tell me much about Whitefish."

"Didn't want to scare you off, I 'specs," Mike said with a twinkle in his eye.

Todd laughed. "Tell me about my parishioners."

"Not much to tell. We're just a bunch of Irish Catholics from the Boston slums. Not big on book learning and we are just finding out what it takes to farm in these parts, yet these are honest, hardworking folks. We miss the Sacraments and a priest to tend our souls, and you, Father, can supply both. This summer and fall we intend to build a church. Bishop Byrne and Fr. Quinn wrote a letter explaining that you were coming and telling us that the new parish advocate is St. Patrick. They intend to come up here next spring and dedicate the church to him."

"That's what Fr. Quinn also explained to me. What are our plans for tomorrow?" Todd asked.

"Our horses are across the street in the livery. We should get an early start tomorrow. It will be a long hard ride to Whitefish, which is 40 miles northwest of here and longer than that by trail. It will be a good two-day's ride and we will make camp tomorrow night at the halfway mark. I hope you're comfortable on a horse."

"No problem there. I was raised on a farm in western Pennsylvania. I know how to ride and take care of horses."

"I'm sure glad to hear that. I was afraid Fr. Quinn might have sent us a city greenhorn."

They finished their beer and went back to the hotel for dinner. Todd slept well that night but a knock on the door woke him while it was still dark outside. He opened the door to see Mike all dressed and ready to ride.

"Better get ready and gather your stuff. Meet me at the livery stable."

Todd dressed, went downstairs, and checked out. The clerk, who was also the postmaster for the community, had sorted the mail and set aside a stack of letters.

"These letters are for Whitefish," he said. "Please take them to Mike who will be sure to deliver them.

Mike waited impatiently for Todd at the stable. He held the reins of three sturdy horses, each a dozen or more hands high. He nodded to Todd as he came inside and noticed that besides the stack of mail, he only carried a backpack and one valise with him.

"Is that all you have with you, Father?" he asked as he stuffed the mail in his saddlebag.

"Yes, this is it. The rest of my stuff will arrive here in Grand Rapids in another week or two."

"I guess I can pick your things up when I next come to town, but that might not be until next month. I hope there is nothing that you will immediately need."

"No, I have all the essentials with me."

"Tie your stuff onto the packhorse and we'll be ready to go."

Todd's horse was a five-year-old palomino mare named Molly. Mike claimed she was well trained and gentle. "I thought you might not know how to ride, being a priest and all, so I picked the gentlest horse in Whitefish for you."

"I appreciate the thought, but I know how to ride," Todd assured him as he rubbed Molly's nose and then placed his foot in the stirrup and deftly swung his leg over the saddle.

"I can see you do," Mike commented, half expecting the priest to try to mount Molly from the wrong side.

Mike mounted his horse, a grey mare he called Bandit, and led the way out of town.

The trail followed the Mississippi River, now only a hundred feet wide or so as it flowed from the northwest through the gently inclined countryside. A short distance upriver, the entire Mississippi emerged from narrow cannon and cascaded over a series of small waterfalls, each two to four feet high. Spray from the resulting white-water rapids dripped from nearby moss-covered rocks. A vivid rainbow arched across the river, beginning on the western shore and ending over the trail on the eastern shore. Mike turned around and said something about the rainbow, yet Todd following several yards behind couldn't hear him over the thunder created by the falls. Todd caught up to Mike and asked him what he had said.

"This is the Grand Rapids," Mike repeated, "which marks the northern extent of Mississippi navigability. All the country to the west and south of the falls belongs to the Dakota Ojibwa Indians and, according to the treaty with them, white folks are forbidden to trespass, hunt, or fish on their lands. Unfortunately, many immigrants have done just that and caused a lot of trouble for the Army by doing so."

They followed the river north for a few miles and then rounding a curve, a large rock-strewn stream joined the Mississippi from the north and the main river continued in a westerly direction. They rode in silence for several more hours until the trail came to a large deep blue lake that emptied into the river. Mike called it Winnibigoshish Lake, a primary source of the Mississippi and a good spot to rest the horses and have lunch. He dug around in his saddlebag and found a hunk of cheese, a loaf of sourdough bread, and a bottle of wine. After lunch, the trail skirted the eastern shore of Winnibigoshish Lake until it veered away and then continued north, gradually gaining altitude and passing through thick woods of red pine, black spruce, and isolated stands of birch and aspen. From the top of a pass, the trail wound down to another lake, much smaller than Winnibigoshish, with an outlet stream that flowed north.

"We've now crossed over the continental divide," Mike said. "All the rivers south of the pass flow to the Gulf of Mexico, while all the waters north of here eventually flow into Hudson Bay. The trail we are now on follows the Big Fork River that flows into Canada."

Later that afternoon they came to a large meadow dominated by a shallow pond. Three moose, one with a huge rack, were munching on weeds that they tore from the pond in bunches that hung from their mouths. The trail ran across the meadow skirting the pond but passing only yards from the moose.

"Best we stay away from those critters," Mike warned. "At times, the bulls can be real cranky."

They skirted the meadow and rejoined the trail that had become barely visible as it meandered through the thick woods.

At dusk, they came to the edge of another meadow. Mike halted and climbed down from his horse.

"We've come about halfway, and tomorrow we will have a bit of a climb to cross over the Mesabi Range. This is a good spot to make camp for the night," Mike said. A brook made its way through the clearing and disappeared into the forest. A fire ring confirmed that others had camped in this spot.

Mike staked out the horses and then announced, "I'm going to go catch some dinner. Please get a fire started while I'm gone." A half hour latter Mike returned with a string of 8-inch brook trout. He cleaned and covered them with flour and then laid them in a greased fry pan and placed it on a folding wire grill over the fire.

After dinner, they retrieved bedrolls from the packhorse and as night fell, they climbed into their bedrolls and wished each other goodnight. Coyotes yelped in the distance making Todd thankful for the fire. He lay on his back and scanned the firmament. Countless stars blazed in the moonless sky looking like little jewels set on a velvet tapestry. An especially bright star shone without twinkling as all the others did. *This must be a planet*, he thought, remembering that planets did not usually twinkle. *Perhaps it is Jupiter or Venus*, he thought, and his pondering soon put him to sleep.

Mike shook him awake in the predawn twilight. "Time to get underway," he said.

After a quick breakfast of flapjacks, which tasted a bit fishy because Mike fried them in the same skillet that he had used to cook the fish, they broke camp and resumed their journey on the narrow, indistinct trail. Riding in single file, Bandit led the way with the packhorse in tow. At first, Molly followed close behind Bandit and the packhorse, but this morning she seemed in no hurry and even with Todd's gentle prodding, they were soon a hundred feet or more behind Bandit and the packhorse. The morning chill penetrated Todd's coat and shirt and soon he was shivering. Walking would warm him, so even though they were a bit behind, he climbed down from Molly and led her along the faint trail. Mike seemed unaware that Todd was on foot and when he disappeared around a bend, he was too far ahead to hear Todd's cries to wait up. When Todd rounded the same bend, Mike was nowhere in sight. He remounted Molly and spurred her to catch up, but after a quarter of a mile and a few more bends in the trail, they came to a fork and Mike was nowhere to be seen. He had no idea which trail Mike had taken. He called out again for Mike, but the thick woods only served to muffle his cries. He knew that Mike would soon discover that he was no longer behind him and come back looking for him. Rather than take the wrong trail, he thought it best to dismount and wait for Mike to return to the fork. Todd sat down on a log and waited. A half hour went by and then an hour with no sign of Mike.

Bandit and Mike must have gotten a lot further ahead than I imagined, he thought. Panic began to grow in Todd's gut. Why hadn't Mike noticed Todd and Molly were no longer behind him? By now, he should have returned. He called out again, but as before the woods swallowed his shouting. It was cold in the dim, damp woods and after sitting still for over an hour, he again began to shiver. He needed to get moving, but a tough decision faced him. He could shiver and wait here for Mike to return, or warm up by walking out. Nevertheless, if he chose the wrong trail it could lead him even deeper into these unfamiliar woods. He searched each trail for signs of recent tracks, but both trails showed recent prints and Todd had no experience as a tracker. Hid panic deepened and he began to imagine what it might be like to be lost in these dense, unfriendly woods. He let go of Molly's reins, said a quick prayer, and flipped a coin. If heads, he would hike the left trail, and if tails the right one. Heads it was, so he left an arrow of pebbles pointing to the left trail, mounted Molly, and started down the trail, urging Molly to go a bit faster. After a half hour with still no sign of Mike, he began to regret leaving the fork. Perhaps he should go back. Just then, he noticed a pile of fresh horse manure on the trail. Wisps of steam floated up in the morning chill. God had answered his prayer and Todd had made the right choice. Mike had to be somewhere close by along this trail, but how had he gotten so far ahead without discovering that Todd was no longer behind him? He encouraged Molly to hasten down the trail before Mike got any further ahead. Rounding a bend, he almost ran right into Mike who was backtracking to find him.

"What the devil...!," Mike yelled as he spied Molly and Todd. Sounding exasperated, he barked, "Where in heaven's name have you been?"

Todd defended himself. "I was cold and decided to walk Molly for a while to warm up. I yelled for you to wait up but you didn't hear me. In no time, you were far ahead and never looked back to see how I was doing."

"The truth is that I dozed off in the saddle, as I often do on the trail. Bandit knows the trail home, so I usually just let her plod along. When I finally woke up and discovered you weren't behind me, I started back praying that you didn't take the wrong trail at that fork. And here you are, by the grace of God safe and sound."

Todd took off his hat and wiped the sweat from his brow with a bandana. "To say I was upset and angry with you would be an understatement," Todd emphasized. "I could have never found my way to Whitefish."

Mike spit out a stream of yellow tobacco juice, deftly hitting a nearby tree.

"You should have just let Molly choose the trail for you. Like Bandit, she knows her way home."

Todd noticed that Mike had wrapped his hand in a kerchief that was now soaked with blood.

"What happened to your hand?"

"In my haste to find you, I let Bandit run under a low hanging branch. I tried to push it out of the way and cut my hand."

"Let me have a look at it"

"Aw, it's nothing," Mike claimed.

"I was a premed student in college and worked in a hospital for over a year caring for wounded soldiers. I know a bad wound when I see one. Let me see your hand."

They dismounted and Mike reluctantly extended his hand. Todd gently unwrapped the kerchief. A three-inch gash crossed Mike's palm.

"I'm going to have to suture this," Todd said. "Do you have a medical kit?"

Most riders carried a medical kit in their saddlebags, and Mike retrieved his and handed it to Todd. Inside was some cotton, a folded handkerchief, a needle, pig sinew, and small bottle of brandy. The bottle was empty. Todd held the bottle up and scowled.

"Drank it on the way into town," Mike said sheepishly.

Todd got his Mass kit out and found a small cruet of wine. "This will have to serve as an antiseptic," he said. Mike cringed as Todd poured the wine on the wound and deftly sutured it.

Mike smiled as Todd wrapped the wound in the clean handkerchief. "You're a man of many talents. Didn't know I had a doctor and priest on the trail with me."

"I'm not a doctor," Todd protested. "I've just had some medical training and experience."

"Nevertheless, I can see that you know more about doctoring than most folks. The only one with any medical knowledge in Whitefish is our barber. Thanks for fixing my hand."

They rode in single file until noon, when Mike decided to stop beside a small lake for lunch. He retrieved another hunk of cheese and bread from his saddlebag and handed some to Todd.

"This cheese is good. Did you buy it in town?"

"Naw. We make and age it ourselves. It's churned from the heavy cream our cows give, and aged in barrels."

"And the sourdough bread? Did you bake that as well?"

"I did. I got a starter from a trapper and Jerry built us a stone oven. Mary bakes all our bread from wheat that I grow on my farm."

"Jerry? Mary?" Todd asked.

"Mary's my wife, and Jerry Kagan is our closest neighbor and the proprietor of the Mercantile. You'll meet them tonight when we arrive home. In fact, you'll meet the entire parish tonight. Mary has planned a big welcoming party for you."

"How much further is it to Whitefish?"

"Oh, I'd say about four or five hours ride from here. We should be getting in about supper time."

Chapter 4
Whitefish

Late April 1872

The climb over the Mesabi mountain range that extended across northern Minnesota from northeast to southwest required a gradual one-thousand-foot climb that Mike and Todd summited by early afternoon. Todd looked down on a shallow green valley covered by patches of forest separated by wide meadows and a few small lakes. A small stream wandered down the center of the valley and emptied into a large lake situated at the eastern end of the valley. Mike took out a pair of binoculars and handed them to Todd.

"That's Whitefish Lake down there, the large one at the end of the valley," Mike said. "My farm is in that meadow about two miles west of the lake."

Todd counted several dozen farms in clearings, each well separated from their closest neighbors by surrounding forest.

"The half-dozen buildings bordering the western end of the lake is the town of Whitefish," Mike said with obvious pride, "and the smoke column about a quarter mile away is coming from the lumber mill. Our town has a mercantile, a community hall, livery stable, blacksmith's, barbershop, and a saloon. There is even some talk about opening a hotel in the saloon, although I don't see the need for one today. We don't have many visitors to Whitefish, except for a few transient lumberjacks who are only in town for a few weeks to cut and transport lumber to Grand Rapids. They usually camp out or take room and board with one of the families."

They made their way down the switchback trail to the valley floor and rode to Mike's farm. Two log cabins graced the farm, one much smaller than the other, a barn, a corral, three sheds, and two outbuildings. Log fences surrounded two acres of plowed meadowland, where neat rows of emerging green plants contrasted against the red-brown soil. Three horses wandered about the corral, and several cows and goats munched grass inside a larger fenced yard next to a muddy sty where several pigs wallowed. A few free-roaming chickens and white ducks scattered to get out of the way as Mike and Todd rode up to the main cabin and tied their horses to the hitching post. A mongrel dog ran out of the barn barking excitedly.

"Welcome to my home and this is my dog, Max," Mike said as he petted the tail-wagging dog.

A young woman holding up folds of a generous taffeta skirt ran out the cabin door and flew across the porch into Mike's waiting arms. After giving Mary several hugs and kisses, Mike turned to Todd. "Father Bose, meet my wife, Mary."

Petite and a decade younger than Mike, her long blond hair escaped from a blue bonnet that hung in graceful curls over her small shoulders. Mary turned to Todd, smiled bashfully, and extended her hand. Todd took her soft, delicate hand into his and gently squeezed it. Her blue eyes sparkled as she smiled sweetly in response to Todd's touch. His heart skipped beat and a warm glow enveloped him.

"Welcome to Whitefish, Father Bose," she said shyly.

"I'm pleased to meet you," Todd responded.

"How was your trip from Baltimore?"

"Long and tiring, but it is great to be here."

As Mike led the horses into the barn, Mary took Todd's hand still in hers and guided him to the front door.

"Please come inside, Father, and meet the children."

The interior of the single room log cabin was small but tidy and comfortable. A large front window filled the room with bright sunlight providing a pleasing and cheerful ambience. A full-size stone fireplace and hearth in the center of the room opened to both the front and back of the cabin. A black kettle simmered over glowing charcoals and filled the entire cabin with the fragrant smell of dinner. The back of the cabin separated by a colorful drape served as a bedroom, and a quilt-covered bed peeked from behind the partially pulled back curtain. To the left of the fireplace was the kitchen. A pail of water and dishpan sat on top of a hewed birchwood table surrounded by six wicker chairs, and against the wall was a cast-iron cookstove. Shelves to the left of the stove held stacks of dishes and to the other side cast iron pans hung from hooks in the wall. A large birchwood food storage cabinet completed the kitchen. To the right of the fireplace in the front room, a desk and chair, a wicker couch, a captain's chair, and maple rocking chair complemented the no-frills cabin furniture

The sound of giggling drifted from the loft above. Todd looked up to see three children watching his every move.

"Ann, Tom, Frank. Come down here and meet Father Bose," Mary suggested.

Mike hadn't said anything about his children except that he and Mary had three youngsters. Todd smiled as three youngsters climbed down the ladder and lined up in front of him. The three blond children all wore big smiles. Frank, a head taller than Tom or Ann, stood at attention while his brother and sister nervously shifted from foot to foot.

"Father Bose," Mary said with obvious pride, "these are our children. Frank is twelve years old and the twins, Tom and Ann, are nine." Todd shook hands with Frank and then Tom, but when it was Ann's turn, she stepped forward and gave him a big hug.

Mary continued her introductions. "I homeschool here in our cabin with my children and ten other youngsters three days each week. Frank has finished his eighth-grade studies and Tom and Ann are finishing sixth grade."

"I am very pleased to meet each of you," Todd said. All three children beamed. "Mary, do you also conduct Sunday school for the children?"

"No, Father, I haven't yet been able to do so."

"This is something that we will have to correct," Todd said. "The children must have their bible lessons. After Mass on Sunday, with your help I will conduct religious training for all the school-age children."

Mary smiled. "Speaking of Mass, Mike and Jerry have set up a temporary church in the barn. I hope you won't mind saying Mass with the smelly farm animals, but it is the only place large enough to accommodate the entire Catholic community."

Father Boise laughed. "I grew up on a farm, and the smells in a barn are perfume to my nose. Jesus was born in a stable surrounded by a bunch of farm animals, and if the Holy Family didn't mind the animals, neither will I."

Mike came inside after taking care of the horses. "I see you have met my family."

"Yes, and a fine family they are," Todd responded.

"I suppose Mary told you about the barn where we will hold Sunday Mass until we can build a proper church."

"Yes, she did, and I'm sure the barn will make a fine temporary church. I would also like to say daily Mass in the barn, but I will need an altar server."

"That can be arranged," Mike said as he nodded at Frank and winked. "Tonight, I have invited the entire parish to a welcoming supper in the barn. Everyone is looking forward to meeting you."

"I would like to say my first Mass in Whitefish before the supper tonight. Would that be all right?"

"No problem. Mary made a beautiful linen cloth for the altar. I have an old breadbox-size safe that we could use as a tabernacle. I hope you have brought along all that you will need to say Mass."

"If you will bring my valise in from the packhorse, I will show you my Mass kit."

Mike sent Frank out to get Father Bose's valise and he was back with it in a couple of minutes.

The Mass kit consisted of a ten-inch-high crucifix; a leather-bound Bible, a Sacramentary (Mass book), a stole (a scar-like cloth, the sign of a priest's office), an alb, a cincture (a ropelike belt), and a thin white chasuble (the priest's outer vestment). The kit also contained a small gold chalice to hold consecrated wine, a covered ciborium for consecrated hosts, a 6-inch white cloth stiffened with a piece of cardboard with the relic of a saint sewn inside, a 16-inch square linen cloth called a corporal to cover the altar, a box of thin unleavened wheat wafers, and a small cruet of red wine, a second cruet of holy water, a small bell, and a bottle of blessed oil (chrism) completed the kit.

"There is a trunk on its way from Baltimore with my other clothes, some medicines, books, vestments and other altar items for Mass, but it will not arrive for two or three weeks. I assume you have wine here in Whitefish, and I trust some of the women can bake unleavened wheat wafers for Communion. I believe this kit will do for Mass until the time Mike can make a trip to Grand Rapids to retrieve my trunk."

"That will be no problem," Mike said. "Jerry Keegan runs the small mercantile in town and sells wine. He and Peter Murphy make weekly mule-train trips to Grand Rapids to purchase supplies, post letters, and retrieve our mail. He will be glad to bring your trunk back on one of these trips."

"Now you haven't yet asked where you will be staying," Mike said. "Come, let Mary and I show you to your cabin."

They led Todd outside to the small cabin twenty yards away from the main house. The single room inside seemed comfortable and well appointed. Two windows on the south side, each framed by hand-sewn curtains, looked out onto the cultivated farmland and the Mesabi Mountains. Another window on the east side let in the morning sun and beneath it sat a small table and chair that could serve as a desk. Above the desk on the wall were three empty shelves.

"These are for your books when they arrive," Mike said as he pointed to them.

A kerosene lamp hanging from a chain above the desk served to light the room at night. A small potbelly stove and a stack of split wood stood on the west wall and next to the stove was a storage cabinet. Under the eastside window was a bed covered by a thick quilt and feather pillow. A Crucifix and alarm clock sat on a small table next to the bed and on the other side was a three-drawer dresser with a basin and pitcher of water placed on top.

"The outhouse is behind the main cabin, and you will find the well and hand pump next to the barn. If there is anything else you need, please don't hesitate to ask Mary or myself. You will be taking most of your meals with our family, but I expect you will have many dinner invitations from the entire community."

"Thank you. I am sure I will be quite comfortable here," Todd said.

"Oh, and there is one more thing," Mike offered. "You have to be able to get around Whitefish, so Molly and the saddle are yours."

Todd smiled. "Thanks, Mike. I think Molly and I will become great friends."

At six that evening, several horses, carriages, and wagons began to pull up outside the Dunn barn. Soon thirty-three men, women, and children all dressed in their Sunday best filled the barn. Folks seated themselves on planks spread between wood crates or sat on single bales of hay. Others milled around the barn eagerly waiting to meet Father Bose. Mike and his family entered the barn with Father Bose trailing behind, and as he entered, the entire congregation got to their feet and erupted with enthusiastic applause. For the next half-hour, Father Bose stood in a reception line with Mike and Mary who introduced him to each parishioner. The first couple in line was Jerry and Jill Keegan who owned and operated the Mercantile, accompanied by their two teenage sons, Sam and John. Todd greeted each family with enthusiastic handshakes. He met Tom and Teresa Kelly and son Patrick, Gus and Beth O'Neil, Marty and Alice Stein with their children Clara and Jason, Albert and Connie Reilly. He shook hands with the Murphys, Callahans and Donahues, and many others. When the introductions concluded, everyone took a seat as Todd vested for Mass and Frank Dunn prepared the altar. Todd stood in front of the makeshift altar, spread his corporal on top of the white lace tablecloth that covered it, and addressed his parishioners for the first time.

"I am so pleased to be here and meet each one of you. I am sorry, but I am not good remembering names. Yet I will grow to know each one of you, and in the next few weeks I plan to visit each of you to bless your homes. There is a time and date signup sheet for my visits, and be sure to include directions to your homes. I'm honored to be your pastor and that you have allowed me to make my home here with you folks. I am not a formal man, and it will please me if you could call me Father Todd. I will say my first Mass here this evening and will say Mass at 6:00 a.m. every morning and on Sunday at 8:00 a.m. in this barn. As soon as possible, we will begin discussions about building your church, and Bishop Byrne will come next year to dedicate it to St. Patrick, the saint he has designated to be our patron. I encourage everyone to attend Mass every Sunday and every weekday if you can. I will hear confessions each Saturday afternoon and hold Sunday school for the children after Mass on Sunday. Now if I could ask Frank Dunn to assist me, we will begin Mass."

His first homily was about baptism and the gospel story from the previous Sunday. Jesus was tired and thirsty and while resting at Jacob's well outside the town of Sheehem, a Samaritan woman came to draw water. Jesus did not have a bucket with which to draw water from the well and asked the woman for a drink. She was surprised that Jesus, a Jew, would ask her for a drink. Normally the Jews would have nothing to do with Samaritans, and especially a Samaritan woman. As the nephew of the temple priest Zachariah, Jesus was a Rabbi. This Rabbi was breaking Jewish tradition by speaking to a Samaritan woman. Jesus then has a long conversation with her, explaining, "Everyone who drinks this water will be thirsty again, but whoever drinks the living water I give him will never be thirsty." The woman was confused by this pledge and asked Jesus for some of this "living water." Jesus was talking about baptism, Father Todd concluded. "It is through the living water of baptism that your sins are forgiven and you become members of Christ's Church. I know that since coming to Whitefish you have not had access to the Sacraments. I noticed several new babies and toddlers in the congregation. Please arrange with me to have your children baptized if they have not already received the sacrament."

After Communion and the final dismissal, everyone gathered beside the long table in the back of the barn for dinner. Mary and Margaret served a lamb stew complete with biscuits and honey. After the meal, the men moved the improvised seats to the side of the barn, covered the altar with a drop cloth, and Robert Callahan took out his fiddle and began to play a lively tune straight from the old sod. Soon everyone was dancing to the square-dance calls of John Donahue. Father Todd sat on a bale of hay and gleefully watched the festivities and clapping his hands in rhythm. The dancing went on well into the evening, until Tom Kelly came over and offered, "You look tired, Father, and if you want I will take you over to your cabin." It had indeed been a long trip and a long day. Father Todd gladly accepted Tom's offer.

"Mike tells me you have some doctoring skills," Tom said. "We can sure use that around here."

Todd answered shyly. "Well, I am not a doctor but I did serve in a hospital during the Civil War and learned a thing or two."

That night Todd enjoyed the best night's sleep that he had had in two weeks. He awoke at the sound of the alarm clock at 5:00 a.m. The sound of roosters announced first light.

Six women attended Mass that morning, but Mike was the only man. As he later explained, the other men were tending their animals this time of the morning, and it was wise to hold Sunday Mass at eight. Frank served Mass, and afterwards Mary provided breakfast while Mike and Frank performed their chores.

Mike returned from his chores and said, "Father, today we are going to go into town for a short tour and to meet some of the proprietors. You will also meet most of the townsfolk who are not parishioners but are anxiously waiting to greet you at a Community Hall meeting later in the day. I also want to show you something just outside of town."

They saddled up Molly and Bandit and headed toward town. The rutted road led from Mike's fenced yard to the edge of a thick spruce forest and then wandered for two miles through dense stands of conifers until it came to a branch marked with a sign, "Lumber Mill." A hundred yards off the main road, they came to the mill that sat alongside a boulder-lined creek feeding a large waterwheel that creaked and groaned as it emptied its buckets back into the stream. A large incinerator behind the mill belched white smoke and the noise of a buzz saw filled the air. They entered the mill and found a stout man wearing railroad coveralls and wide-brim hat, his eyes protected by thick glasses. He was busy feeding an 18-inch diameter red pine log through the spinning circular saw powered by belts driven by the waterwheel. The ear-piercing noise from the saw made it impossible for Mike to let the man know that they were there. Sawdust flew in clouds from the saw coating the man, his clothes, and the floor with chips of wood and copious piles of sawdust. Mike stood back a respectable distance until the log exited the saw.

"Hey Jack!" he shouted. "I've got the padre with me." The man engaged the clutch that disabled the saw, removed his heavy gloves and earplugs, and extended a hand to Todd.

"My name is Jack Sprier," he said with a smile that extended from ear to ear.

"And I am Father Bose," Todd said as they shook hands, "but I would prefer to be called Father Todd."

"Then Father Todd it is. I belong to the Lutheran community in Whitefish, but we Lutherans have been as eager about your arrival as the Catholics have been. Welcome."

Todd looked at the stacks of finished lumber piled against each wall. "It looks like the lumber business is booming."

"It is, and I imagine you'll need some of this lumber for your church."

"That we will," Mike interjected, "and we will need it as soon as we can raise enough cash to build the church."

"Father Todd and Mike, you don't need to wait for cash money. When you are ready to build the church, I will supply the lumber and your credit is good with me.

"It is not only a pleasure to meet you, Father, but because we don't have a Lutheran minister hereabouts, the closest one being in Brainerd, it is so good to have a priest here with us."

"Brainerd is indeed a long way from here," Todd said. "Nevertheless, last Saturday I met Deacon Everett at St. Martin's, and he invited me to attend his Sunday services. I would have done so but the *Itaska* was leaving that very morning."

Jack's eyes widened. "You met Deacon Everett? Well, I'll be a droop-ear coyote. You sure get around, Father Todd. You've only been in this state for a few days and you've already met the only Lutheran Minister in northern Minnesota, and were even willing to attend his service to boot. I've never heard of a Catholic priest willing to attend a Lutheran service."

"It was the only church in town and I knew it would please God if I made a visit. I don't have a problem praying in a Protestant church, and I don't think God would object either."

"You are a most unusual Catholic priest. I'll just come out with it then and ask what has been my mind. We Lutherans were wondering if you will allow us to hold services in your church."

"If you will help us build the church, you certainly will be welcome to use it," Todd promised.

"Jack is a master builder and he and his Lutheran friends have offered to help us design and build the church," Mike added.

Todd took the plans for St. John's church out of his saddlebags and spread them out on a table for Jack and Mike to inspect.

"These are the plans that my grandfather designed for St. John's church in my hometown of Spartansburg, Pennsylvania. Do you think we can build St. Patrick's church from these plans?"

After Jack and Mike took time to examine the plans, Jack smiled and said, "These plans are very detailed and complete. Yes, we can build your church from them."

"The church will be called St. Patrick's after the patron saint of Ireland. I will leave these plans with you so you can study them. Will you be our master builder?"

Jack beamed with the offer. "Thank you, Father. I am honored that you would ask me and I accept. I can't wait to tell my Lutheran friends about your offer to use the church, and I'll show others in the town your building plans. We have been holding services in the Community Hall. Mark Gottwald the proprietor of the saloon is our deacon. The very idea of having our services in a real church is … well it makes me feel warm and fuzzy all over. Later, after you have had time to adjust to your new surroundings, let's look over your plans and discuss how we are going to build St. Patrick's."

"We're headed into town to introduce Father to the townsfolk," Mike explained. "I understand that they are holding a town hall meeting this afternoon. This will be a good time for Father to meet everyone. Do you plan to be there?"

"You can bet on it I'll be there."

Jack smiled and said, "Now if you don't mind, it's time for Father and me to be on our way and let you get back to work."

"Goodbye then, and I'll see you later at the Community Hall."

Jack reinserted his earplugs, adjusted his protective glasses, and placed his large hands back into his gloves.

Once they were back on their horses and headed toward town, Mike questioned Todd.

"Don't you think you were a bit hasty offering Jack the title of master builder and the Lutherans the use of St. Patrick's? What will Bishop Byrne think of this idea?"

"I judged that Jack is a capable builder. Just look at the sawmill he designed and built. And I was impressed by how he powers the saws from the little creek that runs beside the mill. The waterwheel is a thing of beauty and I noticed all the gears that drive the various belts, all designed and built by someone who knows what he is doing. Jack never hesitated to accept my offer to build the church. If he and the other Lutherans are willing to help us build the church, we should be honored to let them use it."

Mike thought awhile and then furrowed his brow. "You make a good point, Father. Jack is the most qualified person in town to build our church, and he and his people are my friends. They welcomed us when we arrived in Whitefish four long years ago and helped us settle in. They even helped raise my barn. When our crop failed that first fall and winter weather dumped eight feet of snow on us, we ran short of food. Even though the townsfolk were also short of food, they did not hesitate to share what little they had with us. If the Army hadn't showed up with emergency supplies, we would have all starved to death. Those good Lutherans have hinted that they would like to use our church once it is built, but I didn't think it was my place to approve or disapprove that request. Nevertheless, I wonder if our bishop will think it such a good idea. There has been animosity between some Catholics and Lutherans in St. Paul in years past."

"I have no problem with this policy and I will argue the point with Bishop Byrne should he object, but I don't think he will."

They rode into town and hitched their horses in front of the Whitefish Saloon. A covered porch extended the full width of the two-story clapboard building. Simple benches on either side of the swinging half-door entrance graced the porch, and above each bench were six-by-four-foot glass windows made from multiple small panes. A man looking half-asleep sat on one of the benches and silently tipped his hat to Todd as he followed Mike inside. The saloon was small, perhaps 80 feet wide and 120 feet deep, yet well-lit by the two large front windows. A moose head sporting a huge rack adorned one wall and on the other wall two elk heads, each with eight-point racks, glared down on the patrons. Rusty farm implements, beyond their years of productive service, hung on each wall serving as someone's idea of decorations. Two large wagon wheel chandeliers, each with eight oil lanterns, hung from the main log beam rafter. A stairway led up to the second floor. Simple plank tables guarded by wicker chairs were randomly placed about the room. All the tables were empty except for one occupied by four men who were playing cards. The card players took no notice of Mike and Todd as they walked across the creaking sawdust-covered floor and made their way to the empty "bar" that consisted of two six-foot-long oak planks suspended waist-high by two sawhorses. A large mirror surrounded by a gilded frame adorned the wall directly behind bar and various bottles of liquor and glasses crowded the shelves that lined the wall on either side of the mirror. On the wall above the mirror, an open mouth grizzly bear head filled with yellow teeth snarled at all those below.

A man behind the bar dressed in an apron was busy washing glasses in a large galvanized tub. Mike sat down on one of the bar stools and greeted the barkeep.

"Mark Gottwald, I'd like you to meet Father Todd Bose."

Mark dried his wet, soapy hand and extended it to Todd.

"Pleased to meet you, Father Bose. Welcome to Whitefish," he said with a generous smile as he pumped Todd's hand.

"Father Bose sounds too 'East Coast' for Whitefish. Please call me Father Todd."

"All right then, Father Todd, I'm mighty glad you accepted Bishop Byrne's offer to settle here."

"Your saloon is bright and friendly," Todd said. "What is upstairs?"

"Right now, there's nothing up there," Mark answered. "It's unfinished, but someday Sue and I plan to rent some rooms and perhaps change the name to Whitefish Saloon and Hotel. Can I offer you folks a drink?"

Mark looked at Todd and blushed when he realized he had just offered booze to a priest, but Mike came to his rescue.

"No thanks, Mark. Father likes a glass of beer now and then, but right now we are just introducing him to the townsfolk. We'll take you up on that offer later, perhaps after I show Father around town. The Mercantile is our next stop and then I have something else to show him." He winked at Mark.

Just then, a slight young woman came in through the back door carrying a bucket of water and placed on the floor behind the bar. With her golden hair fixed in a bun and dressed in a plain green dress and yellow apron, she looked the part of a saloon mistress; a pair of mud-caked shoes added to her barmaid appearance.

"Sue, meet Father Bose ... er ... Father Todd," Mark said.

Sue's face lit up like the morning sun. Her light blue eyes sparkled as she smiled.

"Father Todd, I am so pleased to meet you. Welcome to Whitefish," she said as she offered him her hand.

Todd took her hand in his and smiled back.

"And I am pleased to meet you, Mrs. Gottwald."

"Please, from now on call me Sue."

He nodded, and after a few minutes of conversation with Mark and Sue, Mike and Todd walked across the street to Jerry and Jill Keegan's Whitefish Mercantile. Father Todd had met Jerry and his family at his first Mass. The store was empty except for a man perched on a ladder busily stocking shelves.

"Jerry, I have Father Todd in tow!" Mike shouted out.

Jerry climbed down from the ladder and grinned at Todd. "Welcome to our store, Father."

Rough-hewn ten-inch thick spruce logs each 60 feet long formed the sidewalls of the 40-foot wide store. Two large plate glass windows dominated the front of the store, and ten red pine beams supported the twelve-pitch roof. Planks cut from sugar maples covered the floor and creaked as one walked across them. Shelves sparsely stocked with household items and canned goods, glassware, cookware, hardware, and other goods occupied six center aisles. Several tables and stand-alone shelves crowded with various items lined the back of the store. Todd was about to ask about Mrs. Keegan when Jill walked through the front door. She looked startled when she spied Todd, but composed herself and greeted him warmly.

"Father Todd, it is good to see you again. We didn't expect to see you in the store until tomorrow, but it is so good to have you visit us. Please have a look around."

She watched intently as Todd wandered up and down the various aisles looking at all the items. Bushel baskets of fresh corn, potatoes, squash, green beans, turnips, and radishes lined the front of the store. Placed in insulated boxes filled with layers of sawdust and crushed ice, butchered meat looked fresh and delicious.

"You have a bit of everything in your store, even fresh meat," Todd commented.

"Venison and elk," she explained. "We're a bit low on inventory right now, and hunting has been sparse this past month. Mike's trip to Grand Rapids was only intended to bring you to Whitefish, so he didn't bring the mules and wagon along to fetch goods. Our twice-a-month mule train trip to town will not be until next Monday, and when they return with our order we will have all these shelves filled."

The store impressed Todd. "I'm surprised," he admitted. "Considering how remote Whitefish is from the rest of civilization, I didn't expect to find a complete mercantile in town. I can see that through hard work you and Jerry have established a fine store to meet the needs of the community."

Jerry and Jill explained their ambitious plans for the store and for Whitefish, emphasizing the immediate need for a church. "Someday we may even have a railroad here," Jerry added.

Jill rolled her eyes. "A railroad? That's quite a dream, Jerry. Right now, I would be happy with a good wagon road to Grand Rapids. A railroad? Indeed."

Their next stop was at the barbershop across the street from the saloon. The barber, Dick Partridge, was busy giving Tom Kelly a shave. Todd said hello to Tom whom he had met the previous evening, and then Mike introduced Todd to Dick.

Dick shook Todd's hand. "Welcome to Whitefish Lake. We certainly need a priest in town, and I understand from Tom that you also have some doctoring skills."

"I was taught doctoring while serving in a Baltimore hospital," Todd said. "However, I am a priest and not a doctor."

Dick wiped some shaving cream from his straight razor and looked intently at Todd. "As the town barber, I have learned a thing or two about suturing wounds and setting bones. All the same, your medical skills will be a damn sight better than mine. Folks will be glad to know that someone with real medical knowledge is in town."

They said good-bye to Tom and Dick and went across the street to unhitch their horses.

"Father, there is something that I am eager to show you."

They mounted Molly and Bandit, rode a quarter mile along the road leading east of town, and arrived at a plot of land next to the lake. Marked by flagged stakes and peppered with a few pine trees, the ten-acre property extended 600 feet along the road and then extended 800 feet deep all the way to the lake. In the middle of the marked lot, another set of ribbon flags marked a plot 100 feet wide by 200 feet long.

"This is where we will build St Patrick's church," Mike said with obvious pride. "The small plot marked with flags in the center will be the site of the future church, provided it agrees with your architectural plans."

The site pleased Todd and he walked around the lot perimeter taking special note of the marked plot intended for the building. "I think this plot is about the correct size for the church, yet the sanctuary may be a bit larger than what is marked."

A small freshly painted sign placed beside the road read, *Future Home of St. Patrick's Catholic Church.*

"With your permission, Father, next Sunday we will have Mass here and place the cornerstone for the church," Mike suggested as he pointed to a 2 x 4 foot spot marked out by rocks at the left front corner of the property.

Todd walked into the center of the marked plot and stood at the spot where he imagined the church would stand. A sudden feeling of peace and contentment overwhelmed him. He stood there transfixed by the experience until a noisy flock of honking geese rising from the lake interrupted his thoughts.

Mike walked over to Todd. "Are you all right, Father?"

"Yes, I'm fine. For a moment, I just felt so warm and contented that the rest of the world faded away."

Mike looked puzzled. "So, what do you think about the site?"

"It's absolutely lovely. Do you think we could have a picture window behind the sanctuary that would look out onto the lake?"

"Sure, we can do that. Tomorrow Jack, you, and I will go over the architectural plans and mark out the church perimeter. But now we should return to town as it's almost time for the Community Hall meeting."

As Todd and Mike hitched their horses to a post in front of the town hall, a balding man with a white beard walked up and shook Todd's hand. He reminded Todd of Santa Claus

"Father, my name is Lloyd Brevick and I own the livery stable. I'm also the self-proclaimed mayor of Whitefish."

"A title conferred by the town council," Mike added.

Lloyd smiled at Mike and then continued. "I want to welcome you to our town, and I suppose Mike already has showed you the church site."

"That he has," Todd said. "It is a beautiful site and I was overwhelmed by it."

"Good. The town council and Mike carefully selected this site. Your church will be a welcomed addition to Whitefish. Come inside and meet the rest of our citizens."

About thirty men and women milled around the hall waiting for the meeting to start. Other than the folks he had met this morning and the parishioners at Mass the previous evening, the rest of the people in the hall were folks he had not yet met. One by one they introduced themselves and welcomed Todd to the community. After everyone sat down, Lloyd asked Todd if what Jack had told him was true. "Did you say that you will allow Lutherans to use St. Patrick's for our services?"

"Yes, you bet I did," Todd said. "I asked Jack to be the master builder, and if you help us build the church, you can use St. Patrick's for your own services."

"Even on Sunday?"

"Yes, even on Sunday. We will have Mass early Sunday morning, and afterwards you can hold your services there."

"And for our baptisms and funerals?"

"Certainly."

"Father Todd, we will be so grateful to have a church in town," Lloyd said with a big friendly smile. "Mark has been holding our services in this Community Hall, and our Lutheran community will appreciate holding them in a real church."

Mark led Todd and Mike to seats in front row. Lloyd Brevick began the meeting by introducing Todd and asked him to say a few words. He stood up and addressed the crowd.

"I am Father Todd Bose from Baltimore where I served as the assistant pastor at St. Catherine's church. I was born and raised on a Pennsylvania farm, graduated from Rutgers University, served during the war as an orderly in a Baltimore hospital and then, after five years in the seminary, last year I was ordained as a Catholic priest. I am so happy to be here with you folks in this beautiful valley. I am committed to be your priest and servant to all of you and you both Catholics and Lutherans will be my people. Bishop Byrne in St. Paul sent me here to form a parish and build a church. Together and with God's blessing, we intend to build St. Patrick's church within a year. I have asked Jack to be the master builder, and Mike and other townsfolk are invited to help build our church."

Todd sat down and Lloyd took over the podium and thanked Todd for his encouraging words.

"Folks, I'll get right to the point: we are thrilled to build a church, but there are two other projects that we desperately need for this community to survive. We badly need a doctor and a road to Grand Rapids. The nearest doctor is in Brainerd, and for him to travel here it is at least two days on the river to Grand Rapids and another two days on horseback to Whitefish. That's not counting the time it takes to get a message to him. Travel from Brainerd to Whitefish is impossible during the winter months. Last fall a tree fell on poor Hector Smith and by the time the doctor arrived, he was long since buried. I wrote to the hospital in St. Paul asking for a doctor who would be interested in moving to Whitefish. I even offered a place for him to stay and promised the townsfolk would build a clinic, but so far no one seems interested in our offer. Dick has acted as town medic, but he only knows how to suture wounds and set bones. Father Todd said that he worked as an orderly in the Baltimore Hospital during the war and learned a bit about doctoring. It is great to have someone in town with some doctoring skills and for this we are most grateful, but it would be even better to have a full-fledged doctor around."

A buzz of agreement circulated around the crowd, and then Lloyd continued. "The second need is for a wagon road to Grand Rapids. Mike and Jerry make the two-day mule-train trip to town every other week to pick up supplies and the mail, but the trail is the only way to get from Whitefish to the outside world. If we are to grow as a community, we need a wagon road to Grand Rapids. One commodity we have plenty of around here is trees, and not just those spindly saplings that grow in the lower part of the state, but large red pine and black spruce, some over 150 feet tall. If we had a road with proper bridges, not only could we get supplies and mail up here on time, but we could bring our logs and milled lumber to Grand Rapids to be shipped downriver to the mills and lumberyards in Minneapolis. Such an enterprise will produce revenue for the town and put cash money in your pockets. The plan is to widen the existing trail, build some bridges, and straighten out those hairpin curves. Much of the trail goes through thick forest, so we will need to clear trees as the road advances and those trees that we don't need for bridges we can take to Jack's lumber mill. I've surveyed the route and estimated that we will have to build about a dozen bridges. Jack's lumberyard can cut some of the logs into thick planks for the bridges. Last summer, we completed the two miles of the road from town to Jack's lumber mill and on to Mike's farm where the trail to Grand Rapids begins. The construction took six men five days to complete. At that rate, it will take over two months to extend the road forty miles into town. This must be a town priority, and one that we must complete by this summer if Whitefish is to survive. I know that most of you cannot afford several weeks away from your farms and families, but I suggest that we form a crew of two dozen or more men and split that crew into two gangs that will rotate weekly. Do I have any volunteers?"

Twenty-six hands went up, enough to create two gangs of thirteen workers each. Lloyd took down their names.

"It is best that we begin this project immediately while the weather is favorable"

He then addressed Dick Partridge, "I'd appreciate it if you would pick and lead the first team. Your team can begin construction tomorrow morning." Then he turned to Marty Stein, "Marty, if you would organize and lead the second team you can begin by relieving Dick's team early next week.

No one else had any further comments on the road project, so Lloyd looked at Todd and asked, "Father, tell us more about your doctoring skills."

Todd looked a bit embarrassed. "Thank you but I am your priest and not your doctor. Nevertheless, I will do my best to help anyone who needs medical attention. I took premed in college and served as a medic in a Baltimore Hospital during the war where I worked for a year treating wounded soldiers. When the war ended I completed my seminary studies and was ordained."

Lloyd responded, "Dick has been our town surgeon and medic around these parts for years, but his skills are better suited to barbering than to doctoring. Your medical knowledge and experience will be a sight better than Dick's. I trust we can call on you when the need arises?"

"You can, and I will do everything within my limited skills to help folks. I don't have many medicines or instruments with me now, but my trunk contains a few instruments, medicines, and other supplies. It should arrive in Grand Rapids in a week or two. My priority is that I am here as your pastor and only secondarily as a medic, but I will gladly see patients at Mike's farm. You are all welcome to attend the laying of the cornerstone for St. Patrick's next Sunday after the 9:00 a.m. Mass."

That Sunday, almost everyone in the Whitefish community showed up at the St. Patrick's building site for Mass. Mike had fashioned a makeshift altar and bales of hay as seats with a view toward the lake. In an unusual change of tradition, Father Todd stood behind the altar facing the congregation, a revision that would become permanent at St.

Patrick's. Father's homily was about faith and perseverance as shown in the New Testament story of the paralytic man who could not get through Simon's crowded house to see Jesus, so his friends lowered him on a stretcher from the roof where Jesus cured him.

"Now that was faith and perseverance," Father Todd concluded.

After Mass, Mike, Jack, Lloyd Brevick, and Mark Gottwald laid the cornerstone that Mike had chiseled and polished from a solid block of black granite. On it was chiseled, *St. Patrick's Catholic Church 1872*. Jack rolled out the architectural plans on a table for everyone to inspect. The construction of St. Patrick's Church had begun.

Chapter 5
Priest and Healer

June 1872

Over the next few weeks, Father Todd settled in as pastor of St. Patrick's parish. He visited and blessed the homes of his parishioners and came to know each of them by name.

"My flock knows me and I know them," he quoted from the New Testament.

Two weeks after Father Todd arrived in Whitefish, Mike and Jerry made the twice-a-month mule-train trip into town and brought Todd's trunk back with them. Once delivered to his cabin, Todd opened the trunk and sorted through the contents. Including several changes of clothes, the trunk held a warm sheepskin coat, two pair of boots, bedclothes, medicines and medical instruments, priestly vestments, items for the altar, and dozens of books.

The medications in the trunk were basic items, those found in any apothecary in St. Paul: alcohol and mercurochrome disinfectants; Calomel (mercurous chloride), a laxative; gum camphor, zinc oxide and calamine lotion to treat skin rashes; laudanum (opium in alcohol), morphia (morphine sulfate) and salicylic acid (aspirin) for pain and to reduce fever; quinine sulfate to treat malaria; Fowlers solution (potassium arsenate) for diarrhea; lobelia (an emetic); wax myrtle, a powerful antibiotic; chamomile to reduce fevers; and ginger to treat nausea.

From the day Todd's trunk arrived, folks started to come to Mike's farm for medications and treatment. Todd's cabin was too cramped to allow him to treat patients properly, so he asked Mike to build a small room walled off from the rest of the barn to be his infirmary. Mike cut a large window in the side of the barn to let as much light into the room as possible. They placed a woodstove, bed, storage cabinet, and a large oak plank suspended by two sawhorses as a treatment worktable. Todd treated minor wounds and illnesses and gave out medications from the infirmary.

One morning after Mass and breakfast, Mike asked Todd if he would like to go fishing with him in Whitefish Lake. Todd loved to fish and accepted the invitation without hesitation. Mike led him to the north end of the lake where an eighteen-foot rowboat remained tied to a small dock. The boat looked sturdy and well made, but would have been very difficult to transport on the narrow trail from Grand Rapids.

"How in the world did you get a rowboat up here?" Todd asked.

"I didn't. I built it right here," Mike said as a matter-of-fact.

They rowed the boat offshore a hundred yards, and wet their lines.

"So, what do we expect to catch in this lake?" Todd asked.

Mike looked at him as he would an inquiring child, "Whitefish and perhaps a few other species like muskie or pike. But mostly whitefish, which is why the lake is so named."

"I never gave the name much thought. We don't have whitefish back in Pennsylvania. What do they look like?"

"They have a body the same shape as a trout, silver sides with large fins, a yellowish tail and underbelly, and a small soft mouth. Hold the rod gently in your hand and wait for a small tug. Let the fish mouth the bait and then set the hook.

Nothing happened for a few minutes, but then Todd felt a barely perceptible tug on the line. "I felt a nibble," he said. Mike watched the line. "That doesn't look like a whitefish bite, perhaps it is a pike or sauger mouthing your bait. Let him swallow the bait first, and then set the hook."

"What's a sauger?"

"Kind of like a small pike."

Todd had never caught either a pike or sauger. He waited.

"Now hook him!" Mike yelled.

Todd jerked the rod upwards and his rod bent almost in half.

"I think I've snagged a log," Todd remarked. Then the "log" began to strip line from his reel.

"That's no log. It's either a pike or muskie."

Todd spent the next half hour fighting the fish, gaining a few yards of line, and then giving it back when the fish made another run. For a time it became a question of which fighter would tire first, the fish or Todd, yet eventually it was the fish. He swam belly up to the boat and Mike threaded a small rope through his gills and hauled him in.

"A fine 20-pound pike," Mike beamed. "Be careful of that toothy mouth as you remove the hook. These fellows can remove a finger."

When it was time to go back to the pier, they had caught a pike, six whitefish, a sauger, and a muskie.

"Today was a good day for fishing," Todd remarked.

"A very good day indeed," Mike added.

*****

Mike's barn filled with parishioners each Sunday morning, and occasionally a few who were not parishioners attended to hear his homilies. After Mass each Sunday, Mary and Jill would fetch pots of hot coffee and warm corn cakes from the house. Folks ate, drank, and socialized until well past noon. Father Todd was drinking his second cup of coffee one Sunday in May when he heard a wagon hurriedly pull up to the front of the barn. Marty Stein rushed inside and said there had been an accident at the road construction site this side of Mesabi Pass.

Todd and Mike rushed outside to find John O'Laughlin covered by a wool blanket and bleeding from his leg. He groaned as he lay in the wagon. Marty explained that while he and John were bringing a load of logs to Jack's lumberyard, the wagon brakes proved inadequate to slow the wagon, resulting in a missed curve that spilled John out onto the road and a log from the fully loaded wagon ran over his leg. Three men brought John into the infirmary and carefully placed him on the exam table. Father Todd cut away John's pant leg and examined his broken and bloody left leg. It was bad news. He had a compound fracture of the lower leg with the exposed white end of the bone protruding just above the ankle. Todd had seen worse wounds before while serving at the Baltimore hospital, yet he knew without immediate treatment John's leg would soon become gangrenous and he would eventually lose it. Todd asked Mary to get a fire going in the stove and set a pot of water to boil so he could sterilize his instruments.

Todd knew that this was not going to be an easy operation. He gave John a bottle of whiskey and told him to take a good drink. He turned to Marty and asked, "How long ago did this happen?"

"Late yesterday afternoon. I had to wait until this morning when I had enough light to drive the team safely down the mountain," he explained.

That was not good news because it was likely that deadly infection had already set in. Todd nodded and gave John another generous swig of whiskey and poured the rest on the wound. He winced but the alcohol was already taking effect to lessen the pain. He gave John a piece of leather to bite on. "John, I'm sorry but if I am to save your leg, I must set it right now. This is going to hurt a lot, but it will all be over in a few seconds."

He asked Mike to get a pulley and rope and to tack one end of the pulley to the wall of the infirmary. He then tied the free end of the rope to John's foot and gave the other end to Mike.

"When I say 'Go,' pull. Pull slow but firmly until I say to stop." Todd readied himself and then told Mike to pull. John screamed, bit down on the leather, and then fainted. Todd said to stop pulling and gently pushed the broken bones back into line, making sure the broken ends matched. He then doused the open wound with more whiskey, sutured the wound, and bandaged it with a splint. Since he didn't have any plaster of Paris, he tied two stout splints to the leg, one on each side and wrapped rope tightly around the splints. Although awkward, the splint would immobilize the leg bones while they healed.

John opened his eyes filled with pain. "Have another drink of whiskey," Todd said. After John consumed a quarter of the bottle, despite the pain he was smiling. Todd handed a package of morphine powder to Marty. "Tell John's wife Ann after he sobers up to give him a teaspoonful of this medicine in water four times each day until it is all gone. It will ease his pain. The leg will take at least six weeks to heal before we can take off the splints, and for the first two weeks he must not get out of bed. I will come to John's house tomorrow to dress the wound and make sure that it is not infected."

When Todd visited the next day to dress the wound, John had sobered up and, thankfully, there was no sign of gangrene. In the following weeks, John's leg healed and the accident left him with only a slight limp. Immediately after the operation, everyone in the community began to talk about Todd's doctoring skills. Each day patients came to the infirmary and Todd treated them with whatever skill and medications he had on hand. He set broken bones, sutured wounds, treated burns, cured skin rashes, removed a fishhook from a child's finger, and treated various internal and external ailments. Soon his medications, initially limited to a few supplies, ran short. On his next trip to town, Mike took a list of medications Todd needed to Captain Pinot of the *Itaska*. The hospital in St. Paul filled the request and a week later, the medications were waiting in town for the bimonthly mule wagon to Whitefish.

The Whitefish summer of 1872 was mild with ample rainfall and, as a result, crops were abundant. By the end of August, fields of hay, alfalfa, corn, wheat, barley, and various vegetables were ready for harvest. All September and most of October the folks in Whitefish spent their days harvesting, processing, and storing the bounty produced by each farm. They cut and baled hay, milled wheat and barley, and filled their corn bins to the brim. They harvested and stored potatoes, squash, carrots, turnips, and onions for the winter months and each household cut timber and split rounds for firewood to keep their cabins warm throughout the coming winter months. Every family was encouraged to cut, split, and stack at least eight cords of firewood.

By early summer church construction had progressed, but at a snail's pace. Most of the available men, horses, and equipment were needed for construction of the road, which by now extended over Mesabi Pass and to within 25 miles of Grand Rapids. Although progress was slow, with Jerry's help Jack Sprier and Mark Gottwald managed to dig out a shallow church basement and prepared the ground for the stone and concrete foundation. Mike, Lloyd, and Dick Partridge gathered stones from the dry Williams Creek bed and erected a four-foot-high stem wall, cementing the stones in place with a mixture of water, sand, and crushed limestone. They installed pine floor joists and nailed under-flooring plank floorboards in place. Then they fit two tiers of logs on top of the stem wall.

That September the road crew opened the wagon road to Grand Rapids. It passed through 42 miles of thick woods, climbed over two mountain passes and countless hills, crossed dozens of creeks and rivers, and skirted soggy bogs. The road crew constructed six long bridges to cross over wide streams and dozens of other bridges to traverse creeks and span gullies. The completed road reduced a two-day horseback or pack-mule ride into town to a one-day trip and allowed wagons or buggies to travel from Grand Rapids to Whitefish. Jack Sprier hired several men to work at his lumberyard to saw the logs left over from construction into construction lumber. Since the road made it possible for freight wagons to travel to and from Grand Rapids, he purchased a stout freight wagon in St. Paul and had it shipped to Grand Rapids. With the wagon drawn by four mules, Jack began weekly lumber wagon trips to Grand Rapids, where he shipped his lumber on a barge downstream to the Minneapolis lumberyard. This enterprise brought cash to the Whitefish community and soon several families had earned enough money to order their own wagons or carriages from the Minneapolis Carriage and Wagon Manufacturing Company.

One morning after Mass, Mike asked Todd to step outside; he had a surprise for him. Once outside, Todd found Molly hitched to a buggy. "It's a used buggy, but in good shape," Mike said with a huge smile. "Your parishioners bought it from a doctor in Grand Rapids. We felt it more fitting for our pastor to travel around in a buggy rather than on horseback."

Father Todd climbed into the buggy and Mike handed him the reins. "Take Molly for a little ride," he encouraged. Todd rode a mile or so down the newly completed section of the road to Grand Rapids, then he turned around and trotted Molly back to the barn.

"Thank you, Mike, and my thanks to all the parishioners. It's a fine buggy, and Molly does not object to pulling it."

*****

Now that the road was finished, men and equipment were available to work on the church. Soon the log walls and roof beams were in place, the windows and doorframes installed, the front steps and porch in place, and by late October they covered the roof with Jack's cedar shakes and the floor with maple planks. The goal was to have the church protected from the weather by the time the first snow flew in mid-November. When construction began in August, there wasn't enough money to order the twelve colored glass windows designed to enclose the church, so they planned to cover them with translucent oilcloth, which would make the interior dark and gloomy but keep the weather out. Mark Gottwald and Jack Sprier came to the rescue and provided the down payment required to order windows from the St. Louis Glass Works. The colored glass windows, sectioned into sixteen-inch squares, arrived in Grand Rapids the last week of October and by mid-November, workers had glazed them into the window frames. A few days later the first snowstorm of the year covered Whitefish with a foot of wet snow. Mike and Jack had been working since August to build the twenty-two wood bench pews, and by the end of November they had installed all of them. Jerry donated a potbelly stove procured in Minneapolis and Mike and Jerry constructed and polished the black granite altar quarried from the Mesabi Range foothills. Jerry ordered a bronze life-size corpus of the crucified Christ from New Orleans, fixed it on a cross that he fashioned from cedar, and hung it on the wall behind the altar. A breadbox-size safe covered by a silk cloth served as a tabernacle.

Father Todd said the first Mass in St. Patrick's on the first Sunday of Advent, 1872. Nearly the entire town and surrounding community attended that first service. Ninety-five men, women, and children packed the pews including a few folks who had never attended a Catholic Mass. Father Todd took his vestments from the trunk, consisting of an alb with chasubles and stoles fashioned in white, red, green, and violet, and carefully hung them in the sacristy closet behind the altar. Since it was Advent, a time of fasting and penance in preparation for Christmas, he wore the violet stole and chasuble. A gold chalice, ciborium, and paten arrived in late October, blessed gifts from Father Quinn and Bishop Byrne, and Todd used them for the first time at this Mass. Bishop Byrne and Father Quinn sent along a note promising to come in June to dedicate and bless St. Patrick's church. Father Todd said the Mass in Latin, but pamphlets in each pew translated the prayers into English. Because it was a two-mile ride into town from Mike's cabin, Father Todd continued to celebrate daily Mass in the barn and only on Sunday celebrated Mass in the church. True to Todd's promise, the Lutherans conducted their own service in St. Patrick's each Sunday morning after Father Todd dismissed his parishioners.

The Wednesday after that first Mass, Father Todd and Mike were making repairs to the roof of Mike's cabin when a wagon hurriedly drove through the muddy snow and pulled up to a stop. From their perch on the roof, Mike and Todd could see on the buckboard was a man and woman and a person wrapped in blankets lying in the back. Mary ran down from the porch to meet the wagon as it pulled up. Dick Partridge the barber and Alice, a parishioner and wife of Marty Stein, climbed down from the buckboard and met Mary at the back of the wagon. Todd was already climbing down from the roof as they opened the wagon gate and allowed Mary to pull the blanket away from their passenger's face. Todd recognized Clara, Alice's twelve-year-old daughter. She broke into a fit of raspy coughing that wracked her entire little body. Dick said that Alice had brought the child to him but there was nothing he could do except to bring the child to Todd. Mary said to take her into the warm house and place her on the extra bed in the front room next to the stove. Once inside, Todd felt Clara's forehead. She was burning up with fever. He took out his stethoscope, listened to the child's chest, and then turned to Alice.

"I'm afraid she has pneumonia," he whispered to the distraught mother. Alice hid her tears from Clara and looked pleadingly at Todd. Pneumonia was a killer, respecting neither the young nor the old, and nothing Todd could do could cure it. He gave Clara a swig of laudanum to quiet her cough and salicylic acid to bring down her fever. There was little else he could do, only pray. Everyone except Alice, who remained by Clara's side, followed Todd into the chapel in the barn and knelt in front of the makeshift altar as Todd led them in prayer. Afterwards, Alice wanted to stay with her daughter, but Mary insisted that she could nurse the child and it was best if Alice let Dick take her home and then come back with Marty first thing in the morning.

"Keep her warm and feed her chicken broth and a lemon tea to break up the mucus," Todd instructed Mary. "As often as possible make her sit up and clear her bronchial tubes of phlegm. All we can do now is make her comfortable and trust that her little body has the strength to cure itself."

Despite Mary's excellent nursing care, Clara had a bad night and by the next morning, when Todd examined her, the child's labored breathing and weak pulse signaled the end was near. When Marty and Alice came to see her that morning, Clara sat up but barely managed a weak smile. As Alice hugged her, Marty noticed that Clara's skin had taken on a sickly bluish tinge. Todd listened to her chest again and gave her more medications. They improvised a tent around Clara's bed and placed a large pan of steaming water under it. Todd said that the steam would help Clara breath. Mary whispered to Todd that Clara's breathing was so labored she didn't think the child would live through the day. After Mass, Father Todd brought Eucharist to Clara and gave her the last rites as her mother and father tearfully watched. She was barely able to sit up and swallow the Eucharist, and she seemed unaware that Father Todd was administering the last rites. When Todd placed his thumb in the vial of Chrism (blessed olive oil) and prepared to administer the sacrament, he felt the same warmth that he had experienced years ago as he knelt beside the prone form of the soccer player. He made the sign of the cross with chrism on Clara's forehead and, placing his hand on her, he prayed. His shoulder tingled and he felt warmth travel down his arm and into his hand. It was an indescribably pleasant feeling that invaded not only his arm and hand but filled his entire body with warmth. It was a sign that Clara was safely in God's hands. The sensation reminded him of when he was a child and needed comforting. His mother would wipe away his tears, take him into her lap, wrap her arms around him, and then gently rock him back and forth and assure him that all would be okay and then repeat that he was a wonderful son. Todd removed his hand as Clara opened her eyes, smiled, and then fell into a deep sleep.

"It is best if we quietly leave now and come back in the morning," Mary suggested.

Alice objected. "I cannot leave Clara. I don't want her to die without me."

"Alice, I understand," Mary said. "She will probably sleep all day and throughout the night. You can sleep on a cot beside her tent. However, it is best that Marty return home. I will keep close watch over her and replace the pan of steaming water each hour. I will send Mike to fetch Marty should Clara take a turn for the worse." Mary made Alice comfortable on the cot and the distraught mother immediately fell asleep.

Clara and Alice slept all that afternoon and into the night. As Clara slept, Mary noticed that her breathing was no longer as labored and raspy as it had been that afternoon. About midnight Alice awoke, got up, and lit a lamp to check on her daughter. Clara sat up in bed, her color and breathing normal, and her forehead cool to the touch.

"Hi Mom," she said brightly as Alice removed her hand from the child's forehead. "Can I have something to drink, and maybe something to eat too?"

Alice woke Mary who upon examination was dumbfounded by her patient's improved condition. Clara showed no ill effects whatsoever from the pneumonia, no temperature, and her breathing was normal. She took down the tent.

"Well, child, now you're hungry," Mary said. "This is a very good sign. It seems that your fever has broken."

"Was I sick?" she innocently asked.

"Yes, child, you were very sick. So sick in fact that Father Todd gave you the last rites yesterday."

"He did? I don't even remember that he was here. Mom, where is Dad?"

"He will come to see you in the morning. Father Todd will be here too."

Mary gave her two glasses of warm milk, then warmed up some chicken broth and sat on Clara's bed as she fed it to her a spoonful at a time. Alice watched as Clara ate the entire bowl, and then fell back asleep.

At first light the following morning, Father Todd knocked on the front door, half-expecting to see Mary open it with dire news.

"God be praised. Clara's fever broke last night," Mary told him as she invited him in, "and this morning it is as if she was never sick at all. I fed her a whole bowl of chicken soup and two glasses of milk when she woke up at midnight, and then this morning she ate a bowl of porridge."

Father Todd received the news with great joy, but also with some hesitation. "As I gave her the last rites last evening, I didn't expect she would survive the night. Her present condition just proves that God answered our prayers. She is a tough child with a strong will to live."

"No, Father," Mary argued. "It is much more than her will to live and a simple answer to our prayers. It is much more. I think it was a miracle. The moment you placed your hand on her when you gave her the last rites, she stopped coughing and her breathing improved. She smiled at you and then relaxed and fell asleep. No, it was a miracle. God cured her through your hands, I am sure of it."

Father Todd didn't know what to say. He thought for a moment, and then offered, "Mary, God works in his own way. If it was a miracle as you claim, it was not by my doing but through the power of the Holy Ghost. Only God can perform miracles. Please don't continue to say that I cured her because I didn't."

"But Father, you did cure her. I witnessed it," Mary insisted.

Todd recognized there was no use arguing with Mary. He was preparing to go upstairs and visit Clara and Alice when there was another knock on the door. Mary opened it to see Clara's father standing at the threshold, his face twisted in anxiety.

"Clara is fine this morning," she blurted out, almost giddy with joy. "Alice is upstairs with her and the child is sleeping peacefully right now, but she had two glasses of milk and a bowl of soup at midnight and some porridge this morning. Her temperature and breathing are normal now."

Marty relaxed, as if a great weight had been lifted from his shoulders. He turned to Father Todd. "Father, how can this be? Last night she was at death's door. We fully expected to hear bad news this morning."

"It was a miracle," Mary interjected. "Father Todd won't admit it, but this was a miracle. Clara improved the minute he blessed her with the Holy Chrism. I have nursed many pneumonia patients before, but have never seen that awful sickness completely disappear from a child or older person overnight. Usually by the next morning they are dead."

Marty and Todd followed Mary upstairs. Alice was rocking Clara in her lap. She smiled at Marty and addressed Todd when he entered the room. "Father, how do you explain this? Did you cure her?"

Todd answered with complete conviction. "No, I did not cure her. I have no such power to cure anyone. God answered our prayers, and that is all there is to it. Clara lives because she is a strong child and God willed her to live. I am but a minister of the Holy Ghost's grace. If you choose to believe that this was a miracle, then so be it but know it was all God's doing and none of mine."

Chapter 6
The Blizzard

Father Todd's fame as a healer spread throughout the valley. Some folks thought he had performed a miracle by curing Clara; others simply appreciated his willingness to share his medical skills. Todd denied he had any miraculous powers, and in a sermon cautioned his parishioners that he was simply an ordained priest sent to Whitefish to heal souls. Yet if God wanted him to use his limited medical knowledge to heal bodies, so be it. Nevertheless, he had no power to perform miracles. Men, women, and children from Grand Rapids and the surrounding countryside, his parishioners, Whitefish Lutherans, and those who did not belong to an organized religion sought Todd's help at Mike's farm. Folks came with broken bones, serious cuts, festering sores, chicken pox, fevers, and countless other maladies, and Father Todd treated every patient in the same way regardless of where they lived, their ethnicity, or personal beliefs. When necessary, he made house calls in good weather or bad. Soon it became obvious that Mike's barn was inadequate to serve as an infirmary, and in a town meeting, the proposal for a clinic in town drew applause. Mike Dunn, Jerry Keegan, Jack Sprier, Dick Partridge, and Mayor Brevick sought funds to build a clinic and rectory for Father Todd on the property next to St. Patrick's church. Money for the project poured in and they vowed to start construction as soon as the ground thawed in the spring.

In January of 1873, a storm blew out of the Canadian Arctic, a storm unlike any other the folks of Whitefish had experienced. The temperature dropped to below zero, the wind howled, and snow piled into 5-foot drifts that blocked the road. The blizzard continued unabated for three days and nights. It wasn't safe for Father Todd to drive Molly and his carriage into town for Sunday Mass, nor could patients make it to Mike's farm for treatment. Residents hunkered down inside their cabins and kept their stoves and fireplaces blazing. On the second day of the storm, Todd and the Dunn family had gathered around the fireplace when there was a knock on the door.

Mike opened it and a half-frozen Albert Reilly who owned the next farm about one mile down the road stood half frozen at the threshold. Icicles hung from his beard and mustache and snow coated his face, jacket, pants, gloves, and hat. He almost fell into the house as Mike led him over to the fireplace and helped him remove his frozen outer clothes. Albert stood before the fire and shivered as the snow melted from his face and hair and dripped onto the floor. Mary covered him with a wool blanket and gave him a hot cup of coffee. He shivered so violently that he couldn't speak or hold onto the cup, so Mary held it to his lips. After a few minutes, he warmed up enough to tell Mike why he came to their cabin in such weather.

"Mike, my family...." His voice trailed off.

"What about your family?" Mike inquired.

"Connie and the children are freezing. I ran out of wood yesterday, and it is so cold in the house...."

"You have no wood for the fireplace?"

"I do have another cord but it is in the shed next to the barn which is 30 yards from the house. I had a few days worth stacked on the deck, but we burned it all up by yesterday. Six feet of snow drifted between the shed and house and covered the wood stack. I couldn't get through the snow to bring a few pieces of wood inside, and almost froze trying. It was all I could do to get over here. Without your help Connie and the children will freeze to death."

"Of course, we'll help," Mike said. He remembered the admonition that all families should stock at least eight cords of wood and their remaining cord certainly would not last the winter, but thought better at saying anything. "I have plenty of wood stacked in the barn. Frank and I will load a couple of cords onto my wagon and drive over to your place right now. You stay here and warm up."

"No, I'm going with you," Albert insisted.

"Albert, look at you. You're half frozen and you'd be more in our way than to be of any assistance. Stay here with Todd and Mary. Frank and I will take the load of wood to Connie and the children."

The snow was blowing so hard that although the barn was only twenty yards from Mike's front porch, it was barely visible. Mike and Frank hitched the wagon to Molly and Bandit, loaded two chords of wood, and headed down the road in the thick of the storm. It was blowing so hard that they had to yell to one another in short sentences to overcome the howling wind. Fortunately, the wind had blown most of the snow off the road and formed berms along the fence lines, but it was still difficult to know where the edge of the road was. If they ended up in a ditch, there would be no way to get the wagon out. Molly and Bandit struggled to drag the heavy wagon over the one foot of snow that still covered the road.

"Keep your eyes on the depression that marks the road edges," Mike shouted. "And warn me if we stray too close."

Mike cautiously drove the horses forward and a half hour later they pulled into the Reilly farmyard. Once inside the house they found Connie and her two children huddled together in a bed in the loft, shivering under several layers of blankets. Connie managed a weak smile, and Mike told them to stay put while he and Frank warmed the house. They carried several armloads of wood from the wagon into the house and started a roaring fire going in the fireplace. Mike also started a fire in the Franklin stove so he could heat some coffee, but the house was so cold the water bucket in the kitchen was frozen solid.

"Frank, please go out to the pump and draw some water for coffee," Mike asked. Be careful because although the pump is only a few yards away, you could become lost in this whiteout. I noticed a rope on the north side that leads from the house to the pump, and another on the south side of the house going to the barn. Be sure to hold on to the rope that leads to the pump."

Mike busied himself with stoking the fire in the stove and feeding the fireplace. After a few minutes when Frank hadn't returned, Mike began to worry. He went out to the front porch, and there near the door was a filled bucket of water but no sign of Frank. The blowing snow had reduced visibility to only a few yards, and he couldn't see Frank. Cupping his hands around his mouth, he shouted for Frank over the howl of the wind, yet after several shouts Frank did not respond. He reasoned that Frank must have gone to the barn, so he grabbed the rope and made his way to the barn. He found Frank in one of the stalls dumping a bucket of water into a frozen water trough.

"Frank, I thought I told you not to go out to the barn," Mike fumed.

"Dad, you didn't say not to go to the barn, just not to confuse the barn rope with the pump rope. I knew the horses would need water, so I brought them each a bucket or two. In addition, look, there is less than a half-chord of wood stacked here in the barn. The two chords we brought along will only last them a week or two." It was hard to stay angry with Frank, who was only trying to do a good deed. Nevertheless, it was a dangerous thing for Frank to do.

Soon the coffeepot of water was perking on the stove. Mike fed cups of hot coffee first to the children and then to Connie who cupped her hands around the tin cup to warm her stiff fingers.

"Thank you so much, Mike. You are a good neighbor, but where is Albert?" Connie asked after her first sip of coffee.

"He is warming up back at our farm," Mike answered. "He walked all the way over to our house and when he arrived he was almost frozen. I made him stay there with Father Todd to warm up, and then Frank and I came to take care of you and the children and bring you some more wood."

Their fireplace was efficient and Albert had designed it with a copper heat exchanger to capture the heat that normally went up the flue. Less than an hour later the house was warm enough for Connie and her children to climb out of bed.

Mike and Frank stacked the entire two cords of wood on the front porch and then prepared to go back home. Mike had parked the wagon by the side of the house out of the blowing wind, but Molly and Bandit were shivering from exposure.

"We have to get these animals moving so they can warm up," Mike said.

Mike had to brush several inches of snow off the horses and buckboard before he urged the wagon back on the road. The trip back home took even longer than the wagon ride to Albert's farm. Molly and Bandit were barely able to pull the wagon.

Mike used the whip on Molly and Bandit to drive them forward, something he never did.

"If either of these horses should fall, they will not be able to get up and we will be in big trouble," Mike warned. However, the horses didn't fall and trudged on until a temporary lull in the whiteout allowed Mike and Frank to make out the ghostly outline of the Dunn house and barn. Frank went inside as Mike unhitched Molly and Bandit and led them back into the relative warmth of the barn, and then threw horse blankets over each animal.

"Are Molly and Bandit all right?" Frank asked as Mike came back inside.

"Yes, they will be fine."

Albert was anxious to return home to his wife and children, but Mike dissuaded him. "It would be suicide to try to walk home in this weather." Mike argued. "I'd let you take Molly or Bandit, but they have about had it and barely made it back here. Stay with us until the storm dies down. Connie and the children are fine. We brought enough wood inside to keep the fire going for a day or so, and there are two chords stacked on the front porch."

Albert was unable to return home until late the next day when the storm finally blew out. The Reilly family was not the only folks in Whitefish who suffered in the storm. At church the next Sunday, they learned about the death of Peter Callahan. At the height of the blizzard, he trudged outside to care for his three cows. Disoriented by the whiteout, he got lost. A neighbor found him the next day frozen stiff in the snow, only 20 yards from his house. His funeral was the first one held in St. Patrick's church. Peter was well known and liked in the community and the little church was crowded with mourners. Four of Peter's friends carried the simple pine box into the church and placed it at the altar rail. Father Todd said Mass and his homily centered on the biblical story of Jesus ascending into heaven. His wife and son sat in the front pew holding hands as Dick Partridge gave the eulogy. It was a sad day for the parishioners. The frozen ground forced them to wait until spring to bury Peter, so they stored his coffin in the back of Dick's barbershop.

Chapter 7
Leech Lake

April 1873 arrived and brought with it a hint of spring. Mike and Todd were repairing barnyard fences when they saw three men ride bareback up to the house.

"Indians!" Mike yelled, and ran toward the house with Todd only a few steps behind.

Mike went inside and fetched his rifle while Todd remained on the front porch. The three Indians dismounted and quietly stood next to their horses. When Mike came back out on the porch, he cocked the rifle and waved it at the Indians. "These people can be a heap of trouble," he said. "Father, best you get into the house while I find out what they want."

Todd immediately recognized one of the Indians. He was Running Bear, the Indian he had met on the *Itaska*. Todd did not know the other two Indians.

"Mike, I know one of these Indians," he said breathlessly. "They are friendly."

"How do you know they're' friendly?" Mike protested. "We've had trouble with these Indians before."

"The big fellow is Running Bear," Todd said. "I met him on the *Itaska*. He speaks English and he's not here to harm us."

Todd raised his hand, "Tecumseh, welcome to Whitefish."

"Good to see Black Robe again. We ride long way to parley."

"Parley about what?" Todd asked.

Running Bear explained. "Tribe bad sick. Many die; more die unless Black Robe come to village. We know his medicine very powerful. I watched while he cure sick boy on boat, and I hear he cure others in Whitefish. He can cure tribe."

Mike looked at Todd. "They want you to go with them to their village? It is at Leech Lake, a two-day ride from here. It would be dangerous for you to go with them. They might even kill you."

"They will not harm me. They are Ojibwa people and they need my help. I cannot refuse them."

Mike was skeptical. "I don't trust them. You don't even know what ails his people. It could be syphilis, or the pox, or whooping cough, or even scarlet fever. You have no idea what illness they have or how to cure it. Just tell them no and send them on their way."

Running Bear sensed a refusal coming so he interjected, "If Black Robe come to village and help my people, we let Whitefish men fish and hunt our land forever."

Todd smiled. "Tecumseh, I will come with you. I am not sure I can help your people, but I will try."

"Mike, please help me gather my things and saddle Molly."

Mike balked. "You're not going to go alone with these Indians. I will saddle Bandit and come with you."

"No, you will not," Todd said emphatically. "Your family needs you and there is not much you can do to help me in their village. It is best that I go alone with them."

Mike tried to dissuade Todd from going with Running Bear and his companions.

"Father, we need you here in Whitefish," he argued, "and you can't trust these Indians. I don't care about their promise to let us hunt and fish on their lands. Besides we do that anyway with or without their permission."

Todd ignored Mike's arguments and saddled Molly. He filled his saddlebags with some clothes, camping gear, and the few medications he had on hand. Todd mounted Molly and said good-bye. Mike watched helplessly as Todd and the three Indians rode away.

If you are not back in two or three weeks, I'll form a posse and come after you," Mike shouted after him.

The three Indians led Todd along the road over Mesabi Pass and then west along the Big Fork River to Lake Winnibigoshish where they left the road and traveled on a trail around the lake's northern perimeter where they made camp for the night. The next morning, they rode southwest through a thick forest of spruce and pine. The trail faded and became hard to follow. Todd let Molly follow the other horses, and by the afternoon of the second day they came to Leech Lake and shortly thereafter arrived at the Ojibwa village. A pack of barking dogs rushed to greet them as they rode into the village. Despite Todd's expectations, there were no teepees. Two dozen domed wigwams framed by willow branches and covered with layers of birch bark and deer hides comprised the village. Half a dozen birch-bark canoes lay overturned on the sandy beach. The dogs made enough commotion to rouse two women and a boy from their huts. All three ran to greet the party. They smiled and began jabbering with Tecumseh in a tongue Todd didn't understand. Thankfully, these folks looked healthy. They were overjoyed that Tecumseh had returned with the Black Robe. Todd dismounted and Tecumseh introduced him to one of the two women.

"This Tamara, my sister. She white man squaw and talk white man tongue. She teach me white man talk."

Tamara smiled faintly and bowed her head. Her coal black hair, arranged in loose braids, hung over her shoulders partially hiding her otherwise naked breasts. Her face was honey-brown and accented with sparkling black eyes and snow-white teeth as she smiled. Todd thought she was strikingly beautiful.

Tecumseh continued, "Bear kill Tamara husband long time ago. She in my wigwam now. The boy is Waleke, son of Chamaska, my dead brother."

A gray-haired well-built Indian stepped out from the largest hut in the village and as he hurried toward them, he raised his open hand, saying, "an-neen," which by his tone Todd interpreted as a friendly greeting. Tecumseh introduced Todd to the "gimaa" or tribal chief whose name was Sekota (Diving Hawk as he later learned). The chief's wrinkled face, large callused hands, and moist somber eyes suggested his advanced age. He had braided his hair and wore a leather headband adorned with a single eagle feather. An elaborate beaded vest covered his chest and a deerskin apron hung from his waist to below his knees. A pair of soft moccasins covered his feet. Sekota's air and dress identified him as a leader. Todd touched the man's raised open hand with his and repeated "an-neen."

"Shekine," Sekota motioned with his hand as he led Todd toward his wigwam. The village seemed deserted except for the dogs, the gimaa, a boy, and the two women. Outside the gimaa's wigwam wisps of smoke rose from a cooking fire, the only cooking fire in the village that showed any sign of life.

"Where are all your people?" Todd asked Tecumseh.

"Warriors not sick go hunting. Women and children stay in huts … most bad sick. Come see," he pleaded and motioned Todd inside the gimaa's hut. He had to bend over to get through the 3 x 4 foot door covered by a piece of bear hide. A fire ring took up most of the center of the six-foot-high, ten-foot diameter domed hut. Smoke curled from the fire and exited through a hole at the top of the dome. An old man, his white hair tied in a ponytail and his face weathered by age, stood to one side of the Sekota's hut. Tecumseh nodded to the man who glared at Todd and then turned his back to them.

"This Neenah our shaman," Tecumseh explained. "He not happy to see Black Robe in village. He say you bring bad magic, but I say not so."

Spread around the hut Todd counted four Indian women each covered by colorful woven blankets. He knelt beside the closest person, a young woman who stared back at him with frightened eyes. Dime-sized pustules and beads of sweat covered her frightened face. She turned away as Todd reached out to feel her forehead, but Tecumseh said something to her and she allowed Todd to place his hand on her forehead. She was burning up. He recognized the classic symptoms of smallpox. Usually, an otherwise healthy European patient would recover from smallpox. The resulting pockmarks were often the only reminder of this terrible disease. Yet American Indians had never developed immunity to the pox, and hundreds of thousands died of this and other European diseases carried to the New World by the first white men. The very young and old were especially susceptible to the pox, and often more serious bacterial infections like pneumonia followed a pox infection. There wasn't much a doctor could do except to make his patients as comfortable as possible, reduce their fever with medicines, and lessen the itching pustules with calamine lotion. It was also best to cut a patient's fingernails short to prevent scarring.

Todd examined the three other patients, two children and a young woman. One child was a young preteen boy, the other a five- or six-year-old girl. The boy's curly red hair and light skin surprised Todd. His breathing was erratic and he did not respond to Todd's attempt to rouse him. Tecumseh whispered to Todd with a pained look on his face. "This gimaa's only son, Antikum. The woman his squaw. You cure them."

"I don't know if I can cure them. They are very sick," Todd shot back.

"You cure," Tecumseh repeated.

Todd asked Tamara to fill a pot with water and set it on the fire to boil. Then after the water boiled, he opened his saddlebag and mixed wax myrtle powder (an antibiotic) and chamomile (a fever reducer) with the boiling water to make a medicinal tea and fed a cup to each patient. Unfortunately, Todd couldn't wake the boy to give him the tea. He swabbed calamine lotion on his patients' pustules and cut each patient's fingernails. Then he went to each wigwam and treated two dozen other patients in the same manner. All were in various stages of the disease, some recovering and others dying. Sadly, in one wigwam a woman and her baby had died, but he was able to treat her other two children.

Tecumseh pointed to a dozen fresh mounds 20 yards from the village. "They all dead," he said softly.

Todd returned to Sekota's hut to treat his son. The boy couldn't have been any older than twelve or thirteen. He did not respond to Todd's repeated attempts to arouse him and get him to drink a cup of tea. Todd wet the boy's lips with tea and wiped his face with a cool cloth. The boy's breathing was erratic and his pulse slow. *It will be only a matter of a few minutes,* Todd told himself.

"I am afraid Antikum is dying," he told Tamara.

Tamara glared at Todd and said emphatically, "Antikum not die. You cure."

She doesn't understand, Todd thought. *I have no magic medicine. All I can do is pray for the boy and try to make him comfortable.* He took out his bible, opened to the Psalms, and then knelt beside Antikum and placed his hand on the boy's forehead. As he began to read the 26th Psalm, Todd's shoulders tingled and that now familiar pleasant warmth traveled down his arm to his hand. When he first placed his hand on the boy's forehead, it felt hot, dry, and feverish, but after a few minutes, now if felt somewhat cooler. He removed his hand, opened his Bible, and began reading the 27th Psalm. Antikum opened his eyes and looked intently at Todd. He took a deep breath, and then slowly exhaled. Todd thought this must be the boy's last breadth, and continued reading the 27th Psalm. Then a minute later, the boy inhaled and opened his eyes. The shaman entered the tent and Sekota, who had been standing at the foot of the boy's bedroll, began to chant a song and sway rhythmically back and forth with Neenah. Todd closed the bible and stepped back. Tamara lifted the boy's body to a sitting position so he could watch his father and shaman dancing at his feet. With a bewildered stare, he looked from his father to Todd and then back to his father. When the dance ended, Todd offered Antikum the cup of tea. He swallowed half of the cup, and then put his head down and fell into a deep restful sleep.

Todd sat cross-legged next to the sleeping boy and watched his chest rhythmically rise and fall as he took in deep measured breaths. He looked at Sekota who smiled.

"I think Antikum will live," Todd said. Neenah, who had been standing next to the door, said something to Sekota and then went outside.

Todd felt two soft arms come from behind him, cross over his shoulders and end on his chest pressing his body to hers. It was Tamara, who whispered in his ear, "Thank you, thank you, Black Robe." The next day Antikum took nourishment and could stand up.

The week after Todd arrived at the village the hunting party returned, yet none of the men including several young bucks showed any signs of smallpox. For several days Todd and Tamara nursed the sick villagers, but none of the men would lift a finger to help nurse the sick or even help around camp. Tamara said that such labor was squaw work. Neenah convinced the men that helping Todd tend the sick was bad medicine, and claimed his shaman dance, not Todd, cured

Antikum. The only work the bucks did was to bury the dead and butcher the game that they brought into camp. The women, even those recovering from the sickness, did the cooking and all the other camp chores.

Todd's few medications were mostly ineffectual, although the chamomile tea helped soothe stomachs and the wax myrtle lowered fevers. He trimmed the fingernails of sick villagers, painted calamine lotion on their skin, and made his patients as comfortable as possible as their bodies healed. He boiled up four guinea hens and made a large pot of broth that he and Tamara fed to the sick villagers. Tamara was a willing and competent nurse, attending to the sick, feeding broth to them, and giving them wax myrtle medicine and chamomile tea. She bandaged the children's hands to keep them from scratching their pustules that would leave scars. For two weeks Todd remained in camp tending the sick. The women and children began to recover, but by the time the disease had run its course, nineteen mounds dotted the impromptu cemetery.

Curiously, all the men and teenagers who had gone hunting as well as Tecumseh, Neenah, Sekota, the two men who accompanied Tecumseh to Whitefish, and Waleke all appeared healthy. The disease had infected most of the women and children villagers including ten young boys and seven infants. Todd did not understand why most of the village men and teenagers were immune, while most of the women and children became sick. Then in the first few days after Todd arrived, Waleke also came down with the pox. While attending the boy, Todd noticed the colorful Navaho blanket that covered him.

"Where did the boy get this blanket," Todd asked

"From a dead squaw," Sekota said. "He not have his own."

Todd became suspicious of the Navaho blankets that warmed the women and children, while the men and most of the boys used the plain blankets characteristic of Sioux or Algonquin nations. He carefully examined one colorful blanket and discovered that it was infested with fleas hiding in the folds. He examined several other Navaho blankets and fleas infested every blanket.

"Where did you get these blankets?' he asked Tecumseh.

"White man come and trade with us for beaver pelts two moons ago. We call him Pachina, or man with noisy wagon."

That revelation disturbed Todd, for the description sounded a lot like the many tinkers who traded with the Indians. He had heard a rumor back in St. Paul that some traders were going around the west trading Navaho blankets infested with pox-ridden fleas. Such a practice was a deliberate attempt by the Army to wipe out Indian tribes that some white men felt were a danger to homesteaders. Undeniably this atrocity had victimized the Leech Lake tribe and, apparently, the Indian men who disdained using the colorful blankets remained healthy. They knew the Navahos wove these blankets and no self-respecting Lakota warrior would adorn himself with blankets made by his enemies. However, the women and children felt no such masculine pride and covered themselves with the infested blankets.

"Do you know the Pachina who traded these blankets?" Todd asked.

"The one on the boat," Tecumseh explained.

Todd thought back to his trip on the *Itaska* from St. Paul to Grand Rapids where he first met Tecumseh. He had also met a fellow passenger and his family who got off in Brainerd. The man, Seth Meriwether, said he was a tinker, a salesman of various items like pots and pans, various cookware, utensils, clothes, and tools. Could Seth have deliberately traded chicken pox-infested blankets with the Leech Lake Indians and sold his wares to the folks in Whitefish? Todd thought this was a strong possibility and the tinker may have done so deliberately. The next time he was in Brainerd he vowed to register a complaint with the local sheriff. Such a despicable practice amounted to genocide, yet it was well known that the US Army encouraged such practices. "A dead Indian is the only good Indian," was the Army attitude toward these native Americans.

The villagers held a thank-you ceremony for Todd. All the able-bodied men, women, and children gathered around a huge campfire as the men sang and danced.

"They are singing about the Black Robe who performed his magic to chase the evil spirits from our village," Tecumseh explained.

"It was neither magic nor evil spirits. I have no such powers," Todd protested. "It was through the power of prayer and Jesus Christ that these villagers were cured."

Tamara and Sekota sat next to Tecumseh listening to the conversation. Tamara translated what they were saying to Sekota.

Sekota stood up and addressed Todd, and Tamara translated his words.

"Many moons ago, Black Robes come to our village and poured water on many foreheads. They spoke in white man's language different from you, and told us about your Jesus Christ who performed much magic. Most of my ancestors including my grandfather did not listen to them and continued in their traditional ways. Now I have seen for myself that Black Robes speak the truth. This Black Robe's God has strong medicine and He cured my son who would have died from the pox fever. He help other villagers get well. Your Jesus Christ is a good man, and someday I will come to know more about him."

Over the next two days Waleke grew weaker, and nothing Todd did seemed to help him.

"You must come with us on sprit journey," Tecumseh pleaded. "It the only way Waleke will live. Neenah and Sekota come too."

Early the next morning Tecumseh, Neenah, and Sekota led Todd on a trail that wound north from Leech Lake through thick spruce forests. They rode for most of the day until they came to an outcropping of large and small granite stones all piled askew, one on top of the other forming a mound several hundred feet high and a mile long [a glacial moraine].

"Come, we show Black Robe ghost rocks," Tecumseh said.

They dismounted and climbed to the top of the mound topped by a white granite stone as large as a house. A rectangle notch hewed out of the white stone at eye level measured 3 by 4 feet. Within the rectangle were dozens of ciphers in neat rows written in a language unfamiliar to Todd. He rubbed off some of the yellow-green lichen growth that partially hid some characters and then taking a pad of paper and a pencil from his saddlebag, he carefully rubbed an impression of the writings onto the paper.

"This place very old and sacred to my people," Tecumseh explained as he watched Todd work. "We not show to any white man. My ancestors tell of a people with red beards came here in large canoes and made this writing many moons ago. We not know who they were, only that they come from far away."

Todd thought about Antikum's curly red hair and fair skin. While in college Todd read about rumors of Vikings who rowed their ships through the Great Lakes and could have portaged to the rivers that fed the Mississippi, but he did not trust those stories. The Vikings supposedly explored this area hundreds of years before Columbus, but most scholars considered this story only a Scandinavian myth. Yet the Indians claimed a people who arrived in large canoes and had red beards made these centuries-old inscriptions. No Indian could have inscribed this message, written in a script unknown to modern scholars. He knew that lichens were extremely slow growing, perhaps taking 100 years or more to grow to the size of a silver dollar, and yet these lichens had partially covered the inscription, taking centuries to reach this size.

When Todd finished his tracings, Tecumseh said, "Come, I take Black Robe to a place of big magic."

They mounted their horses and Todd followed the three Indians as they led him on a path that wound northeast and higher into the hills. It ended at the foot of a hundred-foot sandstone cliff that loomed over the forest. Dozens of scaffolds stood at the foot of the cliff, each six by two foot and erected ten feet off the ground. Decaying rags hung from the racks, and yellowed bones including a few skulls littered the area underneath the scaffolds. Tecumseh pointed to a 30 by 20-foot niche on the cliff. Dozens of brilliant petrographs decorated the niche, each figure painted in ocher, red, yellow, and white hues. The petrography represented the most complete and undisturbed Indian wall paintings that Todd had ever witnessed or even read about. Nor had any other nineteenth century archaeologists had any others as extensive and well preserved as these been studied by nineteenth century archeologists. The drawings depicted familiar animals, strange spiral symbols, and humanoid figures armed with spears, bows, and dressed in robes and strange beehive-shaped hats. Antelope, bear, elk, deer, and cougars chased one another across the face of the cliff, yet other animals indigenous to Africa and not North America roamed across the cliff face. For instance, facing the human figures, several elephants with long trunks stood at one end of the paintings. Todd recognized that they were not like the African elephants he knew but were covered in long, shaggy fur and their long ivory tusks curved upward almost completing a half circle. The drawings also included small three-toed horses, several camels, and six animals with long necks and legs looking like giraffes. Baffled by these pictographs, Todd realized that early American Indians knew nothing of these African animals. Other drawings were even stranger, consisting of parts of different animals that only existed in the imagination of the artist. Todd took a closer look at a cougar depiction and noticed that unlike normal cougars, long fangs protruded from its upper jaw. Another drawing at first looked like a bear with its front paws leaning on a tree, but on closer inspection he saw it had long hooked toenails and its head was long and narrow with a protruding tongue.

[Scientists now know that ten thousand years ago sloths, mammoths, sabretooth tigers, camels, giraffes, and three-toed horses roamed North America. These animals became extinct after the glaciers retreated and man first hunted them in North America. In the nineteenth century, Todd would have known nothing about these extinct North American animals. Undoubtedly, the artist painted them when they existed ten to fifteen thousand years ago.]

Perplexed and overwhelmed by the pictographs, Todd asked Tecumseh, "Why have you brought me to this place?"

"This a sacred place. It sacred for all Ojibwa and Dakota people and a place of big magic," Tecumseh explained. "My ancestors left their dead here on these platforms, to be close to the gods who painted the pictures. We no longer place our dead here for we not know what the symbols mean. Our shaman says it is bad medicine, but we not know. We bring Black Robe here so he can tell us if it is good or bad medicine. If good, you and Neenah can both pray to the gods for Waleke. If not good, you can pray to your God for Waleke and Neenah will pray to his."

Todd tried to explain in a way that Tecumseh would understand. "I do not have the power to know if this place is good or bad medicine. I do not think gods painted these pictures. I think your ancestors painted them many, many moons ago."

Tecumseh looked at the paintings and said, "Black Robe performs big medicine, he talk with his God and cure my people. Neenah also has big magic, but not strong like yours. He asked our gods to cure Waleke, but they no answer him. Your God will tell you if this a good medicine place. Ask him for Waleke to get better. Your God powerful and he will listen to you."

"God does not always answer our prayers," Todd explained. "Nevertheless, I think the people who painted these pictures were good, and therefore this place is good. I do not believe in magic, I only believe in the power of God the Creator and His son Jesus Christ."

"Perhaps then you can ask your creator God to talk to the other gods," Tecumseh persisted, "and tell them to cure Waleke."

"There are not many gods, only one God the Father," Todd objected.

"I hear you pray to the Jesus Christ God, and I hear you pray to the Holy Ghost God. You have many gods too," Tecumseh protested.

Todd knew this was not a good teaching moment. He didn't want to get into an explanation of the Trinity, so he simply repeated that he could not ask God to explain the paintings, but he would pray for Waleke.

Neenah and Todd sat together before the pictographs and each prayed in his own manner. That night they camped together under the stars in a meadow not far from the petrographs cliff.

"You think your God lives among those many stars?" Tecumseh asked as he pointed upward.

"God lives everywhere," Todd said. "He lives among those stars, here on Earth, in the woods and mountains, and on the prairie. He also lives in your heart, and in mine. God is everywhere."

"If everywhere, why not you see him?"

"He is a spirit ... invisible."

"Your God very strange; you say one and yet three, he's here and there, everywhere, but you no see him. You look up to heaven when you pray, but then if he is everywhere why look to the sky. If he loves you, why he no talk to you? Your God is a strange God, a very strange God indeed. I don't think I can get to know Him." Tecumseh rolled over and went to sleep.

The next morning, they rode together back to the village. When they arrived, Tamara ran to greet them saying that Waleke's fever had broken.

Tecumseh grunted and said to Todd, "Your God no talk, but he listens to you."

Two days after they returned, Tecumseh and Tamara led Todd and Molly back to Whitefish Lake. Mary and Ann came running out of the house as soon as the geese announced the travelers' arrival and embraced Todd. As Tecumseh and Tamara prepared to leave, Tecumseh promised that he would allow all Whitefish men to hunt and fish on Leech Lake tribal lands. The Ojibwa land south of the Big Fork River and west of the Mississippi River extending south to a line running from Brainerd west to Deer Creek would be theirs to hunt and fish. An 1856 treaty between the US government and the Leech Lake Indians forbade white men from trespassing on their tribal lands, and until Todd's visit, no other white men had ever been given permission to hunt, fish, or log on tribal lands. However, this didn't stop many white men from trespassing, which had caused incidents between Minnesotans and Ojibwa and Dakota Indians. Moreover, those lands held abundant game, minerals, and forests, all ripe for exploitation; a temptation that white men couldn't resist. The news of Todd's safe return spread throughout the region, and Mike's farm hosted dozens of visitors who came to welcome Todd back home and have their ailments treated.

Chapter 8
The Dedication

May 1873

It had been over a year since Todd first laid eyes on Whitefish Lake from Mesabi Pass. He had fallen in love with the folks of Whitefish Lake and they in turn loved and admired him. As a priest, he ministered to his congregation's souls and because he was the only medic for a hundred miles, he nursed their bodies as well. Many folks were convinced he performed miraculous cures and refused to listen when he protested such adulation. In addition to Clara's unexpected and sudden recovery, there were other incidents where either through Father Todd's expert doctoring or through his prayers, most folks he treated recovered, often miraculously.

After Todd's visit to Leech Lake and despite the two-day trip on horseback to the Indians from that tribe often came asking his assistance. He would treat their wounds and illnesses, set broken bones, and give them medications to take home. That fall a Leech Lake Indian and another tribe member brought his young son, a boy six or seven years old, for treatment. An arrow had pierced the boy's shoulder and a sharp obsidian arrowhead partially poked through his skin. It was fortunate that his father hadn't tried to remove the arrow, for if he had done so the boy would probably have bled to death. When Todd carefully removed the arrow, the wound bled profusely until he cauterized it. After Todd stopped the bleeding, he sutured the wound. Throughout this procedure, the young boy didn't cry out and hardly even flinched. The Indians had brought along a large bag of red berries which they gave to Todd and instructed him to make a mash from the berries and place it on the boy's wound before he bandaged it. He didn't recognize the berries, but did as the Indians asked. He gave the boy's father a packet of wax myrtle to retard infection. Todd later heard that by the time the Indians arrived back at Leech Lake, the boy's wound had closed and the boy almost had full use of his arm. A new rumor circulated throughout the Indian village and in Whitefish that this incident was another of Father Todd's miraculous cures.

Jimmy Callahan hammered a rusty nail clear through his palm and came to Father Todd with the nail still protruding from his hand. Father Todd tied Jimmy's hand to the table and removed the nail with a pair of pliers. Then he washed the wound with alcohol and covered it with a paste made from the red berries that the Indians gave him, bandaged it, and gave him wax myrtle to place on it. Todd's greatest concern for Jimmy was tetanus or lockjaw, which often resulted from rusty nail wounds. By the next day, Jimmy's wound began to heal and when Father Todd removed the bandage three days later, the wound showed no signs of infection. Weeks later Jimmy showed no symptoms of tetanus and there was only a hint of a scar.

"No wound normally heals as quickly as this," Jimmy told everyone who would listen, and claimed his hand had healed miraculously. Again, Father Todd denied a miracle and credited the rapid healing to the Indian berries and the zinc oxide he used to thwart infection. Yet Jimmy would hear none of it and kept insisting it was another Father Todd miracle.

One skeptic of the miraculous healing stories was Perry Funston who worked at the lumber mill for Jack Sprier. Perry was not a member of a church, and despite Jack's efforts to convert him, he claimed to be an agnostic and proud of his reputation as a pragmatist. "Show me" he would often say of rumors. For every story of miraculous healing, Perry offered a natural explanation.

"Aw, I've seen even faster cures," he would say when someone would describe one of Todd's so-called "miracles." Perry was sawing a large maple log to fashion a ridge beam for the clinic when the blade hit a knot and a large splinter speared his upper thigh. He climbed bareback on his horse, rode to Mike's farm, and found Todd in the infirmary. Todd removed a splinter the size of a number two pencil and sutured the wound. However, the wound would not stop bleeding.

"It must have nicked your femoral artery," Todd surmised. I am going to have to suture the artery or you will bleed out."

"Father, I've always been a bleeder. When I was a child one time a kid gave me a bloody nose and it bled for hours. Even a small nick from a razor blade will bleed and bleed. Nothing will stop the bleeding from shaving except a septic pencil."

"I can't very well use a septic pencil on a leaky artery now, can I?" Todd said.

"No, I don't suppose you can."

Todd tied a tourniquet around Perry's thigh, found the nick in the artery, and sutured the wound. As soon as he released the pressure from the tourniquet however, the wound began to weep.

"You certainly are a bleeder all right. This will never do," Todd said in frustration. "I have to find some way to stop the bleeding." Perry's mention of a styptic pencil gave him an idea. He mixed alum with beeswax and applied a generous amount to the wound. The bleeding soon diminished and stopped.

"Another one of your miracles, eh Father?" Perry chided.

"No miracle," Todd said, "I just improvised."

Perry smiled, thanked Todd, and then limped back to his horse. The next day when he came back to have Father examine the wound he barely limped at all.

"Seems like you are doing fine: the wound has clotted, there is no sign of infection, and the healing has already begun," Todd said with a smile.

After that incident Perry became a believer of Todd's medical skills, but still did not attribute his healing to a miracle. Just the same he asked Todd to baptize him. After weeks of instruction and after Mass one Sunday, Todd baptized him in front of the entire congregation.

"The church doesn't seem complete without a bell," Perry commented.

"Now where in the heck are we going to get a bell," Jerry Keegan protested.

"We can make one," Perry claimed. "I know how to do it. First, we will make a form out of sand and clay. I know where we can mine copper and tin, and then melt it all down in Jack's kiln and pour the molten brass mixture into the mold."

Although the bell was small, two feet wide at the fluted opening, it still weighed several hundred pounds. They had to build a scaffold to lift the bell into place so it could hang from the church ridge beam that extended three feet beyond the front façade. In early June, parishioners gathered around the front of St. Patrick's and watched as they lifted the bell in place and then rung it for the first time. The sound it made was unusually loud for such a small bell, and the vibrations were melodious and continued to ring for several seconds after the clapper stopped hitting the bell. Folks as far as a couple of miles said they could hear its song.

    In the past year, the community had accomplished much, completing the road to Grand Rapids, building St. Patrick's Church, and establishing a thriving lumber and transport business operating out of Jack Sprier's lumberyard. Last month they began to erect the combination clinic and rectory next to the church.

    Toward mid-May, Todd received a letter from Father Quinn saying that in the second week of June he and Bishop Byrne wished to visit Whitefish Lake to dedicate St. Patrick's church. Todd sent an invitation to them asking them to come the weekend of second Sunday in June, and then announced to the congregation that Bishop Byrne would soon visit and dedicate St. Patrick's church.

    On June 14, Father Todd hitched Molly to his wagon and made the drive into Grand Rapids to meet the Bishop and Father Quinn. Mike wanted to go with him, but Todd insisted that he should go alone. He arrived in Grand Rapids on Thursday, four days before the scheduled dedication, in time to greet the Bishop (whom he had never met) and Father Quinn as they disembarked on Friday morning from the *Itaska*. He then drove them to Whitefish, arriving that Saturday afternoon. Prompted by this special occasion, Mark and Sue Gottwald prepared the now finished rooms over the Whitefish Saloon and added the word "Hotel" to the overhead sign. They welcomed Bishop Byrne and Father Quinn as their first ever hotel guests. Sunday morning Todd drove the priests out to St. Patrick's where a dozen parishioners eagerly waited to greet them. They rang the bell when they spotted Todd's buggy coming down the road. Father Quinn was dumbfounded when he heard the bell ring and sighted the church. He was at a loss for words.

After Todd introduced the Bishop and Father Quinn to all the bystanders, Father Quinn smiled and gaped at the front of the church. "Father Todd, I am amazed. You have only been here a year, and yet managed to erect a magnificent church, even with a beautiful bell ringing to greet us. When I sent you on your way last year and promised to visit the following year with the Bishop to dedicate your church, I fully expected you would write and tell me that it would take longer than a year to build the church. Then I received your letter before Christmas that the community had celebrated the first Mass in St. Patrick's. I couldn't believe it and imagined a dirt floor and sod-roof log cabin with a cross, yet here is a church that St. Paul or Minneapolis would be proud to have on any city block."

"Don't congratulate me but applaud these dedicated parishioners and many members of the community. It is through their hard work and generous contributions that the church exists."

Bishop Byrne looked confused. "When you say, 'the parishioners and the members of the community,' do you mean that non-Catholics contributed money and helped build this church?"

"Yes, it was a community project."

Bishop Byrne smiled and then said, "This is a historic first in Minnesota, and such a Christian spirit of cooperation is to be commended."

Then Todd led the Bishop and Father Quinn up the front stairs and into the church. Festively decorated for the occasion, with colorful religious banners hanging from the rafters, the inside felt warm and inviting. The sun flooded the interior with amber light as it passed through the twelve cathedral-style glass windows. The polished black marble altar gleamed as the Christ figure on the crucifix looked down on the church. Parishioners and townsfolk filled the little church to overflowing. Father Quinn, Bishop Byrne, and Father Todd were vesting in the sacristy when a wide-eyed teenager burst in.

"Father Todd, there are four Indians on horses in full war paint in front of the church. They want to see you."

Todd followed the boy through the church and out onto the front porch. Indeed, there were four Indians sitting on their horses, yet they didn't wear war paint but wore their best ceremonial dress and paint.

Todd immediately recognized Tecumseh and Sekota. He climbed down from the porch and greeted his friends in Indian style.

"We hear about prayer house and come to celebrate with Black Robe and his people," Tecumseh explained.

"You and your friends are most welcome," Todd said with a big smile. "Please come inside."

They climbed down from their horses and cautiously followed Todd into the church. The church buzzed in amazement as the four Indians entered the church and Todd made room for them in the front pew.

"Who are they?" Father Quinn asked.

"It's a long story that I will relate later, but these Indians are friends of mine from Leech Lake. I helped their tribe recover from the pox this past spring."

"Leach Lake Indians are friends of yours?" Bishop Byrne said, somewhat shocked. "I hear those Indians have caused a lot of trouble and you've treated their illness and kept your scalp?"

"You're amazing," Father Quinn added, slowly shaking his head.

The three priests co-celebrated Mass. During Mass Father Quinn used another gift that he brought along for the church, an incense burner and incense that he used throughout the dedication Mass. The Indians could not understand the ceremonial Mass, yet the use of incense was one part of the ceremony that they recognized. Their shamans performed similar rituals with sweet-smelling smoke. After Mass, everyone gathered in front of the church for a group photo taken with Lloyd Brevick's recently purchased daguerreotype camera.

The community held a celebration luncheon in the Whitefish Saloon & Hotel. The mood was festive and even the Indians took part in the celebration by performing a traditional dance. When Lloyd passed around the developed daguerreotype print to share with the crowd, the Indians seemed uncomfortable, although they said nothing. Later, as they prepared to return to Leech Lake, Tecumseh told Todd that Sekota was upset because his spirit was now captive in that picture. Todd assured him that it was only a picture, much like a painting or those petrographs, except done with light. Todd's explanation did not convince Sekota, and as they rode down the road, Sekota sang a sad song.

The following morning Todd drove Father Quinn and Bishop Byrne back to Grand Rapids and saw them off on the *Itaska* the following morning. While traveling home to Whitefish, as his buggy bounced down from Mesabi Pass 15 miles from the town, a black bear scampered onto the road and panicked Molly. She took off in a full gallop, ignoring Todd's efforts to regain control by pulling hard on the reins. Molly refused to calm down and when the buggy rolled over a large rock in the road, the axle snapped and the left wheel came off and rolled down an embankment. The buggy suddenly stopped, spilling Todd into the dirt. Molly broke free from her harness and galloped off, leaving Todd and the disabled buggy stranded on the road. Todd slowly got to his feet only to discover that his left ankle was severely sprained. He began to hobble down the road after Molly, but she was nowhere in sight.

"This will never do. I'll never catch up to Molly at this rate," he said out loud. "I'm going to have to stabilize my ankle first."

He found a small stick, then tore part of his shirt into strips, and fastened the stick to his lower leg and ankle. He found a stout walking stick and hobbled off down the road. When after a quarter mile there was still no sign of Molly and with only a couple hours remaining until sunset, he thought it best to return to the buggy where he had a few supplies and some camping gear. He would camp there tonight and pray that someone from town would come looking for him in the morning. There was no way he was going to walk back home, not with a sprained ankle and at night. Without Molly, he was stuck in the woods.

When he returned to the buggy, the bear had obviously visited and strewn his stuff all over the road, smashed some of Todd's gear, and helped himself to the bread, cookies, and fresh fruit Todd had with him. Fortunately, the buggy contained a tarp, a jug of water, matches, a good camp knife and ax, a bedroll, and a can of beans. He improvised a shelter by tying one side of the tarp to the buggy, made a fire, opened the can of beans, and then watched the sun set over a mountain. Worried that the bear might return, he remained on guard keeping the knife close at his side as he ate. The night enveloped his improvised camp like a dark shroud and without light from the new moon, he couldn't see his hand in front of his face. He lit a candle and crawled into his bedroll to try to get some sleep, but sleep wouldn't come easy that night. Coyotes howled in the distance and his ankle throbbed. As he lay wide awake watching his candle burn down, he heard something moving around his camp. He tightened his grip on the knife, expecting the bear had returned intent on another raid. Then he heard a soft neigh. Thankfully, Molly had returned. He got up, took the candle, and found her peacefully standing in front of the broken buggy as if nothing at all had happened. He tied a rope around her neck and then to a tree, and crawled back into his sack for a mostly sleepless night.

As soon as the sun rose in the eastern sky, Todd rode bareback on Molly toward home. As the road climbed down Mesabi Pass, he met Dick Partridge and Jerry Keegan driving a wagon, and Mike, Lloyd Brevick, and Jack Sprier on horseback.

"Father, what happened to you? Mike asked.

"A bear panicked Molly and she took off at full gallop. My buggy hit a rock, broke an axle, and threw me onto the road. I sprained my ankle and spent the night camped out. Molly eventually came back, but the disabled the buggy is still about 5 miles from here."

Jerry said that he and Dick would bring back the buggy while Mike, Lloyd, and Jack led Molly with Todd back to Mike's farm. As it turned out, Todd's foot was more than sprained; according to Dick who splinted it, some ligaments in his ankle were torn.

"Sorry, Father, but you are going to be hobbling around for a bit," Dick said as he taped up the broken ankle. Not slowed down by a broken ankle, Father Todd returned to his duties the next day.

Chapter 9
The Clinic

August 1873

Toward the end of the month, the workers finished and outfitted the combination clinic and rectory. Todd moved his few possessions, medical equipment, and medications from Mike's farm to the new clinic and announced the Whitefish Clinic was now open for business. They outfitted the two backrooms as an office and bedroom for Todd.

Fund-raisers had provided the money to build and outfit the clinic with an autoclave, medicines, and a few medical instruments. Mike made a trip to St. Paul and purchased state-of-the-art medical apparatuses from the St. Paul hospital, including an alcohol gel-fired autoclave. Now that Todd was living at the clinic next door to the church, he could celebrate daily Mass at St. Patrick's. Todd was thrilled with his new rectory and clinic. June Brevick, Lloyd's wife, volunteered to be his rectory housekeeper and assistant at the clinic. Although June had no formal training as a nurse, folks appreciated her skills at caring for the sick and assisting Dick Partridge with medical emergencies. Sue Gottwald served Todd meals at the Whitefish Saloon & Hotel or brought them out to the rectory.

The first patient in the new clinic was Gus O'Neil who arrived on horseback and in so much pain in his belly that he needed help to dismount. Todd laid him on the examining table and prodded his abdomen.

"It looks like your appendix is about ready to rupture," Todd told him. "It has to come out or you will die of septic poisoning."

Todd was not a surgeon, although while serving in the Baltimore hospital he assisted in many surgeries, including an appendectomy or two. Last month Todd had received the autoclave to sterilize his instruments, and the clinic had all the needed instruments for a proper surgery. Todd's biggest problem was a lack of anesthesia, and he dared not give Gus any whiskey to lessen his pain for an appendectomy. He asked Sue Gottwald and Dick Partridge to assist, strapped Gus on the table, and began to operate. Making a small incision, he found the infected appendix and removed it. It was swollen and about to burst as he expected. Had it done so, Gus would have died of septic poisoning, but the operation saved his life. Months later, Gus, who had never joined a religion, began to attend Sunday Mass, and on Easter Sunday Todd baptized him, along with several other adults and children.

The clinic was always busy, sometimes with one or two folks waiting for Todd's attention.

Patients who came to the clinic for treatment were seldom able to pay with cash money. Few folks in Whitefish had any. Lloyd's lumberyard sales in Grand Rapids provided some cash when Lloyd paid his employees with greenbacks, and those few bills circulated around town. Most of payment was in bartering. The few outside visitors to Whitefish paid with cash at the Whitefish Hotel and at Rich Parson's lodge across the lake, but barter was the method of choice in Whitefish. The hardware store would trade chickens or corn for a case of nails or trade a sack of barley for ammunition. Dick Partridge would give a customer a haircut and shave for the price of a chicken or a dozen eggs. As the farmers harvested their crops, they bartered with one another, trading a few sacks of corn for squash or watermelons. Many folks built root cellars to store their vegetables. Mark Gottwald used a nearby deep cave to serve as a meat locker. The temperature inside the cave remained constant, just above freezing all year. Mark cut blocks of ice from the lake during the winter and filled the cave chamber with sawdust and ice. Fall was the primary hunting season, and each man hunted deer or elk for his own family. Successful hunters stored their butchered meat in Mark's cave and then traded the surplus meat for other goods at the Merc or with neighbors.

The clinic also operated mostly on the barter system. Folks would bring Father Todd venison or a basket of vegetables, or couple dozen eggs in payment for his doctoring services. On one occasion Margaret Donahue brought her eight-year-old son John Junior to the clinic for treatment. Todd set the boy's broken arm and wrapped strips of cloth around a splint. John hardly cried, making his mother proud of him.

"Father, I cannot pay you, but I do have something for you," Margaret said. She went out to her wagon and returned with a large jar of pickles and a puppy.

"You need a companion," she announced, "and this little puppy will more than fill the bill." Father Todd stared at the puppy in her arms. "He needs you and you need him," Margaret decided.

Todd didn't know what to say in response. He never had considered owning a dog, and didn't think he had the time to raise a puppy. Nevertheless, he couldn't refuse Margaret's kind offer, and took the jar of pickles in one hand and the puppy with the other. The puppy snuggled into the crook of Todd's arm like this was where he had always belonged.

"I don't know about his pedigree; he's probably just a mongrel," Margaret explained, "Yet he's spirited and smart. A roving bitch birthed him in our barn and after weaning him, took off. Our sheepdog eventually adopted him."

Todd thought he looked a bit like the sheepherder dogs favored by the Basque people, but he obviously was the product of undistinguished parentage. Todd examined his paws. "These paws will produce a medium-size dog," he surmised.

Margaret ended with a final sales pitch, "He sure seems to have taken to you."

"He's beautiful; thank you," Todd finally said.

Only a few months old and gifted with big shoulders and ample hind end, Todd thought the puppy would mature into sturdy medium-size dog. Thick black and white fur, large floppy ears, a hairy tail, long pointed nose, and big brown eyes completed the description.

"What are you going to name him?" John asked.

Name him? Todd thought for a moment. The puppy remained nestled in one arm and his free hand still grasped the jar of pickles.

"Pickles," he said. "Pickles will be his name."

John laughed. "That's a fine name, Father."

Over the next few months Pickles grew into the companion Margaret had envisioned, and Pickles and Todd became inseparable companions. As Todd made his rounds around Whitefish with Molly pulling the buggy and Pickles either followed or rode in a seat next to

Todd. On cold winter days, when it was too cold to leave him outside, during Mass Pickles curled up next to the potbelly stove in the vestibule of the church and no one minded having a dog witness Mass.

*****

The spring rains expected in April and May were scant in 1873, and the month of June began hot and dry. The weather continued warmer and dryer well into the summer months. By mid-August, the forest was tinder dry and the emerging crops withered in the summer heat. A small creek flowed across Mike's farm and he and Todd built an impoundment dam and spent most of July digging irrigation ditches to water the summer crops, and were thankful for the rain that a few thunderstorms gifted. Yet with the welcomed thunderstorms came lightning.

Shawn and Margaret Donahue's ranch was located on cleared forestland west of Whitefish Lake, about two miles from Mike's ranch. One afternoon Shawn came riding up on his horse as Mike and Todd labored clearing irrigation ditches. "There's a fire in the hills above our cabin," he cried. Mike shielded his eyes and looked to the hills above Shawn's ranch. A mushroom column of black and white smoke rose ominously over the forest.

"It's a forest fire all right," Mike agreed, "and a big one at that."

Yesterday the valley had received the first substantial rain of the season and Shawn suspected that lighting had started this fire. Todd, Mike, and his son Frank rode with Shawn over to his ranch. Fanned by the wind, the fire was moving toward Shawn's cabin and only a ridge above the cabin separated his ranch from the fire.

"We have to get Margaret, Lori, and your livestock out of path of the fire and over to the safety of my ranch. At the rate that fire is advancing, we don't have much time," Mike warned.

Todd told Frank to hitch up Shawn's buckboard to his two horses and then take Margaret, Shawn Junior, and Lori over to his farm. After that, he should ride into town and alert Lloyd and others to ride out to Shawn's ranch. On the way into town, Frank stopped at the lumberyard and asked Jack Spier to ride with him into town. They found Lloyd in the livery stable and he suggested that the fastest way to alert the townsfolk was to ring the church bell. They rode out to the church and rang the bell for a solid five minutes. Fifteen minutes later most of the townsfolk had gathered in front of the church.

"There's a huge forest fire heading toward the Donahue ranch," Frank said. My dad wants as many men as possible to ride over there with axes, saws, shovels, and rakes and help construct a firebreak."

Fifteen men and wagons headed toward the ranch. In the meantime, Mike and Todd helped Shawn and his two dogs round up a dozen cattle, two milk cows, and seven goats, and then herded them along the road to Mike's farm. As they returned to the ranch, they met up with Frank, Jack, Lloyd, and a dozen other men from town.

"We have to construct a firebreak on the ridge about ¼ miles west of Shawn's cabin, otherwise this fire will burn his ranch to the ground," Mike said.

The eastern side of the mountain behind Shawn's ranch was heavily forested, but a past fire had left the ridge with few trees, which made it the best place to construct a firebreak. They worked feverishly on the firebreak, but when fire reached the bottom of the ridge, it raced up toward the workers with surprising speed.

"Everyone off the ridge!" Lloyd shouted. "Regroup at the ranch."

Everyone gathered around Shawn's cabin and watched as the fire raced up the backside to the top of the ridge. Some of the men formed a fire brigade and threw water on the cabin roof, but Mike knew it would be of little use.

"The firebreak will stop it," Shawn said. He knew it was more wishful thinking than a fact.

The fire created its own weather, producing a circulating inferno that caused the trees in front of the fire line to spontaneously ignite like torches and then thrust columns of flames and cinders into the sky. The fire hesitated at the firebreak on the top of the ridge, but only for a few minutes. Pinecone firebombs thrust high into the sky rained down on the east side of the ridge, starting several new fires. Soon the entire ridge was ablaze. The fire, now only ¼ mile away from the cabin, was unstoppable. Mike and Lloyd ordered everyone to retreat a safe distance down the road leading to Mike's farm where they watched as the fire crept toward Shawn's cabin and barn. When the fire was only a few yards away, the cabin burst into flames and five minutes later the cabin, barn, lean-tos, and fences were only charred, smoking remains. The valley floor between Shawn's ranch and Mike's farm was mostly meadowland, with only a few small trees and shrubs that could catch fire. When the fire reached the edge of the meadow, there was nothing left for it to burn, and it began to die out. The meadow protected Mike's farm, yet nothing would stop the fire from attacking the forest north and east of Shawn's ranch. The townsfolk watched in horror as the fire, pushed by a strengthening southwest wind, crept toward the mountain northwest of Whitefish Lake. They realized that even the town of Whitefish could be set ablaze. Nothing in their power could stop the fire, and all that they could do was let Todd lead them in prayer that providence would save the town.

The townsfolk had named the mountain northwest of town Scar Mountain for the wide treeless mark formed years ago by a snow avalanche that left a one-hundred-yard-wide rocky scar on the mountain. As the fire raced toward the treeless scar, the wind suddenly changed direction. The fire slowed as it reached the scar, and Mike watched as a line of dark storm clouds pushed by a north wind appeared over the summit of Scar Mountain. Lightning and thunder soon echoed throughout the valley and sheets of heavy rain drenched the men and the surrounding forest. The mountainside scar halted the eastern advance of the fire, and the rain so dampened the forest surrounding it that it was unable to advance and eventually died out. That Sunday at Mass, Todd led the congregation in a prayer of thanks that God had spared the little Whitefish community from this disaster. Later that summer, the men of Whitefish helped Shawn Donahue rebuild his ranch.

*****

Although several babies had been born and baptized since Todd arrived in Whitefish, one medical procedure that he had never performed was to deliver a baby. Theresa Kelly, a competent and experienced midwife who had delivered dozens of babies in Whitefish, continued in her profession even after Todd arrived. Todd had no desire to replace her, and besides the women in Whitefish seemed to prefer Theresa's services. One day in early September Peter Stewart carried his pregnant wife, Abby, into the infirmary. Sue Gottwald was on duty that day and took Abby, who complained of cramps, into infirmary. Sue told Peter to place Abby on the examination table while she went over to the church and fetched Father Todd who was saying his morning breviary.

Todd entered the exam room and asked Peter when Abby was due.

"Not until the end of October," Peter said.

A month too soon, Todd thought. When Todd examined her she was bleeding, yet other than her cramps there was no other sign that she was about to go into labor. He tried to stop Abby's hemorrhaging by giving her clotting drugs, but the medication did not help. He prayed that God would save this woman just as He had done for some of his other patients. Yet the curative warmth that he felt in past situations did not return and nothing he did stemmed her bleeding.

"I'm afraid that unless I operate Abby may bleed to death, and there is a good chance she may lose this child," he said to Sue. As dangerous as this operation was for Abby and her baby, Todd knew that he would have to perform a Caesarian section to save their lives.

"Did Abby have any problems delivering her first child?" Todd asked Peter.

"No, everything was normal with Catherine," Peter said, referring to their first child.

Todd asked Sue to ride out to the Kelly farm and bring Theresa to the clinic as fast as possible. "Tell her that I need her right away."

As Todd prepared to perform the operation, a medicine bottle fell out of Abby's apron pocket. Todd examined the bottle labeled "Dr. Watkins' Elixir."

Todd opened the bottle and sampled the liquid, which tasted bitter.

"Where did Abby get this medicine?" Todd inquired.

"She bought it from the tinker who passed through town last month," Peter explained.

Todd examined the label on the bottle, but it did not list the ingredients.

"It could be that this medicine contains something that is causing Abby to hemorrhage. Have you taken any of this?"

"No, just Abby took it. The tinker said it would strengthen the baby and make delivery easier."

Abby was becoming weaker by the minute and despite the hemorrhaging that would result from a cesarean, Todd could not wait for Theresa to arrive to assist him. He performed the surgery and delivered a healthy, premature baby boy. He cleaned the mucous from the child's mouth with a suction cup and handed him to Peter as the baby let out a healthy cry. He turned his attention back to Abby and sutured the surgery, yet she had lost a lot of blood that continued to seep from the wound. Unless the bleeding stopped, she would die. Peter cleaned the baby off with warm water and placed him in his dying mother's arms.

"Jeremiah," Abby whispered, "Jeremiah is his name. He's beautiful."

Todd's eyes filled with tears as he went back over to the church to pray and to give Peter a few minutes alone with Abby and his new son.

"Father, please don't take Abby. Her husband and Catherine need her, and now Jeremiah needs her too. Show me what I should do," he fervently prayed.

Sue and Theresa arrived a few minutes later and Theresa took charge of the baby. Todd returned and heard Abby's confession and gave her the last rites as she lay on the examination table. Minutes later, she died peacefully in Peter's arms.

After Abby's funeral and interment in the church cemetery, Sue asked, "Father, you saved others, why couldn't you heal this woman?" It was an impertinent question, yet deep down Todd knew he could not offer a satisfying response to either Sue or himself.

Doubt tormented Todd's soul. He knew that the question of evil, an age-old query without a ready answer, was not privy to human understanding. Yet the death of this young mother troubled him and tested his faith. Why had God chosen not to answer his prayer for Abby? The world would have been a better place with her, and her family desperately needed her.

Father Todd's faith could not supply an answer.

Chapter 10
Confronting Evil

September 1873

    Strangers visiting Whitefish were rare, and when a newcomer wandered into town, he would be the object of intense curiosity.
    One September evening at dusk one such stranger rode into town on a gray mare, tied his horse to the hitching post outside the Whitefish Saloon and Hotel, and then climbed the stairs pushing aside the double swinging doors. The doors nosily swung back and forth as he stepped inside, alerting all the patrons to his presence. Dimly lit by two chandeliers, the saloon provided barely enough light for folks to discern a man of notable stature, over six feet tall with broad powerful shoulders and arms. His unkempt red beard, dusty overcoat, and a well-worn black hat perched on top of his head further distinguished him. No one failed to notice the long barrel Colt 44 slung from the gun belt on his hip. Everyone stopped what he or she was doing and watched as the man advanced inside. Spurs jangled from his mud-covered boots as the man strode up to the bar and ordered a whiskey. He took off his hat and laid it on the bar,, exposing a head graced by only a few wisps of red hair. He downed the drink in a single gulp and ordered another. Then with his second drink in hand, he slowly turned around and surveyed the room. Everyone's eyes remained fixated on the stranger as he frowned and squinted, his eyes permanently narrowed by the years in bright sunlight. Without turning his head, his eyes darted from person to person, remaining on each customer for less than a second. He slung his head back, downed the second drink, and then uttered a low growl as he turned back to the bar. Throwing a silver dollar on the bar, he ordered another whiskey from Mark, who poured him a third drink.
    "Your whiskey tastes like piss water," the man hissed.

Mark looked at him and smiled. "Sorry, but it's the best we have. What's your name and where do you hail from?" he asked in his friendliest tone.

The man stared back at Mark for several seconds without answering, and then his eyes narrowed even further and in almost a whisper he finally answered, "The name's Stillwell, and where I come from is no concern of yours."

"Well, Mr. Stillwell, my name is Mark Gottwald. Welcome to Whitefish."

Mark offered his hand, but Stillwell ignored it. He uttered another low growl and then downed the whiskey.

"What do you folks do around here for entertainment?" he asked as he put his hat back on.

"Entertainment?" Mark pondered. "Well, not much I suppose. Most folks spend time with their families and some play cards here each night. Every other Tuesday night we have a hoedown in the Community Hall, and once a month weather permitting there are horse races and a rodeo down at the corral."

"Sounds thrilling," Stillwell said sarcastically. "I meant do you have any ladies-of-the-night in town?"

"No, it's not that kind of town."

"And a shit hole of a town it is," Stillwell added. He let out another low grunt and then walked over to one of the tables where four men who were playing cards had interrupted their game to watch the stranger.

"What's the game?" Stillwell asked.

"Five-card draw, one-eyed Jacks wild," Lars Postel the dealer explained. "The ante is twenty-five cents, with a maximum bet of $1 and three raises."

"Got room for a fifth?"

Lars nodded and Stillwell drew up a chair and sat down. He sized up his competition by intently staring at each player, shifting his gaze from one player to the other.

The players anteed and Lars dealt five cards to each. Stillwell had nothing and threw in his hand with a disgusted grunt.

Several hands later, Stillwell was down four dollars. When it was his turn to deal, he dealt himself two tens and a Jack. He raised the pot two bits, but only one player threw in his cards. Then he exchanged his two worthless cards for another ten and an ace, a winning hand or so he thought. The first player bet fifty-cents and a second player stayed in. When it was his turn to bet he raised the pot a dollar and both players followed his raise. Two raises later, only Lars remained in and called Stillwell's hand. The pot contained over $10.

"Four tens and an ace," Stillwell boasted as he laid his cards down with an arrogant smile.

"You have only three tens and my three Kings beat your tens," Lars said.

"I have a wild card to go with my tens, so I have four tens."

"You have a Jack of Clubs," Lars said. "Only the Jack of Spades and Jack of Hearts are one-eyed Jacks. You don't have a wild card."

"You said Jacks were wild," Stillwell snorted.

"No. I said one-eyed Jacks were wild," Lars corrected him.

Stillwell stood up, drew his six-shooter, and pointed the long barrel gun at Lars. "You want to argue with my Colt?"

Lars said no and backed down. With his free hand, Stillwell picked up the pot and with his gun still pointing at Lars, slowly backed out of the saloon. Mark had been listening to the argument at the card table, and when Stillwell drew his weapon, he reached under the counter for his Winchester rifle. Stillwell didn't see the rifle pointed at him, but Mark kept his finger ready on the trigger. Stillwell continued to back out of the saloon and as he exited the door, Lars got up and started to follow him.

Mark stopped him. "Let him go, Lars, it is best that he is gone. I knew he was trouble the minute he came in, and no one needs to get killed over a ten-dollar pot." Then they heard Stillwell's horse galloping out of town.

The incident made for active gossip around town, but two days later the incident was mostly forgotten when Sue Gottlieb came to the clinic with Lars's sixteen-year old daughter, Julie Postel. Sue claimed that a man had raped Julie and asked Todd to examine her. After Todd's exam, it was evident that Julie had indeed been forcibly raped.

"What happened and who did this to you?" Todd asked the tearful child.

"It was a big man with a red beard," she stammered between sobs. "I was home alone in the cabin last night when he showed up knocking on the door. Mom and Dad took the horses and wagon and went to Grand Rapids for two days and they said not to let anyone inside that I didn't know. I saw through the peephole that it was a stranger and told him to go away, but he wouldn't go away. He said that he had seen my folks going into town and knew that I was alone. He found a small log and used it to knock the door down. He threw me on the bed and raped me. He stunk and his breath smelled of whiskey. It was awful. I wanted to die. Then he ransacked the cabin and left."

"Do you think it might have been that Stillwell fellow folks were talking about?" Todd asked

"Dad told Mom about this guy coming into town. He said he was mostly bald with a red beard. The stranger that raped me was mostly bald and had a dirty red beard."

Todd asked Sue to take Julie to the hotel and give her a room until Lars and his wife returned from Grand Rapids. Then Todd visited with Mayor Brevick and told him about the rape.

"It sure sounds like the person who did this to Julie was that Stillwell fellow all right," Lloyd admitted. "However, I don't know what we can do about it. We don't have a sheriff in Whitefish, and the closest one is in Grand Rapids, but he is only part-time and the chance of getting him up here is piss poor."

Todd was convinced that this was something the town must deal with. "It is abundantly clear to me that we should have some law in Whitefish. Up to now, we haven't seen the need and the town council took care of minor civil matters, but now apparently we need a sheriff. We can elect one and if Stillwell is still around he can arrest him and take him into Grand Rapids for trial."

Lloyd agreed, and the next day called a meeting of the town council. They elected the Merc owner, Jerry Keegan, to be the sheriff. The next order of business was what to do about Stillwell.

"I heard that he is staying at Rich Parson's place across the lake, and Jerry should form a posse and go over there and arrest him," Mike Dunn said.

"And then what do we do with him?" Loyd asked.

"We'll take him to Sheriff Abrams in Grand Rapids. He can lock him up while we send for the circuit judge," Jerry suggested.

Jerry formed a posse consisting of himself, Mike, Mark, Tom Kelly, and Jack Spier. The next morning they rode over to Rich's lodge prepared to arrest Stillwell, but he was not there.

"He was here a couple of days ago, but the fellow was so menacing that I kicked him out," Rich said. "I think he is camped out at the east end of the lake, leastwise I saw some smoke coming from the beach over there yesterday. You'd all better be careful. This man is dangerous, and I don't want to see any of you get shot."

Jerry scouted ahead while the rest of the posse remained at the lodge. When he came back, he reported that he found the camp. "It was Stillwell all right. He didn't seem me."

At dusk they rode around the north end of the lake, and when within a few hundred yards of the camp left their horses with Mark and approached on foot so as not to spook Stillwell. He was hunched over his campfire cooking lunch. The posse hid in the trees as Jerry called out to him.

"Stillwell, I have a posse with me and we intend to arrest you!"

The man stood up, grabbed his rifle, and fired a couple of wild shots into the trees.

"Come and get me if you can!" he shouted.

Tom noticed the man's gray mare tied to a tree about 20 yards away from the fire. Hidden by the trees, Tom circled the camp and quietly untied Stillwell's horse while his attention was riveted on Jerry. Stillwell heard his horse neigh and spun around. He managed to get a shot off, hitting Tom in his upper arm. Bleeding, Tom led the horse off into the forest as Stillwell cursed and paced back and forth around the fire, waving his rifle wildly at the trees and cursing a blue streak.

"The first damn son-of-a-bitch that comes toward me will get a bullet in the head."

Tom came back to the posse leading Stillwell's horse while wrapping a cloth around his arm.

"You've been hit," Mike said.

"Just a flesh wound," Tom said as he finished wrapping his arm.

"This is not going to be easy," Jerry said as he returned to the posse. "The guy is a lunatic and he'll shoot the first one of us he sees. Already Tom took a bullet and I don't want anyone else hurt."

"Why don't we just shoot him?" Tom asked.

"I've only been sheriff for a couple of days, and this is not how I'm going to do things in Whitefish. I'm not going to shoot and ask questions later. We'll just have to flush him out the hard way."

Jerry decided to try to reason with the man. "Stillwell, there are five of us here and we have your horse. Escape is impossible. Just lay down your weapons and come peacefully with us."

"Stick it in your ear!" Stillwell yelled.

Jerry devised a plan.

"Jack, you circle to where he tied his horse. Mike, take a position closer to the lake, and Tom and I will stay here. We will have him in a cross fire and if he decides to run, go ahead and shoot him."

"Why don't you show yourselves you stinking bunch of dirt farmers?" Stillwell taunted.

Jerry gave Jack and Mike time to get into position, and then made a final offer.

"Stillwell, we have you surrounded. Dead or alive we're going to take you to Grand Rapids and if alive, we'll try you for the rape of Julie Postle. Give it up or we will bury you right here."

"I didn't rape the little bitch, she was all over me!" Stillwell shouted.

On hearing that lie, Jack had quite enough. He shot Stillwell in the leg and the man fell to the ground withering in pain. Jerry ran to him, kicked his rifle aside, and stepped on his hand that held the six-shooter. Then Jack and Mike rolled him over, took his gun, and tied his hands behind his back. Stillwell was badly bleeding from his leg wound, so Jack applied a tourniquet as the man uttered every curse word in the book, and then some.

"Your leg's broken," Jack said unsympathetically. "What a pity."

They placed Stillwell on his horse and then retrieved the other horses from Mark. They returned to town and took Stillwell to the clinic.

Todd cut off Stilwell's trouser and examined the wound while ignoring the man's cursing and profanity.

"Your femur is broken, and the bullet passed within centimeters of your femoral artery. Had it severed that artery you would have bled to death. As it is you have lost a lot of blood."

Stillwell looked at Todd and noted his cassock and Roman collar. "What are you, a doctor or a damn priest?"

"I am a priest and a medic, but if you don't calm down I may have to exercise my priestly duties over your grave."

Todd patched the man's bullet wound, reset his leg, and stabilized it with a splint.

"You got some laudanum, Doc?" Stillwell asked. "The damn leg hurts something awful."

"Let the son-of-a-mud-sucker suffer," Tom said.

Despite Tom's plea, Todd gave Stillwell a swig of the painkiller. He then patched Tom's arm and gave him a glass of whiskey.

"How's about one for me," Stillwell pleaded.

"Not for you ... you sorry excuse of a human being," Tom said.

Todd turned to Jerry and Mark.

"You're not going to be able to take him to Grand Rapids until he regains his strength. Please take him to the hotel and put him up in one of Mark's rooms. The laudanum will put him to sleep for a day or so and he won't be able to get out of bed for a couple of days, but be sure to lock the doors and windows of the room so he cannot escape. I will come and see him tomorrow."

They carried Stillwell into the hotel and placed him in a bed in one of the upstairs bedrooms. He remained dead asleep throughout transport, and was still out when Todd and Sue visited him the next day. As Todd examined his leg, Stillwell began to wake up.

He looked at Todd through fog-blurred eyes and asked, "What happened to me?"

"You were shot in the leg. I'm afraid it's broken."

He stared down at his splinted leg. "Broken you say. Just how long am I gonna be laid up here?"

"A few weeks, I'd guess."

Stillwell swore. "What are you anyhow, a doctor or a dammed priest?"

"Like I told you yesterday, I'm not a doctor; yet I'm the closest these Whitefish folks have to one. At times I treat their bodies, and at times I treat their souls."

"I ain't got no time for a damn priest."

"Right now I'm treating your broken leg. We'll see about the priest part later when you are better."

"Don't bother with that mumbo jumbo you priests like to lay on folks. The devil will take me when it's time."

"My job is to see that you get well and live. Considering what you did to Julie, I'm tempted to let the devil take you, but this would go against my conscience as a healer and a priest. Your soul needs healing even more than your leg does."

"Unless you got some whiskey for me, get the hell out of my room."

With that request, Todd left the room and gave Sue a bottle of laudanum to give to him.

"He'll be asking for some whiskey to dull the pain, but just give him a spoonful of laudanum every few hours. No matter how much he begs, don't give him any whiskey. It will not go well with the laudanum."

"Don't worry," Sue said. "I'll only give him the medicine, but I'm tempted to go stingy with the laudanum. I don't mind much if he suffers."

Suffer he did, to the point where he was begging for more laudanum or whiskey. Over the next week, Stilwell drifted in and out of consciousness. When Todd visited him toward the end of the week, his leg did not look at all good. Rather than healing, as it should have, the bullet wound was festering and Stillwell had developed a raging fever.

Todd told Sue that it looked like gangrene had set in and he would have to amputate Stillwell's leg.

When Stillwell heard this news, he became enraged. "No damn priest pretending to be a doctor is gonna take my leg!"

"If you don't let me take the leg, you are going to die a slow painful death, but die you surely will," Todd said. "If you won't let me doctor you, at least let me as a priest help you repent before you die."

"Go to hell!" Stillwell said and spit at him.

Todd prayed that Stillwell would change his mind and accept Todd's doctoring, or at least accept redemption. Two days later Stillwell died without allowing Todd to administer to either his leg or to his soul.

Chapter 11
A Crisis of Faith

Todd pondered and prayed about the death of Abby and that Stillwell died unrepentant, cursing God with his last breath. Both incidents deeply troubled him. He felt empty, in a dark place, and depressed. He had always felt the arms of Jesus enfolding him, keeping him safe and secure from evil. Now his prayers went unanswered. Did God no longer listen to him? He questioned why good people like Abby suffer, and God why allows the devil to roam the world like a ravenous wolf infecting the souls of persons like Stillwell. For the first time, the standard answers that his faith had always provided since his ordination did not satisfy him. Yes, he knew if God did not allow us the freedom to choose good and evil, then we would not have free will and without free will, we could not fulfill God's plan for us. He also realized that God does answer every prayer, but often not in the way that we expect. Nevertheless, now those answers seemed meaningless and empty. Then another incident worsened the surging doubt rising within him.

Lori Donahue, the twenty-year-old daughter of John and Margaret Donahue, was a petite and bubbly Irish lass with a lovely figure and striking features. Her long red hair and creamy white complexion turned the heads of the young men in Whitefish, yet she did not have a serious suitor. She offered to volunteer her time to help Todd in the clinic and he readily accepted her offer that would give June Brevick some needed time off. Her job as receptionist was to check in patients, prepare their paperwork, record their symptoms, and record their blood pressure, height, and weight. Father Todd found her to be reliable, competent, and hardworking. Soon she became an indispensable member of his volunteer staff. Always busy with patients and other tasks, Todd failed to notice Lori's fawning over him and subtle advances.

Alone with Lori in the clinic one evening, Todd worked at his desk finishing paperwork when he felt two slim bare arms gently wrap his neck and a gentle kiss caress his ear. Startled, he gently removed the arms and turned around to see Lori standing behind him. Her auburn hair fell in long curls about her shoulders and her unbuttoned blouse exposed ample breasts.

"We are alone and I am yours," she said softly.

Todd's heart pounded. He swallowed hard and said, "Lori, please. This is totally inappropriate."

"But Father Todd, I know you want me. I have felt this for months."

Todd's mind raced. *What have I done to give Lori the wrong impression? What signals from Lori have I missed, which signals have I unintentionally sent?*

"Lori, I am a priest and have made a vow of celibacy. To this I am irrevocably committed. There can never be anything between us but friendship."

She stepped away, turned around, and ran out of the office crying.

Todd was neither a prude nor a virgin. While in college, he had experienced the warmth and love of a woman. He even once thought he was in love, but as many young love affairs go, this indiscretion ended with two broken hearts. On his next visit home from college, Todd confessed his sin to Father Taylor and left the confessional forgiven but with a hefty penance.

During his time of discernment before entering the seminary, the issue of celibacy hung heavy in his heart. For a priest, celibacy is not an option. It is a lifelong commitment and a solemn vow required by the Church. He pondered long and hard about the price he would be required to make if he was ordained. As a priest, he would never again experience the physical warmth and love of a woman, and for him such a vow was the supreme personal sacrifice. In the end, he resolved to offer God this precious gift. Over the years since his ordination temptations tested that resolve, but he dismissed them as works of the devil and prayed for the strength to remain strong and loyal to his vocation, and to this he remained true.

Now both his faith and commitment to his vocation were challenged. Subconsciously he had warm feelings for Lori, and although he could not recall ever responding to her subtle advances, he had somehow misled this young woman and let her think a romance could develop between them. He remained committed as ever to his vow of celibacy, but Lori had awakened in him the memory of his college sweetheart and as he struggled to overcome some sexual feelings. Had he unintentionally sent signals to this innocent child? How could he explain this to Lori? Should he even try? Before he could decide, Lori composed herself and embarrassed to tears flew out of the clinic, never again to return.

These incidents were testing his faith. *Perhaps I need some time alone, removed from the distractions of my duties as priest and healer,* he thought. Todd had not had time off since coming to Whitefish, he resolved. He needed a few days away from his responsibilities to pray and ponder these events. *I will go alone to explore the woods to the north of Whitefish he resolved.*

He packed a few items in his saddlebag, including some food, a pot, a grill, matches, a hunting knife and ax, a compass, and a bedroll and tarp. He dressed for the occasion with overalls, wool shirt, boots, a warm jacket, and floppy hat. He saddled Molly and told June Brevick that he would be back by Saturday.

Astonished, she asked "Where are you going, Father?"

"I don't exactly know. I've never explored the mountains to the north of Whitefish Lake. This seems like a good time for Pickles, Molly, and me to do so."

June stood with her mouth agape, but finally composed herself and said, "May God go with you, Father, and please be careful. You haven't had much experience camping out in the woods. If you are not back by Saturday, I'll have Mike organize a search party. Stop at Rich Parsons' place on the way out. He can tell you about the country to the north"

Rich Parsons arrived in Whitefish in 1870 and built a cabin on the north side of Whitefish Lake, next to a free-running hot spring. Slightly arthritic, he claimed the mineral hot spring waters provided medicinal properties that reduced his pain and made his joints move freely. He intended someday to build a lodge and spa there.

Todd mounted Molly and trotted off toward Rich Parson's cabin. He whistled for Pickles to follow.

Rich enthusiastically greeted Todd as he rode up to the cabin. Rich invited him inside for a cup of coffee.

"Father, I ain't seen you at the Lodge since I started coming to your church. What brings you and Pickles to the springs?"

"Just needed some time off," Todd explained, "and I thought Molly, Pickles, and I would head north on that old Indian trail that starts above the hot springs and winds up the mountain."

Rich looked concerned.

"I've only explored that trail for a short distance. It's a good climb up to the top where you can see for miles. The plains beyond the ridge extend clear to Canada with only a few hills to interrupt the flatlands. Other than the occasional Indian hunting party, there are no people thereabouts. Some Indians told me that it is a cursed land into which few of them will venture. I've never explored the area myself and only visited a lake at the bottom of the ridge. Some Hudson Company trappers from Canada visited me and told that it's a wild place, heavily forested, with scattered lakes, and traversed by cold streams. You should be aware that bears, cougars, wolves, and other varmints roam those plains. Do you have a gun with you?"

"No, I don't even own one."

"Father, if you're still intent on going alone into that godforsaken country, you'll need a weapon, that's for certain." With that, Rich disappeared into his room and came back out carrying a Winchester Carbine, a saddle holster, and a box of shells.

Todd knew Rich better than to refuse the loan of a rifle. "Thanks, Rich. I never fired a gun before, but I'm sure I'll figure it out."

Rich frowned and took him behind the cabin, loaded four shells into the gun, and handed it to him. He showed him how to place the stock tightly in his shoulder, take off the safety, and cock the hammer.

"See that can on the stump over there? Place the bead at the end of the barrel in the notch near the trigger and sight in on the can, then slowly squeeze the trigger … squeeze it, don't jerk it."

The explosion rocked Todd back on his feet. The can remained untouched on the stump.

"Guess I missed," Todd admitted.

"Yea, you missed the can all right but ya hit the stump. Not bad for a first try. Aim a bit higher next time. Takes a bit of practice but you'll get the hang of it. Before you head out, spend the night with me and enjoy a dip in the hot spring." Todd fired a few more practice rounds and hit the can on his third try.

Rich had dammed the creek leading out of the hot spring and built a series of pools leading down to the lake. The pool closest to the lake was lukewarm, but each successive pool leading up the hill to the spring grew warmer and warmer until the one next to the spring was scalding hot, so hot that no one could even put a foot into it. They sat in the lakeside pool and then worked their way up toward the spring until the water was uncomfortably hot. The hot mineral water melted away all Todd's aches and pains.

"You really should build that lodge you've always been talking about," Todd suggested as they soaked in the hot water. "Folks will enjoy this spa, and who knows, but it may have curative powers."

Rich thought for a minute. "First I need to find two things: a partner and some money."

"You might approach Jack Sprier. He's a good businessman and may have an interest in your project." Rich responded that he would think about it.

The next morning Todd prepared to go.

"How long do you plan to be out there?" Rich asked.

"Just a few days."

"How much food ya got with you?"

"A loaf of bread, a hunk of lard, a few turnips, a slab of bacon, and a sack of beans.

"How about water?"

"I have a water bottle in the saddlebag," Todd said.

Rich shook his head and went back inside the cabin. He came out with a sack of venison jerky, some hardtack biscuits, a canteen of water, a few small potatoes, and fishing gear.

"You'll need all this to survive in that country. There's plenty of game if you're not too shy about using the carbine. I don't think anyone but a trapper or two and an occasional Indian ever hunts there, so it's the place to be if you want solitude. Don't drink the creek water without first boiling it. Be sure to stop and see me on the way back home. If I don't hear from you in a week, I'll go into town and organize a search party to go looking for you."

Todd thanked Rich for his kindness, and then he mounted Molly and Pickles followed the trail that scrambled through dense stands of spruce and alders and zigzagged up the mountain. Keeping the faint trail in sight was difficult. Molly seemed to know where they were headed so he loosened the reins and let her find the path. Surrounded by the tightly packed trees he lost all sense of direction. North or south became meaningless and as Molly climbed the mountain, the only direction he was aware of was up. As the trail grew steeper, the trees thinned out and Molly began to struggle on the rocky trail. Her breathing grew labored and foam dribbled from her mouth. Todd dismounted and led Molly up the steep path as Pickles ran ahead to take point. After an hour of hard climbing, they scramble above the tree line and the summit appeared immediately ahead. At the top the path split: one trail descended into the flats below, while the other followed the ridge westward. The summit, the highest point for miles around, offered an unobstructed panoramic view of the countryside to the north. The thick forest, interrupted here and there by a meadow or small lake, extended to the hazy horizon, which Todd surmised must be Canada. He had brought along a spyglass that he now dug out of his saddlebag. The view of the countryside through the spyglass was stunning. A mixture of spruce, aspen, and birch trees covered the basin floor as far as he could see. The fall color of maples, birch, and aspens fully arrayed in various shades of red, orange, and yellow painted the landscape. This struck him as unusual, for the trees around Whitefish had not yet turned. Three small lakes rested at the foot of the mountain, the only interruption in the carpeted forest immediately below. Trees hung over the shoreline of each lake, and only one of the three had a visible beach where he could make camp. A small meadow and narrow beach on the north side of the third lake looked inviting, so Todd decided to make that his destination. The ride down the mountain was even steeper and more treacherous than the ride up from the Whitefish side. Only a hint of a trail wound down the mountainside into tree line where it almost disappeared in the thick forest, but

Pickles sniffed out the path. Molly followed her and in two hours, the path ended on the sandy shoreline of a deep blue 15-acre lake. An eerie silence permeated the lake. The absence of a whisper of wind through the trees, or the croaking of frogs, or even the buzz of insects disrupted the ominous silence. He looked around for birds but didn't see or hear any of his favorite creatures. Without their familiar cries, the edgy stillness permeated the setting. Todd walked Molly around to the northern shore where a meadow extended from the edge of the lake well back into the forest. The only sound was that of a small creek that emerged from the meadow and splashed over boulders as it made its way down the embankment and emptied into the lake.

It was late afternoon and the sun already threatened to dip behind the treetops on the western edge of the lake. *This shoreline will be a good place to make camp*, Todd thought, *and this lake deserves a name.* He named it Jenny Lake, after a child in Whitefish that he once nursed back to health. The sandy beach was only eighteen feet or so wide but provided adequate space to make camp. He unsaddled Molly and let her graze in the meadow. Pickles took off into the forest to forage for her dinner. Todd formed a fire ring from boulders he found around the shore and was gathering driftwood for a fire when he heard Pickles barking. He grabbed his carbine and followed the sound into the forest. A few hundred feet into the woods he found Pickles frozen and growling, pointing to a stand of aspens. At first he didn't see anything but then caught sight of a black furry beast hurrying off through the trees.

"Pickles, I guess we have invaded the home of Mrs. Black Bear," Todd said. "I don't think she will bother us, but tonight I will keep my carbine close by."

On the west side of the lake, a large spruce log reached several feet out into the water, a natural dock from which to fish. He chose a willow branch, tied a string with a hook on one end, and then cast a grub he found under a rock into the lake. After a few tries, he landed an 11-inch trout and then another.

Returning to the campsite, he cleaned the fish, started a fire, and set the fish on a stick to cook. Filling his pot with water, he set it near the fire to boil, took two potatoes out of his saddlebag, peeled them with his hunting knife, and then set them in the pot to cook. One fish was enough for dinner, so after cooking both he gave the second fish to Pickles who devoured it bones and all.

He spread his bedroll out on the beach and lay down on his back to view the multitude of stars in the dark, moonless sky. He pondered his mission as a priest and healer and prayed that God would provide insight to the questions that troubled him.

"Father, why did Abby have to die? Why couldn't I get through to Stillwell before he died? Why do you choose to heal some of your children and not others?"

His faith and understanding of free will should have provided the answers to both questions and while such answers had satisfied him in the past, this time they did not. He was not the first or last person to ask such an impertinent question or be so troubled by it. In addition, he was troubled by Lori's attention. He had been blind to her advances and as a result hurt her. Why was this temptation sent to test him at a time when he was already questioning his faith? He asked God for strength and understanding, for such difficulties were part of the life of a priest.

After a few prayers, Todd turned his attention to the ribbon of the Milky Way that spread across the velvet tapestry of the firmament. It glowed brighter and more vivid than he had ever remembered seeing it. He had read that this asterism was an arm of our galaxy that was composed of millions and millions of stars like our own sun. While at Rutgers, he took a class in astronomy. The subject had always fascinated him, so he retrieved his 50-power spyglass from his saddlebag. One look through his telescope revealed that the Milky Way consisted of countless stars, too many to count in the limited field of the scope. Two adjacent stars in the east outshone all others and did not twinkle, as stars should. The lower of the two, brighter than its nearby neighbor, caused him to remember reading in Ben Franklin's Almanac about a rare conjunction of Venus and Jupiter that would occur this fall. This must be those two planets. To the north he recognized the constellation Cassiopeia, or the Lady in a Chair. Cassiopeia looked like the letter W and to the right and a hands length below he noticed a smudge, about the size of a quarter held overhead.

He focused his telescope on it and in doing so, the blotch revealed itself as an elongated cloud with a bright center. His Rutgers astronomy professor had claimed this was a gas cloud resting in the Andromeda constellation, but to Todd the structure didn't look like a cloud at all but something much more complex with a bright center and well-defined structure. Could this cloud be another Milky Way? He thought about this for some time and then concluded that the universe must consist of much more than the Milky Way. It could be unimaginably vast. Hundreds of years ago, mankind concluded that the earth was the center of the universe, and then with better science, astronomers proffered that the sun was the center of the universe and Earth and all the planets and stars circled about it. Astronomers recently decided that such a conclusion was insufficient and the sun was only a minor star in the vast Milky Way Galaxy which consisted of stars that were other suns. Could it be that there were also other galaxies, like this cloudy splotch in Andromeda? Todd contemplated that all this only proved that an Intelligent Creator fashioned all this stuff for a purpose, *a purpose that He has not yet revealed to us. Even more profound, if we were the only object of his creation, why did he create all these stars out there.*

    Todd admitted to himself that this is just one of the many questions humans pondered without arriving at a satisfactory answer. For example, why does God allow good and evil to exist side by side, or why does He allow human suffering and temptation. Such questions are as unfathomable as is the hidden purpose behind all this vast creation. *Perhaps the only answer is that God's ways are not man's way*, he concluded. *God created all these stars and planets according to a plan known only to Him, and seems trivial and arrogant to question His ways or his justice. Who is Father Todd that he should so question God?* This realization so quieted his troubled mind that he felt as if the heavy burden of doubt had lifted from his shoulders. Comforting warmth enveloped his entire body and he fell into a deep untroubled sleep and did not wake until the sun rose over the trees across the lake. He felt renewed, invigorated, and so thankful for the morning and that he had taken this vacation.

While exploring the meadow the day before, he discovered a path that ran through the meadow and then following the creek disappeared into the woods. Horseshoe prints in the muddy path aroused his curiosity. Where did the path lead and who was making use of it? Because of the horseshoe prints, the visitor must have been a white man. He saddled Molly and rode to the end of the meadow where a beaver dam had created a small pond and a cut sapling protruded above the surface. He lifted the sapling out of the water and discovered a wire noose attached to the sapling, evidence that trappers were active in this area. He returned the sapling to its position in the pond and continued to ride along the path as it meandered north through the forest. After a few miles, the trail branched off into three different directions. He took the center path that continued north and to mark his position, he blazed a mark on a nearby tree. Later that afternoon, and what he estimated to be 15 miles beyond Jenny Lake, the sky clouded over, and a cloudburst threatened to soak him to the skin. He came to a lean-to, a fire pit, and other evidence of trapper activity. It didn't look like anyone had made use of the shelter for some time, so he and Pickles made camp under it. He lit a fire to warm up and dry his damp clothes. The rain continued off and on throughout the night, but by morning the sun emerged between dark-grey clouds. After a quick breakfast of jerky, he saddled Molly and continued along the trail.

After a few miles, Todd rounded a bend and saw a man bending over a trap. Pickles barked and the man stood up with a bloody fox hanging from his large hands. The man was tall, lean, and muscular. He wore a pair of dirty overalls held up by black suspenders over a red-checkered shirt. A pair of large ears held a floppy hat in place, a size too big for his rather small head. Startled to see another human, he reached for his rifle as Todd shouted a friendly "Hello."

"Hold it right there, fellow," the man yelled in a not-so-friendly tone as he shouldered his rifle.

Pickle's frantic barking echoed through the woods and Todd told her to stand down. "My name is Father Todd, and you can put down that rifle. I mean you no harm."

The man lowered the barrel but kept his finger on the trigger and the rifle tight against his shoulder. "What do you want?"

Todd dismounted, told Pickles to stay, and then held his hands out in a gesture of peace as he approached the startled man. He repeated, "My name is Father Todd ... from Whitefish ... and who might you be?" He continued to hold his hand out expecting a friendly handshake, but the man just stood there and stared at Todd, his rifle still ready against his shoulder.

"A priest you say ... and from Whitefish? Ya must be that black robe healer I heard about from dem Indians. Sorry, but ya weren't wearing no black robe, so how's I ta know you's a man of the cloth. Wada ya doing in these godforsaken woods?"

Todd withdrew his still empty hand. "I'm not wearing my cassock today, but I am Father Todd. I'm just exploring the countryside, on a vacation you might say."

The man relaxed and leaned his rifle against a tree. He took Todd's hand and cautiously shook it. The man's grip was firm, his hand calloused and rough as an ax-hewn plank. An ugly red scar ran across the back of his right hand as he pumped Todd's arm. His skin was brown and wrinkled, evidence of an outdoor life and advanced age. An unkempt black beard salted with patches of gray hid most of the man's face and neck. Piercing black eyes sparkled from large, deep sockets, and a hooked nose poked through ample whiskers. As he released Todd's hand, his mouth parted into a wide smile, revealing a set of yellowed teeth and a space in front where a tooth went missing.

"The name's Jake, Jake Brown. I don't see many white folks out here in dese woods, so I'm sorry fer the unfriendly greeting. You can't be too careful about the strangers you run into around here."

"Are there any other folks living or hunting around here?"

"Naw, other than a few Lakota hunters, I's da only one around. You're the first white face I've seen in dese parts. I trap fer da Hudson Bay Company and came down from Canada last spring looking for weasel, fox, wolverines, and beaver. I've been trapping all spring and summer, and a fellow gets kind of lonely without other folks ta talk to, so I's glad to see you." He glanced at Pickles who obediently remained sitting behind Molly.

"I see yas got a mutt wid ya, and a well trained one at dat. I had a mutt some time back, but a wolf got him. I has a cabin a short piece up da trail and if you're a mind to having supper wid me, I has a pot of beaver stew cooking."

Todd accepted Jake's invitation and mounted Molly. Jake untethered the gray mare and led Todd and Pickles down the path for what seemed to Todd like much more than a "short piece." They rode for the better part of two hours until they came to a fork in the trail. A faint side path took them to another lake much larger than Jenny Lake. Across the narrow end of the lake, Todd could make out a rough-hewn log cabin, a corral, and a lean-to. A wisp of smoke curled out of a stovepipe sticking from the sod-covered roof. The trail circled the end of the lake, crossed over a stream, and then ended at the cabin. A few chickens scattered in the front yard and a donkey in the coral bayed as they rode up. They unsaddled the horses and then led Molly and the gray mare inside the lean-to that served as a barn. Pelts of beaver, weasel, fox, and a single wolverine were rubbed with rock salt and set out to air-dry on racks. Piles of pelts ready for market were stacked in one corner. "Come inside," Jake offered.

Pickles followed Todd into the cabin and curled up in one corner. The Inside of the cabin was clean but dark and smelled of rancid smoke. The oiled brown paper that covered the two small front windows only allowed a glow of sunlight to penetrate. Sawdust covered the dirt floor and the man's sparse furniture consisted of a rough plank table set between two sawhorses, two wicker chairs fashioned from willows, a cupboard, sideboard made from planks, and a quilt-covered pile of spruce branches that served as a bed. An oil lamp hung from a rafter in front of a large stone fireplace that sheltered a few glowing embers that heated a black kettle suspended from an iron rod. Jake lit the oil lamp and then went over to the fireplace and swung the rod askew so the kettle hung out over the flagstone hearth. He picked up a large wooden spoon, stirred the kettle contents, and then took a taste from the spoon.

"Looks, tastes, and smells 'bout ready," Jake announced. "Grab a tin plate off the table and come help yourself."

Todd took two plates from the table and handed one to Jake. Todd took the large wooden spoon and stirred the pot before dishing himself a spoonful of stew.

"Careful when yous stir dat pot," Jake warned, "old stuff is in da bottom."

Todd understood the warning, for stew pots were seldom if ever washed. He nodded and spooned out a plateful of stew, and then took a seat at the table. Jake filled his own plate and then got a loaf of cornbread out of the cupboard, placed it on the table with a butcher knife, and sat down with Todd.

He handed Todd a chunk of bread and a metal spoon. "Eat afore it gets cold."

"Hope you don't mind if I say grace first," Todd said.

"Well, I sorta does mind. If ya hasta say some words, say dem ta yourself. I donna take kindly ta dat prayer stuff in my cabin."

Jake's refusal to say a prayer surprised Todd, for no one had ever objected to his prayer before meals. Todd blessed himself and silently prayed.

Todd had to admit the beaver stew was delicious, with generous chunks of meat, carrots, turnips, and potatoes in thick, brown gravy. After they ate, Jake opened the door of the cupboard, took out two tin cups, and retrieved a fancy bottle of brown liquid. He poured each of them a generous drink

"Best Kentucky whiskey you'll ever taste," he said proudly, "80 proof an older dan me. I saved it for special occasions."

Todd took a sip. His lips, mouth, and tongue tingled and then grew numb. When he swallowed, the whiskey burned all the way down to his stomach and he almost choked.

Jake smiled and stifled a laugh.

"I guess I'm not used to strong drink," Todd said as he recovered his composure.

"Sorry. I forget you's a man of da cloth. But a bit of whiskey is good for the soul."

Todd's second sip didn't burn as much as the first one did, and he enjoyed his third and the fourth sips. His stomach warmed as he finished the cup and put it down.

Jake poured him a second cup, and it went down even smoother than the first. Jake tried to pour Todd a third cup, but he placed his hand over the cup.

"No thanks, my head is already spinning," Todd said.

"Ain't none of my business, but I's wondering what a fella like you, a black robe nonetheless, is doing out here in dese woods."

His inhibitions dulled by the whiskey, Todd confided, "I needed to get away by myself for a few days. You might say I was having a crisis of faith."

"A crisis of faith ya say. I had one of dem years ago. My pappy was a preacher man, but he had a mean streak when he got to drinking, which was often enough. After taking one of his many beatings, I lit out and never came back. After dat, I decided dat God and me didn't have much to do wid one another, and that's da way it's been all dese years."

It began to rain, the drops softly sounding on the sod roof. "Der ain't much room in here, but if yous wants ta, set your bedroll out on da floor in front of the fireplace an yous can sleep in here out of da rain and cold."

Todd unrolled his bedding and got as comfortable as possible on the sawdust-covered floor. It had been a long day and soon he was sound asleep.

It was still dark in the cabin when Pickles woke him the next morning with a lick on his face. The oil lamp overhead cast a dull yellow glow and deep shadows marked the small cabin. Jake had started a fire in the fireplace and was boiling a pot of water. He threw a handful of coffee into the pot and let it boil for a few minutes as Todd got up and stretched.

Jake took another loaf of cornbread out of the cupboard and placed it on the table with a can of lard. He then poured two cups of coffee and beckoned Todd to sit down.

"I gots ta check my string of traps up north of here today, and if you have a mind to, you and Pickles can tag along."

Todd thought this would be a good way to see the countryside without the danger of getting lost, so he accepted. They rode for two hours north of the cabin which brought them to a beaver pond where Jake dismounted to check a trap.

"Damn, it's empty. I knows ders several beavers living here abouts, but dese damn animals are smart ones. Dey's been avoiding my traps fer weeks. I have another one in the shallows." Todd told him about the empty beaver trap that he found. Jake found the protruding sapling and lifted it out of the water. This trap had spring-loaded metal jaws that had been sprung and the bait was gone. Jake forced open the jaws of the trap and set latch. He prepared two willow saplings as bait and set them inside the trap. Suddenly Todd heard the metallic sound of a sprung trap and immediately Jake swore.

"Hell's bells, it got me!"

Todd dismounted and went over to Jake where he knelt on the ground next to the pond with his right hand caught in the jaws of his trap.

"Get a stout branch and help pry me out of this damnable thing."

Todd found a branch, pried the trap jaws open, and freed Jake. He held his bleeding hand up high and swore a blue streak. Then realizing he was with a man-of-the-cloth, looked apologetically at Todd and said, "I think my hand's busted. That was a damn fool ting fur me ta do."

Todd had no doubt that Jake's fingers were broken and his hand was bleeding from a deep wound. Fortunately, Todd had brought his medical bag with him and retrieved it from his saddlebag. Three of Jake's fingers were severely smashed and broken, and the trap jaws had cut deep into his palm. Todd cleaned the wound with whiskey, stemmed the bleeding with septic powder, and temporary splinted the broken fingers. He then bandaged Jake's hand with strips of cloth from his extra shirt.

"I need to get you back to the cabin so I can properly set the broken bones in your fingers and suture the wound."

"Is yous some sorta doctor?"

"No, I'm not a doctor, but a sort of medic. I've worked in a hospital and I run the medical clinic in Whitefish."

They rode back to the cabin where Todd set Jake's fingers with splints and sutured the wound.

Jake looked at his broken hand, wrapped in a torn-up shirt with three of his fingers splinted with twigs.

"Dis hand is gonna be pretty much useless for weeks."

"Yes, that's right, and you cannot stay here alone. I suggest you come with me back to Whitefish Lake where I can better treat your hand at the clinic. While it's healing, you can stay in the Whitefish Hotel."

"I donna have much money, but I has a lot of pelts dat I was planning to sell to the Hudson Bay Company up in Canada."

"We'll bring your pelts along and we'll see about selling them in Grand Rapids. Let's quickly pack up and go."

They loaded the pelts on the donkey along with Jake's few possessions and closed the cabin.

Todd strangled one of the chickens for dinner that night. "Guess da rest of dem chickens will have to fend for demselves," Jake sadly said.

They rode back to Jenny Lake where they made camp for the night, and the following morning rode back to Rich's cabin.

"What do you have there with you?" Rich asked as he met the two riders outside.

"This is Jake Brown, a trapper that I came upon. He is hurt and I am taking him to Whitefish and the clinic for treatment."

Sue greeted them as they rode up to the clinic.

"Father Todd, you're certainly a sight for sore eyes." She noticed Todd's companion and asked, "And who might this be?"

"This is Jake Brown. He's had a bad accident and I need to treat his broken hand." Once inside the clinic, Todd gave Jake a few swigs of whiskey and then set to work resetting and properly splinting Jake's fingers and suturing his hand for the better part of two hours. Jake sat in a chair barely wincing as Todd worked. When finished, Jake's bandaged hand was twice its normal size.

"How long am I gonna have to wear dese splints and bandage?"

"I'm afraid your hand will be out of use for some time. Your fingers were broken in several places and the ligaments were torn. I'm not sure you will ever regain the full use of your hand. After it heals, I will show you some exercises so you can get back most of your hand's function."

"I'm beholding to you, Father Todd. Dem Indians claims you's a healer, and dey's sure got dat right. If you hadn't come along when you did, I'd been stuck in dat trap for some time, and when I got loose, I wouldn't survive da coming winter out der wid only one hand."

Sue took Jake over to the hotel and set him up in one of her rooms. Todd took Jake's mare and donkey over to Lloyd's livery stables.

"What in the hell you got there?" Lloyd asked as he looked at the donkey and his load of furs. "You been trapping or something?"

Todd dismounted Jake's mare and explained about Jake's accident and that these pelts were the result of his trappings.

"Jake is going to need some money as he heals. Do you think you can take these pelts into Grand Rapids on your next trip and sell them for him?"

"No problem. I'll take them with me on Monday."

A week later Jake walked over to the clinic so Todd could examine his hand.

"Ya knows Father, I never thought much 'bout God or religion and dat sorta stuff, but the last few days as my hand healed I be given it a lot a' thought. God and I had an agreement, I donna bother 'bout Him and He donna bother 'bout me. I 'spect God knows I been a lost soul most all my life, but da thought of Him has been eating away at me as I did my trapping. I just kept chasing dem religion thoughts out of my mind, but they wouldn't go away. Den you shows up. How many black robes knows how to doctor someone? Had you not come along, I would a' had ta leave da cabin en prob'ly go back ta Canada wid dis broken hand. It's just like God to send a doctor into da wilderness ta heals my hand and a priest ta heals my soul. Now dat my hand is doing fine, it's my soul dat still needs mending."

"So, what is it that you want?" Todd asked.

"I want dat baptism ting yous does. My pappy beat religion out of me, and dat's da way it's been fer some time. But now I's seen da light."

Father Todd began instructions with Jake, and by the time his hand healed, Father Todd was ready to baptize him. Todd also pondered this in his heart. The encounter with Jake had healed his shaky faith. As he said the words of baptism for Jake and poured water over his forehead he thought, *God sent me into the woods to reflect on my doubts, but he had another plan to heal me. He made sure that I found Jake who needed me. Because of this encounter, my faith has been restored and Jake has received baptism. God certainly works in wondrous ways that we don't fully understand., His wonders are something to behold.*

Chapter 12
The Tinker

Abby's needless death in childbirth angered Todd. After her funeral, he called a meeting at the town hall.

"Who is this tinker who was selling Dr. Watkins Elixir around town?"

"We don't know his real name," Lloyd Brevick offered, "but we call him Seth the Tinker. He comes around here about once or twice a year selling tools, pots and pans, blankets, utensils and knives. This was the first time he was selling medicines and tonics."

Todd sighed. "Seth the Tinker you say. I met this tinker on the way to Grand Rapids on the *Itaska*. He got off at Brainerd. Anyone who has bought any of Dr. Watkins tonics should throw them out. They are poisonous and most likely responsible for Abby's untimely death."

"Seth seemed like a gentle, harmless person," Lloyd countered. "He comes here with his wagon and mule each spring or fall and we have never had any trouble with him before. With all his pots and pans clanging away you can hear his wagon coming from a mile away. Yet I don't recall him selling medicines before his visit last fall."

Todd had a hard time controlling his anger. "Seth the tinker could be the same man who sold infected blankets in Tecumseh's village at Leech Lake. His real name is Seth Meriwether and since he and his family disembarked in Brainerd, I assume that's where he lives.

"Was he selling any Navajo blankets this time through?"

"No, not that I recall. And I don't think he ever sold blankets in Whitefish," Lloyd said.

"If he ever shows up again, chase him off."

However, in the spring of 1874, Seth Meriwether did show up in Whitefish again. From inside the clinic, Todd could hear the pots and pans clanking and making enough noise to wake up the dead. He went outside as Seth tied his wagon to the hitching post.

"Seth Meriwether?" Todd asked.

Seth looked at Todd and a smile of recognition crossed his face.

"Father Bose from the *Itaska* I presume. I see you have built your church," he said as he stood there admiring the church.

"Yes, we finished St. Patrick's and had it dedicated last year," Todd said in none too friendly a tone.

Seth looked puzzled.

"I stopped by the hotel in town, but Mark wouldn't rent me a room. He said I should come here to the clinic and talk to you."

Todd frowned.

"Did you sell Dr. Watkins's Elixir to Abby Stewart last time you were in town?"

"It could be. I don't keep sales records but sold my medicines to many folks around here."

"Your medicine may have killed her."

Seth looked shocked. "My tonic killed Mrs. Stewart? That's not possible. My medicines are intended to help folks, not kill them."

"That elixir prevents a person's blood from clotting, so when her baby came due she bled to death; all because you sold her a bottle of Dr. Watkins's Elixir. Who supplies your medications?"

"I buy them from an apothecary in Minneapolis. I have only sold them for the past year, but no one has complained about my medicines. Dr. Watkins mixes his medications from herbs, berries, and roots the Indians use for medications."

"His mixtures contain mercury and who know what else. It is poisonous to some folks. Do you have any with you this visit?"

"Well, yes a few bottles," he said sheepishly.

"Stop selling them here or anywhere else. And while we are talking about your wares, did you sell blankets to the Indians in Leech Lake?"

Seth's face turned scarlet. "Could be, and I suppose you're going to tell me that my blankets are poisonous. There's nothing wrong with my medications or my blankets."

"After your visit last spring, many Leech Lake Indians died of smallpox. Fleas transferred the disease from the blankets that you sold to them. Where did you get those blankets?"

"From the Army post at Ft. Snelling," Seth explained. "A Captain Jeremy Johnson sold them to me."

Todd recalled his meeting with Captain Johnson who openly expressed his personal hatred for the Indians. Could he have deliberately offered Seth contaminated blankets to trade with the Leech Lake Indians? It was a strong possibility, for there were many rumors about the Army deliberately providing infected blankets to Indians.

"Did you know those blankets were infested with fleas?"

"No, I did not. Sometimes I trade with the Indians, including those at Leech Lake. If fleas infested those blankets, I knew nothing about it. You should talk to Captain Johnson if you have a problem with the blankets he sold me."

Todd remembered Captain Johnson saying the only good Indian was a dead Indian, and blankets infected with smallpox would be a good tool for genocide.

"Smallpox has killed almost 1/3 of the tribe, mostly women and children. If you still have any of these blankets, burn them."

Seth shrugged his shoulders and offered a weak excuse. "I'm just a poor businessman who sells pots and pans and does some trading for a living. I don't know anything about poisonous elixirs and contaminated blankets."

Obviously, Seth showed no remorse about selling the poisonous elixir to Abby or contaminated blankets to the Indians.

"You ought to be put in jail," Todd hissed. "Take your wagon and poison elixirs and get out of Whitefish. Don't ever come back here again."

Todd watched as Seth drove back toward town, his wagon bouncing on the rutted road and his pots with pans clanging as he went. Later that day, Lloyd said that Seth drove straight through town and down the road to Grand Rapids without stopping.

However, Todd was not satisfied with simply driving Seth out of town. He met with Lloyd, Mike, and Dick and told them that he intended to travel to Brainerd and file a formal complaint of genocide with the local sheriff against Seth and Captain Johnson, and perhaps even file a complaint against Seth for causing Abby's death.

"You're going to charge Seth and the Army with genocide?" Lloyd asked incredulously. "You might get an indictment against Seth for selling the poisonous tonic, but not against the Army for genocide. No way is that going to happen."

"But I must try," Todd protested. "Captain Johnson conspired to wipe an entire tribe of humans off the face of the earth, and Seth was his willing accomplice. If there is any justice in our courts, this could be a test case to stop this despicable practice by the Army."

Todd left Pickles with Mike and drove to Grand Rapids on Wednesday, March 21, to catch the *Itaska*, leaving Molly and his carriage at the J. Yearling Livery Stable. Captain Pinot welcomed Todd as he boarded on the riverboat's return trip to St. Paul that afternoon. He grabbed Todd by the shoulder and said,

"I knows ye finished dat church like ye said ye would, 'cause I brang da bishop and Father Quinn up here last year ta dedicate it. I didn't believe ye could do it in one year, yet ye sure did."

Thursday morning Todd disembarked at Brainerd and went immediately to the sheriff's office where two saddled horses stood hitched to a post alongside a water trough. Located in the center of town, the false front building came complete with a covered porch and two benches placed on either side of the front door. A man with a deputy star on his chest sat stretched out on one of the benches, apparently asleep. A ten-gallon hat covered his face so Todd couldn't be sure if he was awake or sleeping, but he didn't stir as Todd climbed onto the porch. The sign on the front door announced, "Brainerd County Sheriff John Stalwart" and another smaller sign beneath it read, "Office Hours 9-6 Monday through Saturday."

Todd stepped inside. A large picture window that looked out onto the street filled the front office with welcoming sunlight. A large bulletin board plastered with various wanted posters and announcements of events in town hung conspicuously on the wall next to the front door. Empty jail cells were visible through an open door leading into the back room.

Sheriff Stalwart, a thin balding man with a prominent handlebar mustache, sat behind a large desk covered with two stacks of papers and a third pile that he was busily sorting as Todd entered the office. A leather coat, a well-worn cowboy hat, and a belt holding a holstered Colt revolver hung from a coat rack next to his desk. His red checkered wool shirt, a size too big for his body, drooped from his narrow shoulders. A large tin star pinned to his chest identified him as the sheriff. He looked up with the slightest trace of a smile, and then taking off his square reading glasses he stared at Todd for a few seconds before speaking.

"What can I do for you, Padre?" he asked in a gravely voice.

"My name is Father Todd Bose. I am the pastor of St. Patrick's church in Whitefish. I want to file a complaint,"

The hint of a smile disappeared. "A complaint against whom and what for?"

"Against Seth Meriwether for selling poisonous tonics that killed one of my parishioners and for causing the death of Indians at Leech Lake," Todd said.

The sheriff's face morphed into a decidedly unfriendly snarl, looking like he had been weaned on a sour pickle. He leaned back into his chair and mockingly asked, "Selling poisonous tonics and killing Indians? That's your complaint? What did Seth do, shoot a few of those heathen Leech Lake bastards?"

The sheriff's prejudiced response shocked Todd. It was obvious that this meeting was not going to go well.

"No, he didn't shoot any Indians," he said indignantly. "Seth committed genocide by deliberately selling those poor Indians Army blankets infested with vermin that transmitted smallpox to the tribe. The women and children came down with the disease and, as a result, three dozen innocent people died. I spent three weeks in their village trying to cure those poor sick souls and prayed over dozens of graves for those I couldn't cure."

"What makes you think Seth's blankets had anything to do with these deaths?"

"I examined the blankets that he sold to them. They were Army blankets from Ft. Stilwell infested with fleas that can carry the pox, and I think Seth knew this. This was a deliberate act of genocide."

"How would a priest know that the blankets Seth sold to the Indians carried small pox? Are you a doctor?"

"No, I am not a doctor. I served in a hospital during the war and I do know about a disease like smallpox that is carried by fleas."

"And who sold Seth those blankets?"

"He got them from Army Captain Johnson at Ft. Stilwell."

"How do you know that?"

"Seth told me so himself, and embroidered on them was 'Property of the US Army, Ft. Stillwell.'"

Todd waited for a response, but the sheriff said nothing.

"This is not my only complaint against Seth," Todd continued. "He is also guilty of manslaughter."

Todd placed a bottle of the tonic on the sheriff's desk. "Seth sold this Dr. Watkins's Elixir to some folks in Whitefish, including a pregnant lady. His so-called 'tonic' killed that lady, a patient of mine who bled to death during childbirth. I tested Seth's medicine and it contains mercury and strychnine, a poison often used to kill rats."

"Rat poison you say," the sheriff scoffed. "I've taken Dr. Watkins's tonic for months now and have suffered no ill effects whatsoever."

"Then you'd better be careful when shaving. One serious cut and you could bleed to death."

"Well now, those are serious charges you're making, Father. You can't waltz in here accusing one of our outstanding citizens of manslaughter and genocide without proof. Do you have any proof?"

"Yes, I do. As I said, that bottle of Dr. Watkins tonic contains strychnine, and I suggest you immediately send this sample to the St. Paul pharmaceutical lab for analysis. It will confirm my testing. As far as the blankets go, you'll have to take my word that they were infected with fleas and that at least three dozen Indians, mostly women and children, died of smallpox they caught from those blankets."

Sheriff Stalwart cleared his throat and launched a stream of yellow tobacco spittle into a spittoon next to his desk.

"The Army has been passing blankets to the Indians for months to help them keep warm. If some of those blankets were infested as you claim, well they weren't that way when the Army sold them to Seth. The Indians never bathe and are always covered with fleas and lice."

"It is a well known fact that the Army provides infected blankets to some Indians. This is not new news to you or to me," Todd replied angrily.

"I suppose you want to include the US Army in your complaint against Seth and Captain Johnson?"

"If that is what it takes to get some justice for the Indians and force the Army to stop this practice of genocide, I surely will do so."

Sheriff Stalwart sat back in his chair and thought for a moment. Then he said, "I cannot stop you from filing these complaints but I certainly can advise you that to do so is foolish. It will be a waste of your time and mine. Our circuit judge, Judge Mason, will be here next month. I will give him your complaints but it is unlikely that an indictment will follow. Seth is a longtime resident of Brainerd, and has a good reputation in these parts. As for your genocide complaint, Seth was only doing the Indians a favor by selling those Army blankets to keep them warm in the winter. You have no proof that they were contaminated when Seth bought them from Captain Johnson, so an indictment against the Army is without merit. As far as I know, nobody has ever successfully indicted the Army for selling infected blankets to the Indians. That is a nasty rumor designed to discredit the Army. Your genocide accusation will go nowhere."

Sheriff Stalwart handed Todd two complaint forms complete with carbon copies. He sat down at the table and filled each one out, one against Seth and Captain Johnson for genocide, and the other against Seth for distributing toxic medicines. He then handed the top copy of each form to the Sheriff and kept the carbon copy. Stalwart examined each, stamped them with his name and a time and date, and then added then to his stack of papers.

It was obvious that burdened by his prejudices, the sheriff was not about to take Todd's complaints seriously. He would file them with the Brainerd court, but without the Sheriff's proactive support there was little hope that an indictment would follow. Frustrated, Todd left the sheriff's office and went down the street to St. Martin's church where he found Deacon Everett in his office. After a handshake, Todd gave him the copies of his complaints and explained about the death of Abby and the infected blankets that Seth sold to the Indians.

Deacon Everett read the complaints and returned the papers to Todd. "You traveled all the way down here from Whitefish to file these complaints?"

Todd nodded affirmatively.

Deacon Everett sadly shook his head. "I know Seth and his family; they are my parishioners. I find it hard to believe that Seth deliberately sold infected blankets to some Indians or knowingly sold poisonous elixirs to your people. Perhaps he didn't know the blankets were infected and wasn't aware the tonics contained strychnine."

"That will be for a judge and jury to decide; that is, if Judge Mason acts on my complaints. The sheriff was unsympathetic and I have the feeling my complaints will be ignored. I would like to hire a lawyer here in town to represent my complaints in court. Can you recommend someone?"

"Yes; Peter Dean is an honest and competent lawyer, and a member of my church. His office is two doors down from the sheriff's. How long are you going to be in town?"

"The *Itaska* will not return on its upriver trip until Saturday, so I guess I'll be around until then."

"We have a Thursday vespers service at 7:00 p.m., and I hope you will join us."

Todd said he would attend, and then thanked Deacon Everett and walked down the street to Peter Dean's office. A large sign on the front of the building read, "Brainerd Law Offices," and hand-lettered sign on the glass window announced, "Peter Dean, Doctor at Law." As he opened the front door, an overhead bell rang. Knotty pine paneling covered each wall, and the room smelled of fresh-cut pine. Sparsely furnished, the office consisted of a table and two chairs, a small oak desk and leather chair, a visitor chair in front of the desk, an empty coat rack, a multi-drawer set of file cabinets on one wall, and four shelves of law books on the opposite wall. An American flag hung from a pole set to one side of the desk, and a large painting of the signing of the Declaration of Independence graced the back wall behind the desk. In the leather chair, a young man was examining a document. He looked at Todd from behind a pair of thick square-cut glasses that made his eyes look smaller than they were. Smartly dressed in a suit and vest accented by a forest-green tie, he looked too young to be a lawyer. He pushed aside the document and smiled when he recognized Todd's cassock and Roman collar.

"I'm Peter Dean. Please have a seat, Father. What can I do for you?"

Todd introduced himself and immediately decided that he was going to like this lawyer.

"I want you to represent me in these two complaints." He handed Peter the two complaints, took a seat in front of the desk, and patiently waited for Peter to read each. When he finished he looked at Todd and asked, "And you want me to represent you in court regarding these complaints?"

"Yes, that's right. Sheriff Stalwart gave me the impression that he wasn't interested in pursuing my complaints. I am the pastor of St. Patrick's church in Whitefish and must return in a couple of days. I understand that Judge Mason will be in town next week, and I want to retain you to represent my complaints in court and see to it that they get a fair and impartial hearing."

"Please tell me more about these complaints," Peter requested.

"The first complaint is about a tonic that Seth Meriwether sold to one of my pregnant parishioners. That Watkins tonic made her bleed to death during childbirth. I believe the tonic contains strychnine, a blood thinner. I hold Seth complicit in her death.

"The second complaint concerns Seth selling infected Army blankets he bought from Captain Johnson at Ft. Stilwell to the Indians at Leech Lake. I believe the captain, the Army, and Seth knew the blankets were infected with fleas that carried smallpox, and as a result several Indians died from that disease. I nursed many Leach Lake Indians back to health and buried others."

"And your complaint is with Seth, Captain Johnson, and the Army?" Peter asked.

"Yes, I believe Captain Johnson and the Army have a policy of genocide against the Indians, and Seth was a willing accomplice."

Peter thought for a minute. "I don't know about this Watkins Tonic that Seth sells, but he should be responsible for what he is peddling. I'm also aware our sheriff has no love for Indians and is friends with Seth. Moreover, I am aware of the Army policy of genocide against the Indians, but no one has even indicted the Army for this rumored practice. Regardless, your complaints deserve a fair hearing, and Judge Mason is an honest and just juror. If you want to retain me for $5, I can file these complaints with the court and represent them for you with Judge Mason."

Todd gave Peter a $5 gold piece and signed a client agreement. "I gave the sheriff a bottle of Dr. Watkins' tonic and asked him to send it to the laboratory in St. Paul to have it tested for strychnine. I want you to make sure he does that so you can have the results in hand before the hearing."

"I will be sure to do so. What exactly is your involvement with the Indians?"

"I'm not a doctor but I've been attending to the medical needs of the folks in the Grand Forks area for the past two years. Three Indians from Leech Lake came to Whitefish saying that many in their village were sick and dying. They asked me to help them, so I rode with them to their village and found that most of the women and children were sick with the pox, so I stayed in their village for three weeks and treated them. We buried over two dozen people who died from that terrible disease. However, the men did not come down with the pox, and I found this to be very curious. I discovered that because the Navahos made the blankets, the bucks refused to use them, but the women and children gladly used them. I examined those blankets and found them infested with fleas, fleas that can carry smallpox. Seth got these blankets from Captain Johnson at Ft. Stilwell who knew that they were contaminated, and I believe Seth knew this as well. He sold them to the Indians with the Army's blessings."

Peter pondered the issue for a few more moments and then said, "I agree that your complaints have merit. Genocide is the worst form of murder, and the rumor that the Army has a policy of using disease to wipe out American Indians, especially those tribes that have caused them trouble, is well known. Disease has decimated the Sioux tribes across the Mississippi. If your complaint against the Army is upheld in court and should I pursue this genocide complaint against Captain Johnson, the Army will defend him and Seth with their high-powered lawyers. I will be going against powerful people and most likely, I'll lose.

"On the other hand, your complaint about the poisonous tonics has merit, especially if I have the results of the tests. Perhaps I can get an injunction from Judge Mason to ban Seth from selling them. That is the best I can offer you now."

Todd thanked Peter and found a room at the local hotel. That evening he attended the vespers service at St. Martin's, and who should be sitting in the front pew but Seth with his family. Deacon Everett introduced Todd to the congregation and invited Todd to preach, but Todd politely declined. After vespers, Todd also met a lumberjack by the name of Steve Gothard, the foreman at a lumber mill outside town.

"If you have some time tomorrow, why don't you take a ride out to the mill and I'll show you around," Steve offered.

"I don't have anything planned for tomorrow and I'd like to see the area, so I'll take you up on that offer."

After the service, Todd retired to his hotel room and slept soundly.

Early the next morning after breakfast, he rented a horse from the livery stable and rode north out of town on a trail that paralleled the river. About ten miles upriver from the town, he saw a column of smoke rising over the trees. The path emptied onto a large meadow extending from the river and west to the forest beyond. A big clapboard building and a few outbuildings sat in the middle of the meadow next to a large black incinerator that belched a column of grey acrid smoke. A creek meandered through the meadow and fed a large waterwheel fixed to the main building. Todd entered a small outbuilding marked "Office." Steve rose from his desk, shook Todd's hand, and offered to show him around the operation. Their first stop was the river wharf where workers were loading cut lumber onto a barge. Rafts of large bucked logs floated in the river downriver from the wharf. Todd watched as three men selected a log and, with long hooked poles, tied a rope to the log and to a mule that then dragged it out of the river and along a skid to a log crane that stacked each log in neat piles next to the mill. Todd counted six individual stacks of 8- to 12-inch diameter logs, each ten-foot-long and stacked fifteen feet high.

The noise inside the main building was deafening. Two men with grapplers guided individual logs through a hole in the side of the building to a ramp leading to a six-foot diameter saw. The saw sang as workers guided a ten-inch diameter log through the machine, and Todd couldn't hear a thing Steve was saying. The workers guided the bisected log from the first saw to a series of other saws that cut it into smaller and smaller widths until it exited as 4 x 8 x 10 foot cut lumber. Todd noticed a series of belts and pulleys hooked to the main shaft of the waterwheel which powered all the saws.

A warning shout erupted from the log pile outside as Todd and Steve exited the building. They watched in horror as a log being lifted to the top of stack slipped out of the rope noose that held it and fell on top of a worker standing below. Steve ran toward the accident site with Todd in close pursuit. Two men were dragging the lifeless body of the worker out from underneath the errant log. They laid him on the grass and stood around not knowing what to do next. Steve and Todd pushed through the knot of workers standing around and observed the body of a young boy, perhaps fifteen or sixteen years old. He was not breathing. Todd knelt beside him, tore his shirt open, and with both hands placed on the boy's bare chest began to press rhythmically on it and prayed while he administered the CPR that he had learned during the war. The boy's face was ashen gray and his wide-open eyes stared blankly into the sky.

After several minutes with no response, Steve placed his hand on Todd's shoulder. "The boy is dead. You can stop now."

Todd ignored him and continued to pray and give CPR. After another minute the boy coughed, his face turned pink, and bloody foam bubbled from his lips and nose. After a few minutes, Todd helped him sit up and examined his chest that was red and exhibited a large bruise. Steve tried to get the boy to his feet. He looked bewildered and his rubbery legs wouldn't support him. His left arm hung limply by his side. Blood tricked down his pants leg from a three-inch gash in his thigh. They helped him into the mill and laid him down on a table in the office where Todd could examine him.

Steve looked questioningly at Todd. "Father, where did you learn to bring life back to the dead?"

"The boy wasn't dead. I just helped to get him breathing again."

"He was as dead as any man I've ever seen. His name is Jonnie. He is the son of the mill owner. It was a miracle that you visited the mill when you did. Are you a priest or a doctor?"

"I'm a priest, but I have picked up some doctoring skills along the way."

Todd examined the boy as foamy blood trickled from his mouth. He sutured the leg wound with a needle and thread from the medical kit he always carried with him. The boy's bruised chest, fast pulse, and erratic breathing made Todd suspect the boy had broken ribs and possible internal injuries. "Jonnie may be bleeding internally," Todd suspected. "We must get him into town at once to see a proper doctor."

Steve readied the buckboard and his men carefully placed Jonnie in the back of the wagon and covered him with a blanket. Todd followed them back into town on his rented horse. When they arrived at the doctor's office, Todd and Steve carried Jonnie into the infirmary and placed him on the exam table. The doctor took his blood pressure and as Todd suspected, he discovered the boy not only had three broken ribs, but also a possibly ruptured spleen. As he prepared Jonnie for surgery, Steve told him how Todd had brought Jonnie back to life.

"You performed lifesaving first aid out there," the doctor said to Todd. "Had you not got him breathing again, we would be preparing for a funeral rather than surgery."

About this time the boy's father, the mill owner, burst into the infirmary. He looked at his son lying on the examination table and then at the doctor.

"Doc, is Jonnie going to be all right?"

"Yes, I think so. His arm is sprained and he has three broken ribs and some internal injuries that need immediate surgery, but with any luck he will survive."

The boy's father then addressed Steve. "What happened?"

"The boy was stacking logs when one slipped from the crane and fell on top of him," Steve explained. "By the time my men dragged the boy from under the log he wasn't breathing. You need to thank the priest who resuscitated him at the mill. Father Bose is the pastor of St. Patrick's parish in Whitefish, but he seems to know a lot about doctoring."

The mill owner grabbed Todd's hand and began pumping it.

"Thank you, Father Bose. Thank you so very much. My name is Frank Burns. I own the mill outside town. Jonnie is my only son. What brings you from Whitefish to Brainerd?"

"I had business with Sheriff Stalwart."

"I thank God for whatever business that bought you here to Brainerd and that you were at the mill at this critical moment. God certainly must care for all of us."

"That He does," Todd said with a knowing smile, "that He does."

The next day Todd visited Johnnie, who had recovered from the operation and was doing well. He then boarded the *Itaska* for the trip back to Grand Rapids. Tied to the deck of the *Itaska* was a four-passenger stagecoach.

"It's for the new stage line in Grand Rapids," Captain Pinot explained. "Two more coaches are on order from St. Paul. I understand Jacob Yearling of Grand Rapids intends to provide the communities of Hibbing and Whitefish with regularly scheduled stagecoach service. He might even extend the line all the way to Duluth someday, provided they ever complete that road."

A stage line to Whitefish, Todd thought, *our little community is growing to become a real town.*

He got off the *Itaska* and stopped by the livery stable to retrieve his horse and carriage just as the new stagecoach arrived from the boat. Max was hanging a new sign over his livery stable that read, *Yearling Stage Lines* Todd asked what the plans were for the stage service to Whitefish. Max said it would run every Wednesday and Saturday, and would carry passengers and freight. He also had a contract to deliver the US mail. Todd made his way back to Whitefish and stopped by the Dunn farm to visit with Mike and Mary.

He told Mike about his visit to the sheriff in Brainerd, and that the sheriff wasn't at all helpful. He added that he didn't think the circuit judge in Brainerd would do much about Seth, his blankets or his medicines, but he had hired a lawyer to represent his complaints in court. He also shared the news that Jacob Yearling intended to offer weekly stagecoach service between Grand Rapids and Whitefish.

"This means we will have visitors; maybe even tourists will come to Whitefish," Mike said excitedly.

"I wouldn't place too much hope for tourists," Todd said. "It still is a bumpy, dusty ride to Whitefish, and what would they come to see?"

"Rich Parson and Jack Sprier have finished building the North Shore Lodge and Spa across the lake and will welcome the Yearling Stage Lines that will bring customers to their fledging business."

Yes, Whitefish was indeed growing.

Chapter 13
Tecumseh

Summer, 1874

Two months went by before Todd received a letter from Peter Dean. The news was disappointing but not entirely unexpected. Peter said the Dr. Watkins Tonic test results did not arrive in time for the hearing, and based on the testimony of Sheriff Stalwart and friends of Seth, Judge Mason dismissed both complaints. Todd wrote back and asked Peter to send his complaints to the State Attorney in St. Paul. In his return letter, Peter said he was sorry, but considering the dismissal by the circuit judge, he had closed the case. He felt it would be a waste of his time and refused to take Todd's money to pursue the complaints with the state attorney in St. Paul.

The summers in Whitefish were short and by mid-September, the first snow had already briefly coated the ground. One Sunday after Mass, Lloyd came into the sacristy as Todd was taking off his vestments and said that three Indians were waiting outside to see him. Todd thought Tecumseh had come to visit and hurried outside to greet him, but Tecumseh was not one of the three men. Sekota, Tamara, and Neenah sat on their horses waiting to speak with him.

Todd greeted them and asked Tamara where her brother was. She remained on her horse and said, "Tecumseh in Army jail. Soldiers come and arrest him."

"In jail ... for what?"

Tamara's face hardened. "They say he kill tinker man, but he no do."

"Do you mean Seth Meriwether?" Tamara nodded. "Seth is dead?" She nodded again. "What happened?"

"Two moons ago while braves out hunting, tinker man come to village to trade for pelts. We know him as the man who trade blankets that make many Ojibwa people sick with pox. We tell him to go, but he no go. He want food and water and want to trade knives for Ojibwa squaw. We say we no give him food, water, or squaw, but he take food and water, tie up Sekota's niece, and take her with him. He make camp the other side of lake. When Antikum and other braves come back they angry that tinker man come to village and take squaw. They ride to his camp and I go with them. Tinker man shoot at Antikum but he miss. Braves then shoot tinker man full of arrows and he fall dead in front of my pony. When soldiers come looking for tinker man they say Tecumseh kill tinker man. They take my brother to soldier fort. We want you to go to white man city and make the solders let Tecumseh go. Tell them about tinker man and how he kill many Ojibwa with bad blankets and come to village and take squaw and that Tecumseh hunting with braves and no kill tinker man."

"I cannot make the soldiers release Tecumseh," Todd said. "I was not there when Seth was killed, so I cannot testify that Tecumseh is innocent. I assume the Army will turn him over to the civilian court in St. Paul and they will try him for murder. You and Antikum can testify to the truth at his trial, and what I can do is hire a lawyer and testify about Seth trading infected Army blankets. I will tell the jury that Tecumseh is my friend and is a truthful and honest man. This I will do for you."

Without a thank you or good-bye, Tamara turned her horse around and, looking straight ahead, galloped off. Her companions followed behind generating a cloud of dust.

"Those Indians are angry. Are you going to try to help Tecumseh?" Lloyd asked.

"Yes, but all I can do right now is to send a letter to my lawyer, Peter Dean, in Brainerd. I will ask him to defend Tecumseh."

Todd sent that letter, and Peter agreed to defend Tecumseh pro bono. Peter made the trip to Leech Lake and interviewed Tamara and Antikum. He then visited Captain Johnson at Ft. Snelling and obtained the bill of sale for the Army blankets signed by the captain and Seth. He then traveled to St. Paul and demanded the Army turn their prisoner over to the civilian court in St. Paul, which they did without protest. After the Army transferred Tecumseh to the St. Paul prison, Peter met with the defendant and the prosecutor. While there was no doubt that the Leech Lake Indians killed Seth, the State had no direct evidence that Tecumseh committed the crime. Tecumseh vehemently argued his innocence and asked if Todd and Tamara could testify for him. Peter petitioned the court for bail, and the judge set bail at $1,000. Since the tribe had no money with which to post bail, Tecumseh sat in jail awaiting his trial set for early October. Peter subpoenaed Todd, Antikum, and Tamara to testify for the defense. Todd boarded the *Itaska* in Grand Rapids five days before the trial was to begin, and Tamara and her Indian companion joined him in Brainerd. Todd was grateful that the trial date was scheduled before the end of the season when river ice would shut down the *Itaska* service to Grand Rapids.

They went ashore in St. Paul and rented rooms in a downtown hotel. This was Todd's first visit to St. Paul since leaving for Whitefish Lake two years earlier, so he went to the cathedral to visit with Father Quinn and to meet again with Bishop Byrne. At first the bishop seemed miffed that Todd had involved himself in Indian affairs and had even hired a lawyer to defend a tribe member in court. Yet when he heard Todd's story of how he went to the Leech Lake village to treat the outbreak of smallpox from deliberately infected Army blankets, he sided with Todd and praised him for administering to those folks.

"The Indians are God's children and while I was aware of the rumors the Army was distributing smallpox infected blankets to many tribes, I didn't believe that it was true. Now I know better and this is a terrible evil that must be righted, and I admire you for your involvement."

Tecumseh's trial for murder opened on October 10, 1874, in the St. Paul courthouse. The previous week, a reporter from the St. Paul Journal had interviewed Tecumseh and printed a story about the rumored Army policy of trading infected blankets to troublesome Indians. The story raised local interest and when the trial began, spectators filled the courtroom. Todd sat in court behind Tecumseh and Peter Dean who were at the defendant's table. Tecumseh's sister Tamara, and Antikum her companion, took seats next to Todd as Judge Caldwell began proceedings by reading the murder charges.

The prosecutor, Jeff Miller, summarized his case, which was short and to the point. Tecumseh in a fit of rage had murdered Seth Meriwether at Leech Lake. He called only one witness, a Lieutenant Craig, who had arrested Tecumseh at Leech Lake. He testified that when the soldiers arrived at the Ojibwa camp to investigate Seth's disappearance, they discovered a recent grave and exhumed the body of Seth Meriwether. It was riddled with arrows. The lieutenant said he then interrogated Antikum and Waleke who both placed their mark on an affidavit claiming Tecumseh had killed the tinker man.

Peter then cross-examined Lieutenant Craig.

"Antikum and Waleke placed their mark on the affidavit. You don't speak Ojibwa, so how did you question them?"

"By sign language," Lt. Craig replied. "After Antikum and Waleke claimed that it was Tecumseh who shot Meriwether and signed the affidavit, I arrested Tecumseh and took him to the Ft. Snelling jail."

"On just Antikum's and Waleke's word?"

"Yes, but there were others, but these two were the only ones I asked to make their mark on the paper."

"You testified that you used sign language to question Antikum and Waleke. Do you understand Indian sign language?"

"To some extent I do, enough I suppose to get by," the lieutenant claimed.

Peter made a gesture with his left hand placed against his chest, fingers cupped and thumb pointed upward. "What does this sign mean?"

The lieutenant smiled. "That gesture means 'I accept your offer.'"

"No, that means 'You're a weasel.'"

The courtroom exploded in laughter, and the judge demanded order.

Peter continued. "Then we can assume that you do not fully understand Indian sign language. Did you question the woman who Seth abducted?"

"No."

"Why not?"

"She was only a squaw and couldn't speak English, and as you just demonstrated, it is difficult to converse with Indians using sign language."

"Only a squaw," Peter repeated disdainfully. "Then since we cannot trust your knowledge of sign language, is it possible you misinterpreted Antikum's signs, and he and Waleke didn't understand the affidavit he placed his mark on?"

"Could be."

Peter then asked Lieutenant Craig how many arrows were in Seth's body.

"Oh.... I'd say a half dozen or more," the lieutenant responded.

"And were all the arrows identical?" Peter asked.

"What do you mean?" Lieutenant Craig asked.

"Each Indian's arrow is unique. For instance, different bird feathers, identifying markings on the shaft, or shape of the arrowhead will indicate which person made the arrow. Were all the arrows in Seth's body identical?"

"I don't know. I didn't examine them all that close."

"Isn't it likely that with so many arrows in Seth's body, there could have been more than one shooter?"

"Yet you only arrested Tecumseh for shooting Seth Meriwether. Did you assume all these arrows came from the same bow?"

"I suppose so. I never thought much about it."

Peter had no other questions for Lieutenant Craig so the judge excused him.

The prosecutor called no other witnesses, and then after placing Antikum's and Waleke's affidavits into evidence, he concluded his case.

Peter began his defense by calling Tecumseh to the stand. He denied he had shot Seth and claimed that he wasn't even at the tinker man's camp when he was shot. He said when Antikum and Waleke were questioned they said Tecumseh did not shoot Merriweather and when they placed their marks on the paper they didn't understand what it said.

"Antikum no say Tecumseh shoot tinker man. He say many braves shoot him, and he say Tecumseh not with them when tinker man killed."

Then Peter called Tamara to the stand. She had a good knowledge of English and testified that the tinker man came to trade for a squaw, and they told him to go away but he wouldn't go away. Then he forced Sekota's niece to go with him. Tamara testified that she herself was present when Seth was murdered.

"Tecumseh not with braves who shoot tinker man. Braves come to tinker man camp and they very angry with tinker man for bringing pox to tribe and for taking young squaw. Tinker man try to shoot Antikum but he miss. Then many braves shoot arrows at him and he fall dead at my pony's feet. Tecumseh not there and was hunting with other braves. He no shoot tinker man."

When it was Father Bose's turn to testify, he repeated his story about treating the tribe's outbreak of smallpox and despite his nursing, many Ojibwa women and children died of the disease. He said he discovered the Army blankets that Seth traded to the tribe for beaver pelts were infested with fleas that can carry smallpox.

In cross-examination, the prosecutor wanted to know how Todd knew those blankets were the source of the smallpox outbreak

"When I arrived at the Leech Lake village," Todd explained, "most of the braves were away hunting and when they returned, not one of them had come down with the pox. I thought this was very curious. Why were only the women and children in the tribe infected, all the men were healthy and initially the teenage boys were also spared? I noticed only the squaws and children used the colorful Navajo blankets that Seth traded for beaver skins the month before, but the bucks ignored the blankets. I found out that they refused to use those Navaho blankets because the Navaho are enemies of the Ojibwa and Sioux people and no self-respecting buck would use blankets made by their enemies. I examined the blankets and found them crawling with fleas, insects that can carry smallpox."

"Are you a doctor?" the prosecutor asked.

"No, I am a priest."

It was becoming increasingly evident that Jeff Miller had not done his homework.

"Are you qualified to diagnose smallpox?"

"Yes, I am. I worked in the Baltimore Hospital for two years and as a doctor's assistant treated many cases of smallpox. From the pockmarks on your face I assume you must also have suffered from this terrible disease."

"That is not the question here," he said a bit miffed at Todd's personal observation. "You claim the blankets Seth sold to the Indians were infested with fleas. Are you an entomologist who can identify flees?"

"No, I am not, but I know a flea when I see one, and the folds of each blanket were infested with them."

The audience snickered and the judge slammed his gavel down and demanded order.

"Indians are not all that clean and are usually infested with vermin of one kind or another," the prosecutor quipped. "They could have been Ojibwa fleas."

"That is not true," Todd protested. "There are no fleas in upper Minnesota; they cannot survive the subzero winters up there. Fleas do not infest the Leech Lake Indians, their dogs, or their ponies. The blankets had been infested with fleas, like the fleas that infest Ft. Stilwell."

"How did you know those Navajo blankets were Army blankets?"

"By the Army insignia embroidered on them."

Having broken every rule of cross-examination, the prosecutor then asked Todd another question to which he didn't know the answer.

"How would an Army insignia end up on an Army blanket?"

"The Army had a contract to buy blankets from the Navajo Nation. Then to identify them as Army property, it was the practice to add their logo to them."

"And where did Seth buy these Army blankets?"

"He bought them from Captain Jeremy Johnson at Ft. Snelling."

There was an audible gasp in the courtroom.

The judge rapped his gavel again to quiet the crowd down, and then asked, "Father Bose, this is a serious accusation. You say the

Army and specifically Captain Jeremy Johnson knowingly sold infected blankets to Seth Meriwether for trade with the Indians at Leech Lake."

"I am saying exactly that, Your Honor," Todd said without hesitation.

"Have you proof of this?" the judge asked.

"Yes, I do," Todd replied. He took out a piece of paper and handed it to the judge. "I have a bill of sale signed by Captain Johnson to Seth Meriwether for three dozen Army blankets. The price was $12 for the whole lot, and a bargain at that price."

A murmur swept through the courtroom as the prosecutor fumbled for words. "The US Army is not on trial here; Tecumseh is on trial," he argued.

Peter objected. "Your Honor, in a way the Army is on trial here at least by implication as a co-conspirator. Selling the tribe infected Navajo blankets was the reason the Indians were so angry with Seth and coupled with the abduction of Sekota's niece, the Indians were angry enough to kill him. It was foolish for him to come back to the village to trade and then abduct one of their young women. This trial is as much about the Army policy of genocide by infecting Indians with disease as it is about who murdered Seth."

The judge pondered Peter's objection for a moment, and then denied the motion. "While it is true that the motivation for Seth's murder may have been retribution for genocide and abduction, these proceedings are about Tecumseh's indictment for the murder of Seth Merewether. This trial is not about genocide, but about the murder of a white man by an Indian. However, I am appalled about Captain Johnson's behavior and I am going to refer the accusation and evidence presented by Father Bose to the state attorney. It is criminal that the Army encourages this policy of genocide. And if Captain Johnson sold those infected blankets to Seth to trade with the Indians, he will be indicted."

The prosecutor summarized his evidence against Tecumseh. He claimed he had motive and opportunity to commit this murder and that two witnesses had accused him of shooting Seth as attested on the affidavit.

Peter then rose to give his summary.

"We know that Seth Meriwether was murdered by Indians at Leech Lake. Nevertheless, the state prosecutor has produced no evidence whatsoever that it was Tecumseh who killed him. Lieutenant Craig who arrested Tecumseh demonstrated that he doesn't understand sign language and may have misinterpreted the testimony of his only witnesses. Their marks on the affidavit are invalid. All that we know is that some angry Leech Lake braves bent on revenge shot Seth full of arrows. It isn't possible that with so many arrows in his body only one person could have shot Seth. We have Tecumseh's testimony that he was not there and did not kill Seth and we also have the testimony of Tamara that Tecumseh was hunting with the other braves when Seth was killed. I rest my case."

After a few moments of silence, the judge suggested, "I will entertain a motion for dismissal."

Peter rose and said, "I motion that due to a lack of conclusive evidence, the case against Tecumseh be dismissed."

"So ordered," the judge said and rapped his gavel.

Todd shook hands with Peter. "Congratulations and thank you."

Tecumseh looked confused. "You're free," Todd explained. Ever stoic, Tecumseh showed no emotion at those words, but just sat in his chair watching people exit the courtroom. Tamara thanked Peter and Todd and then helped Tecumseh to his feet. Brother and sister then left the courtroom together. They sailed the next day on the *Itaska* to Brainerd and from there returned to Leech Lake on horseback.

After a few days working at the chancery, Todd returned to Whitefish and resumed his duties at the clinic and as pastor of St. Patrick's.

The Yearling Stage Lines now provided scheduled stagecoach service to Whitefish every Wednesday and Saturday, and townsfolk now enjoyed regular US mail deliveries. The US Postal Service selected the Whitefish Hotel as the local post office and named Mark Gottwald as the town's first postmaster. Mark set aside a part of his reception desk to sort incoming mail and built mail slots for each family, proudly displaying a sign that proclaimed *Whitefish U.S.P.O.* Todd visited the hotel each Saturday and Wednesday afternoon to retrieve his mail along with a copy of the weekly St. Paul Journal. Although it was always last week's news, it was only a week old rather than a month old. The front page of the October 27, 1874 St. Paul Journal proclaimed that *Army Captain Jeremy Johnson had been accused of Genocide.* The story went on to say Captain Johnson, the commandant of Ft. Snelling, was indicted by a St. Paul grand jury for selling infected Army blankets to the Leech Lake Indians, and as a result dozens of women and children had died of smallpox. The state scheduled his trial for the spring of 1875, but the Army argued that this was a military matter and Minnesota did not have jurisdiction.

Subsequent newspapers described a decision handed down by the Minnesota Supreme Court. Because Captain Johnson had sold these blankets to a civilian who then traded them to the Leech Lake Indians, it was a civil matter that should be tried in Minnesota courts. The court subpoenaed Father Bose to testify at the trial scheduled to begin on May 22, 1875. Because Captain Johnson and by implication the Army was being accused of genocide, the trial prompted national headlines. Newspapers in Chicago, Baltimore, Washington, and New York made it front page news. The papers printed details of the trial proceedings. This aroused the populace to stand against the Army practice of giving out infected blankets to Indians. The Army officially denied they practiced genocide and claimed that this was a vicious rumor intended to discredit them, but their denial gained no traction. Father Bose's compelling testimony caused a national sensation. His story about how he had saved many of the Leech Lake Indians deliberately infected with smallpox, and how he determined that the Army blankets traded to the Indians were contaminated, raised an awareness in most folks and engendered a national movement against the Army and how they were treating the Indians.

The jury eventually convicted Captain Johnson of genocide and the judge sentenced him to ten years in prison. Although Captain Johnson and not the Army had been on trial, the public awareness of the Army's practices toward the Indians forced the administration to disavow such tactics and encouraged better treatment of the Indians. Even President Grant weighed in and rebuked the Army generals for encouraging the spread of smallpox among vexatious Indian tribes. As a result, the US Army stopped giving out blankets to the Indians and the newspapers credited Father Bose with bringing this outrage to national attention. Todd had become an inadvertent celebrity, especially in St. Paul. He didn't wish for or welcome such attention, and only wanted to get back to St. Patrick's as fast as possible. Before he boarded the *Itaska* for the trip back home, Bishop Byrne summoned him to the chancery.

Bishop Byrne was aware of Todd's doctoring skills and the clinic in Whitefish. When the St. Paul newspaper printed the full story about Father Todd healing the Indians and how he had doctored the folks in Whitefish and even performed a successful appendectomy, the bishop became concerned. Setting broken bones and medicating fevers was one thing, but performing surgery was quite another matter.

When Todd arrived at the chancery, Mrs. Penrose ushered him into the bishop's office where he took a chair and remained silent as Bishop Byrne finished signing some papers and then handed them back to Mrs. Penrose.

"Father Todd," the bishop began as he peered over his reading glasses, "God has blessed you with the skills of a doctor, but you are not a licensed physician. The newspapers write that you have been performing surgeries in Whitefish. The Medical Association in St. Paul has expressed their concern about your practicing surgery in Whitefish without a license. You are a priest, not a doctor. I cannot have my priests performing unauthorized surgeries."

Todd was stunned. He said that he understood the bishop's concern but defended his actions. "The good folks of Whitefish have petitioned for a resident doctor for years, yet no one has ever offered to answer their prayers. When I first arrived, the folks up there soon learned of my medical experience and began to come to me for treatment. I have treated their illness, mended their broken bones, and even helped deliver their babies. Yet this was the only time I performed a surgery. If I hadn't removed Tom's appendix he would have died from septic poising. I assisted with this surgery on several occasions at the Baltimore hospital, and I know how to do it safely and avoid infection. What would the local Medical Association have me do, let the poor man die?"

"No, we do not want that nor do we want to limit your practice at Whitefish, but the answer to this dilemma is possible. What both Bishop Allen and I both want you to do is to enroll in our local medical college, earn your medical degree, and be licensed by the state," the bishop said. "Then you can practice as a doctor which is what the diocese and the medical profession want you to do."

Todd was flummoxed. "But Bishop, this would require me to leave my Whitefish parish for up to four years to enroll in a medical college and study for a degree. Those folks need a priest even more than they need a licensed doctor. I cannot abandon them to go back to school."

"You will not have to," Bishop Byrne said with a slight smile. "We have an excellent medical college right here in St. Paul, and I have spoken to the school administrators about you. They reviewed your Rutgers premed transcript and your work in the Baltimore hospital during the war. They consider this education and experience equivalent to three of the four years necessary to complete the course of study necessary for an MD. Provided you can pass their entrance exam, they are willing to enroll you and then, over the course of four successive summers, you can earn your MD. The folks in Whitefish will miss you for three months, but the community must understand that you must have a medical degree to continue to perform surgeries and run the clinic up there."

Obedient to the wishes of the bishop, in June of 1875 Todd traveled to St. Paul and took the required entrance exams. He passed those exams and enrolled in the St. Paul Medical College, where he spent three months during each of the next four summers taking courses and completing his residency at the local hospital. In 1879, Father Todd graduated and passed the test for a medical license from the state of Minnesota.

Both Bishop Byrne and Father Dunn proudly attended Todd's graduation ceremony. Mike and Mary Dunn also made the long trip from Whitefish to attend Todd's graduation.

Afterwards with a twinkle in his eye, Father Quinn asked Todd,

"How should we address you now ... as Father Bose or Doctor Bose?"

Todd smiled and said, "My vocation has always been as a priest. The folks in Whitefish have always addressed me as Father Todd, and despite this sheepskin, that remains my wish."

Mike laughed. "How about Doctor Father Todd?"

Todd looked sternly at Mike. "Please, just Father Todd."

The next day at sunrise, Todd, Mike, and Mary boarded the *Itaska*. Todd was especially happy to be heading home.

Chapter 14
Family Matters

May, 1880

It was difficult for Todd to realize that it had been eight years since he first arrived in Whitefish. Much had transpired in those intervening years, including earning a medical degree. Fires, hailstorms, bitter cold, locust invasions, drought, and disease conspired to make his ministry in Whitefish a challenge. Father Todd shepherded his flock through all those hard times and continued to operate the clinic and tend to their bodies as well as their souls. With each challenge, Father Todd grew deeper in his faith and the community grew deeper in theirs. The folks in Whitefish, Catholic and non-Catholic alike, loved him and respected his talents both as a doctor and as a priest. He was comfortable in his dual role, but still dismissed the title of Doctor Bose. "I'm just Father Todd," he reminded anyone who tried to address him as "Father Bose," or worse yet "Doctor Bose." He insisted that everyone recognize his priestly ordination was above that as a doctor.

One May afternoon he opened a letter postmarked five days earlier at Titusville and addressed to Father Bose. It was from his father, John Bose. In all the years since he arrived in Whitefish, he had received many letters from his mother, yet he never once had he received a letter from his father. John was just not a letter writer. With shaking hands, he read in his father's barely legible scrawl. It said that on May 13, his mother, Matilda, had died suddenly from pneumonia in the Titusville hospital. Her funeral and internment was to be held on Tuesday May 25 at St. John's church in Spartansburg. John said that one of her last wishes was to have Todd preside at her funeral Mass. Could he come?

Todd looked at the calendar. It was already Tuesday May 17 and it had taken five days for his father's letter to arrive. He did a quick calculation. If he could catch the *Itaska* due to leave from Grand

Rapids tomorrow morning, and if all the trains ran on time, then he might just make it to Spartansburg in time for the funeral on Tuesday. Two days' travel to St. Paul by riverboat, another day by train to Chicago, and a day and a half to Pittsburg, then another day to travel to Spartansburg by a rented horse and buggy. If all went well he should arrive sometime next Monday afternoon. It would be close but he just might make it in time if he left immediately.

Todd walked to the church, climbed into a pew, and between tears prayed. Matilda was a wonderful mother, the one person in this world who was most responsible for Todd being who he was, and even though it had been years since he last saw her, he knew that he would miss her terribly. Of course, he would preside at her funeral, yet the question remained if he could make the six-day trip in time for her funeral next Tuesday. Fortunately, the *Itaska* was scheduled to depart on its weekly voyage from Grand Rapids to St. Paul the next morning. Had the letter arrived one day later, he would have to wait a week for the next riverboat and there would have been no way that he could be home in time for the funeral. He would have to pack and leave this afternoon without having time to say good-bye to his parishioners. He hitched Molly to his buggy, informed his assistant at the clinic of the emergency, and asked her to inform every one of his mother's death and funeral in Pennsylvania and arrange for his absence. He arrived in Grand Rapids that afternoon, boarded Molly at the livery stable, and went down to the dock to purchase passage to St. Paul. However, the riverboat tied to the dock was not the *Itaska*. Much smaller than the *Itaska* and graced with a single black smokestack, the boat's pilothouse sat on top of the single-story deck structure. The forward deck crane was lifting crates from the boat to the wharf. Todd walked around the cargo stacked haphazardly on the wharf and noted the name on the bow "*Natchez*." Climbing up the gangplank, he found the captain busily supervising deck hands as they attached a crate to the deck crane hook.

"Hello, my name is Father Todd Bose. Where is the *Itaska*?"

The captain was tall, lean, and beardless. He wore a full captain's uniform yet looked much too young to command a riverboat. Curly red hair locks escaped from underneath his captain's hat, and although somewhat annoyed at the intrusion, he forced a weak smile when he recognized Todd's Roman collar.

"Father, the name's Captain Richards. The *Itaska* is downriver in St. Louis undergoing repairs; seems her boiler almost blew up last month."

"Can you book me passage to St. Paul for tomorrow morning? I have a family emergency and need to catch a train to Chicago and Pittsburg as soon as possible."

Captain Richards brow furrowed. "The *Natchez* is mostly a cargo scow and doesn't have the fancy accommodations of the *Itaska*. There are five staterooms and four are reserved out of Brainerd, so I guess I can accommodate you to St. Paul. My cook is also my deckhand, so don't expect fancy meals like you'd get on the *Itaska*. You'll be the only passenger until we dock in Brainerd, so go ahead and store your stuff in the stern leeward stateroom. Dinner is at 5:00 p.m., and we'll cast off later tonight. We should tie up in St. Paul late Thursday morning."

"Thursday morning?" Todd said with obvious surprise. "That is good news but the *Itaska* takes almost two full days to make the trip from here to St. Paul, so I didn't expect to be there until late Thursday evening."

Captain Richards smiled. "That old salt Captain Pinot wouldn't run the river at night, so each trip he tied the *Itaska* up overnight in Grand Rapids and in Brainerd. I think he just wanted to visit the local saloons. Considering the nighttime layovers, he could only make one weekly round trip between St. Paul and Grand Rapids, but now by running at night I can make two such trips each week. After a short stop in Brainerd tomorrow, we'll run downriver at night and arrive in St. Paul as I said on Thursday morning. It is quite safe to run the river at night. We have a good gas-powered searchlight on board and my mate and I can view the river ahead for dangers like sandbars and debris."

Todd remembered Captain Pinot's reluctance to run the river at night, and wouldn't do so even if he had one of those new-fangled gas searchlights. The captain worried about running the *Itaska* aground on a sandbar or putting a log through her hull in the dark. Yet Todd was thankful that he would be in St. Paul a half-day early to catch a train to Chicago that afternoon, so he didn't argue with Captain Richards about the dangers of running the river at night. He thought that although this captain may be young, he must know what he is doing. He found his cabin, stowed his backpack, and dined in the small dining room with Captain Richards, his mate and two deckhands. He retired to his cabin early that evening after the *Natchez* untied and the rhythmic throbbing of the engines soon lulled him into a sound sleep. He slept until a long blast from the vessel's steam whistle woke him. Surprised to see that the sun was already up, Todd rose and hurriedly dressed. He arrived on deck in time to watch as the deck hands tied the *Natchez* to the Brainerd wharf. As Captain Roberts indicated, after loading cargo and passengers they left Brainerd later that morning, ran downriver all that day and night, and arrived at St. Paul early the next day. The early morning sun was already well up as the *Natchez* docked. Anxious to get into town to check on the trains to Chicago, he gathered his belongings, said good bye to Captain Richards, and walked down the gangplank.

He looked around for a taxi to take him to the train station, but except for a couple of stevedores preparing cargo to load on the *Natchez*, the wharf was deserted. Todd hiked down the road to the Pigs Eye Saloon, where he saw two carriages parked outside. Their horses were drinking from the trough in front of the porch. Two shapely ladies wearing frilly dresses stood on the porch talking and laughing, their dark hair neatly arranged in buns, and faces painted with heavy makeup. Todd climbed the steps and walked toward the women. They ceased laughing when they saw him coming toward them and both took a step back when they recognized the man wore a Roman collar.

"'Tis a bit early for business, Father," one of the ladies said with a nervous laugh.

Todd blushed. "I was looking for a ride into town, nothing more."

"Ah, Father, we thought you were looking for a lady's companionship," the second lady said. "I'm sure we can arrange a taxi ride into town for you." The first lady turned and went inside, and a few moments later returned followed by a short man dressed as a coachman.

"Janette tells me you need a ride into town," the man said.

"Yes, to the train station," Todd explained.

The coachman hitched one of the horses to a buggy, climbed into the driver's seat, and then invited Todd aboard.

The horse plodded through the city streets as folks prepared for the day's business. Fifteen minutes later, the driver pulled up to the St. Paul Train Station and held out his hand.

"That will be twenty-five cents."

Todd paid him and went inside to the information desk. The big wall clock indicated that it was 10:10 am.

"When is the next train to Chicago?"

"You just missed the 8:00 a.m. train. The next train leaves for Chicago at 2:00 p.m. this afternoon."

Todd purchased a ticket and pondered his situation. He could sit in the train station for the next few hours, but since there was plenty of time, he felt he should visit with Father Quinn. He hailed a taxi outside the station and told the cabbie to take him to the chancery. As he strolled up to the chancery front desk, Mrs. Penrose looked up from her work. A big smile graced her face.

"Father Bose! It's good to see you. What brings you to St. Paul?"

Todd explained about his mother's sudden death and said he was on his way to Pittsburg to preside at her funeral in Spartansburg.

"I'm so sorry to hear that, "she said. "Let me see if Fr. Quinn is available." She disappeared down the hallway and in less than a minute returned.

"Father Quinn says to go right in."

Todd knocked at Father Quinn's office door.

"Come in, come in," Father Quinn bellowed.

The elderly priest stood up as Todd entered and warmly shook his hand.

"Well, Father Todd, I certainly wasn't expecting to see you today. What brings you to St. Paul?"

Todd explained about his mother's sudden death and his trip to Pittsburg to preside at her funeral in Spartanburg.

"I'm so sorry to hear that. I will say a Mass for her in the morning. How long are you going to be in town?"

"My train leaves for Chicago at 2:00 p.m."

"I guess in that case our visit will be short." Father Quinn looked at his watch. 'It's after ten. I assume you have not yet had the opportunity to say Mass this morning."

Todd said that he hadn't, so Father Quinn led him to the chapel inside the cathedral and served for him as he said Mass. Afterwards they returned to the chancery dining room where the housekeeper poured each a cup of coffee. After returning to the kitchen, she came back with a plate of pancakes and eggs. Father Quinn questioned Todd as he ate. It was evident that he had something important on his mind....

"Father Todd, how is it going at St. Patrick's?"

Todd put his fork down and finished a mouthful of pancakes before answering.

"Other than the hailstorm that destroyed part of our crops last fall and a terrible forest fire that burned two farm houses and barns to the ground, we are doing reasonably well. These folks are unbelievably resilient and supportive of their neighbors. The town got together and rebuilt the farmhouses and barns. For the past years the harvest has been abundant, so we stored corn and wheat in silos anticipating such a disaster. This allowed the community to make it through the winter without asking for a rescue from the Army."

"And how's the clinic and your doctoring going?"

"Busy as always with the usual walk-in emergencies such as broken bones, various infections, teeth that must be pulled, and wounds that need stitching. Yet since I received my MD and surgical training, I have performed only three surgeries. One was for a breach birth that required a Caesarean; another was for a child run over by a wagon. I had to remove his spleen. The third was for a parishioner accidentally shot in the abdomen. There is a story about this shooting which I will save for a later time."

"I hear that most of your patients recover nicely, including a few whose cures were quite unusual. Some folks claim you have medical powers that border on the miraculous. One of your parishioners told me about the surprising cure you effected for a person who was dying from TB."

"That would be Rich Parsons," Todd offered. "He came to the clinic suffering with an advanced case of TB. He was only forty-two at the time and I estimated he had perhaps only six months to live, yet today he is strong and healthy. His cure was not miraculous but brought about in large part to the medicinal Indian berries and herbs I gave him and perhaps to the mineral waters of his hot spring. For centuries the Ojibwa have known about the medicinal power of certain herbs and the curative benefits of hot springs and have used them to treat many ailments. The medications coupled with months of complete rest and daily bathing in the Whitefish hot springs aided in his cure. It wasn't miracles that cured him but my recommendation for herbs, mineral water, and complete rest. Sometimes Jesus and His mother Mary listen to my prayers and as a result, my patients get well. Other times despite my prayers they do not. It is all in God's hands, and I am only His tool. The only power I have is my faith and my medical knowledge." Father Quinn smiled yet said nothing in response.

"After Rich Parson's health returned, he and his partner Jack Sprier built the North Shore Lodge and Spa across the lake from the town. Each week a dozen guests arrive by stage from Grand Rapids looking forward to a week in the lodge and bathing in the spa. The town built a dock near St. Patrick's and constructed a 22-foot boat to ferry passengers across the lake to the lodge. Some folks believed that the mineral waters in the hot spring have curative powers, so Rich cools the water in his root cellar, bottles it, and then sells the mineral water in town and in Grand Rapids."

"Well it may be the medicines, herbs, mineral water, and good doctoring as you say, but I've been told about several cases where folks insist you have performed miraculous cures. I am a bit of a skeptic, but I do believe in miracles. Once I even witnessed a miraculous cure myself. Some years ago, I traveled to France and visited Massabielle, near Lourdes, France, where in a small grotto in 1858, the Blessed Virgin Mary appeared to a young girl named Bernadette. Bathing in the water from this grotto is said to have curative powers, and lining the walls of the grotto pool lay hundreds of discarded canes, wheelchairs, and crutches. During my visit, I personally witnessed a miraculous cure of a paraplegic confined to a wheelchair for many years after a carriage ran over his legs. The man's friends helped him into the small spring-fed grotto pool and after a dip, he prayed in the church next to the grotto. His friends carried him into the church, but the next day he walked into the church unassisted. Yes, I am a skeptic but I do believe that God sometimes interacts with humans to work preternatural cures of His choosing. After all, nothing is impossible with God."

Father Quinn took another sip of coffee and then continued.

"Bishop Byrne and I think it is prudent that you document each patient you treat. Keep a detailed journal for each patient, recording his or her affliction, and your diagnosis. Include their medical history, their treatment, and the results. It is most important to keep a record of any changes in their spiritual life that might accompany a cure. For instance, do they attend Mass and receive the sacraments more often after their cure than before? Are they more prayerful? Have any of your patients asked to be baptized after they were cured? Personally I remain skeptical about rumors of your miraculous cures, and I think most of the time you are just a good doctor. However, I also admit that God often does work miracles by using ordinary people as his instrument. Perhaps He has selected you to be His tool. You would not be the first or last person to be so selected."

Todd said nothing but nodded his agreement to keep a detailed journal. After their meeting, he said goodbye to Father Quinn, returned to the train station, and boarded the Chicago Limited at 1:45. The train ride brought him to Chicago Friday morning where he changed trains and continued to Pittsburg, arriving there Saturday afternoon. Sunday morning after attending Mass at St. Mary's Cathedral in Pittsburg, he hired a horse-driven buggy and made his way to Slippery Rock where he spent the evening. The next day he drove to Titusville and marveled at the transformation the town had undergone since his boyhood days. Ever since Ed Drake drilled for water and instead struck oil, the area had exploded from a village of less than 500 persons to a town of several thousand. The hospital where he interned as a premed student had expanded from a one-level wood building to a multistory brick structure occupying most of one block. The downtown area bustled with wagons and horses and new businesses lined the main street. Todd hurried through town and on to Spartansburg, arriving there Monday afternoon. His hometown had visibly changed in the years since his last visit. Several new buildings lined the main street. The old familiar two-story 1780 hotel had burned down, and a new building replaced it. The general store everyone called "The Merc," where as a teenager Todd worked sweeping floors and stocking shelves, had been renovated and although the familiar front porch was no longer there, the original hand-painted overhead sign still announced, "Bryson's Mercantile." He drove past the Merc and down First Street to St. John's church and Father Taylor's rectory. The housekeeper led Todd to the study where Fr. Taylor sat in an easy chair, his legs covered with a blanket. Now about to celebrate his seventy-second birthday, Father Taylor looked old and tired. Crippled with arthritis he sat uncomfortably in his easy chair but managed a broad smile when he recognized Todd.

"Father Todd Bose! I am so glad to see you, but I expected you would come. I was so sad to hear of the untimely death of your mother. She was only a young girl when I first arrived here as pastor of St. John's. Years later, I married her and your father, baptized you and your two brothers, gave you first Communion and heard your confessions. Matilda was a wonderful woman, an attentive mother and wife. We will all miss her terribly, and I don't know how your dad is going to get along without her on the farm, nor is he in the best of health."

Todd's forehead furrowed. "What is ailing Dad and how is he dealing with Mom's death?"

"I think your dad has arthritis and suffers a bit from the palsy. He is lost without Matilda. Can I assume you will co-celebrate with me at her funeral Mass tomorrow morning?"

"Of course I will. Dad wrote that it was her last wish."

"And how is it going at St. Patrick's?"

"Whitefish is growing and so is St. Patrick's. The little church is crowded each Sunday, and I am always busy with baptisms and confessions."

"I understand you built the church from plans your grandfather designed for St. John's."

"Yes, we did, and St. Patrick's looks just like St. John's did seventy-five years ago."

Fr. Taylor shuffled through a stack of newspapers on the table next to his chair and handed Todd a yellowed copy of the Pittsburg Tribune. The front-page headline read, *"Army Captain Johnson Convicted in St. Paul of Genocide."* The article was the last in a series of stories on the trial and conviction of Captain Johnson. Father Taylor had underlined a paragraph in the middle of the article.

"Fr. Todd Bose of Whitefish, Minnesota, is responsible for bringing this injustice to the attention of the Minnesota Superior Court. His testimony about how he treated the Leech Lake Indians infected with smallpox, and how he discovered that Army blankets were to blame for their illness, was critical in solving this case. In the end, the Army discontinued its practice of giving Indian tribes infected blankets thanks to the efforts of Fr. Bose."

Todd handed the newspaper back to Fr. Taylor. "The newspaper gives me more credit than I deserve."

"You followed your conscience and did God's will," Father Taylor said with an understanding smile. "This newspaper story made you into a national hero especially in these parts. The whole town of Spartansburg is proud of you and has adopted you as their native son."

Father Taylor put the newspaper back on the stack.

"And how is your clinic doing? I heard that you are now an official medical doctor."

"Yes. Bishop Byrne heard that I had performed an appendectomy without a license. He insisted that I attend medical school in St. Paul and earn a doctor of medicine degree, which I did. I work in the clinic five days a week; however, my first duty is to my congregation as their priest and pastor."

"And have there been any miraculous cures in your work?"

"Some folks claim so, but I contend that the so-called miracles are exaggerated. To be truthful, some of my patients have recovered from serious illnesses and accidents, but I attribute this to good doctoring and God's will, not to miracles."

"Todd, as long as I have known you I have sensed there is something special about you. I believe God is working through you in significant ways. You are His instrument of healing. Accept this and thank God for such a gift."

Todd nodded and stood up. "I haven't been out to the farm yet to see Dad, so I had better get along. I will be here at 7:00 a.m. tomorrow. Is Mary's interment to follow afterwards in the Church graveyard?"

"Yes, right next to your grandmother and grandfather's graves, under the large oak tree."

"Then I will see you tomorrow."

"God go with you," Father Taylor said as Todd left the study.

The farm hadn't changed much from the day he left eight years ago, except that the trees surrounding the house seemed a bit taller, the swing under the big oak tree hung from only one chain, the barn looked more weather beaten, and the house was in bad need of a coat of paint. He took the buggy into the barn, unhitched the horse, and put him in an empty stall. Todd found John sitting alone in the kitchen nursing a cup of coffee. His face lit up when he saw Todd, and he jumped to his feet and threw a bear hug around his son. Stunned by this gesture, for such affection was a rare event in the Bose household, Todd wrapped his arms around his father. He knew his dad loved him but most Pennsylvania Dutch farmers had difficulty showing affection, even to their sons.

"Can I pour you a cup of coffee?" John offered. Todd said he would much appreciate a cup and took a seat at the kitchen table. He noticed how his father's hand visibly shook as he poured a cup of coffee from the pot.

"I am so proud and happy that you could make it here in time for the funeral," John began. "I had my doubts that you would arrive in time."

"It was a small miracle that I did. The trip usually takes seven or eight days but I made it in six days. I left Whitefish as soon as I read your letter and caught the riverboat to St. Paul that evening. The trains from St. Paul to Chicago and Pittsburg all ran on time and by the grace of God, here I am."

"I imagine you will say the funeral Mass tomorrow?"

"Yes, I will co-celebrate with Father Taylor."

"That was her dying wish." John paused for a while and then continued, "Your mother went quietly. A couple of weeks ago she complained about a pain in her chest, but by the next morning she said it went away and we thought nothing more about it. Two days later, I came in from the fields for dinner and found your mother lying on the kitchen floor. My hired hands, Paul and Luke, helped me get her into the buggy and Paul and I drove her to the Titusville Hospital. The doctor said she had had a heart attack, but the next morning, although she had trouble breathing, she could talk. The pneumonia came on fast and for the next few days, the doctors could do nothing except make her comfortable. Father Taylor gave her the last rites on Saturday afternoon. I sat with her all that night holding her hand as she slept. When the sun rose Sunday morning she opened her eyes and looked at me, and then managed a faint smile and breathed her last. She went very peacefully."

"Dad, I am so sorry. Thanks for telling me about her last days. Somehow, this helps me realize that she is gone. I keep expecting to see her come through the back door any minute now with an arm full of eggs from the henhouse."

John looked at the back door, and then staring into his coffee cup, he said nothing more. It was not a time for conversation but reflection, so both sat silently and drank their coffee. After a few minutes of contemplation, John looked away from his coffee cup and smiled at Todd.

"One thing that was part of your mother's and my daily routine was to watch the sun set out on the porch. Come on out with me and together we will watch it set."

Taking in deep breaths, they sat silently on the porch for a few minutes enjoying the peacefulness of the waning day. The smell of fresh cut hay filled the air, chickens pecked around the grounds, geese strutted about the yard, and birds flittered between trees. The only sounds came from the chickens clucking and an occasional neigh of a horse and mooing of a barnyard cow. As the sun tinted the western sky with a deep orange glow and began to sink toward the western mountains, one of the handymen exited the barn and walked up toward the porch. He bounded up the steps and extended a callused hand to Todd.

"Father Todd. I'm Paul and I'm so pleased that you could make it here in time for the funeral," he said, smiling broadly as he pumped Todd's hand. "Your dad has been searching the driveway all yesterday and today for a sign that you might come. I kept telling him I knew you would." Luke, the younger hired hand, came out of the barn and walked toward the porch while holding a leather tether in his hand, bounded up the steps and introduced himself. Paul and Luke had worked for John for the past seven years, but Todd had never met either one of them. Paul was tall and lean with a well-tanned face that displayed years of working out in the sun. His light blue eyes sparkled as he talked, and his mouth graced by a handlebar mustache showed a faint trace of a permanent smile and several missing teeth. A well-worn cowboy hat covered his head. Luke was a hatless young teenager a head shorter than Paul, not yet old enough to have grown a beard, although the hint of one graced his upper lip and chin. After Todd and Luke exchanged pleasantries, Luke excused himself to take care of the horses.

Paul sat down in the chair next to John. "John, now that Father Todd is here, Luke and I will fix dinner for the four of us. I imagine Father Todd is very weary and hungry after his long trip here." John nodded but said nothing. Then Paul turned toward Todd. "Luke and I sleep in the bunkhouse and there is a bed in the guest room there if you want to stay with us. I felt you might rather sleep in the house, so Luke made up the room at the head of the stairs. I have been told that it once was your room, and will understand if this is your choice."

"Thank you, Paul. It was my room and I much appreciate your thoughtfulness. Yes, I would prefer to sleep there."

Paul adjusted his hat to shade his eyes from the setting sun.

"Neither Luke or myself are Catholic, although your mother has worked on changing our status for years. We're still thinking about it, but we will both be at the funeral Mass tomorrow." Paul then excused himself and went inside to prepare dinner.

After dinner Paul and Luke joined John and Todd for a whiskey as they talked and smoked on the porch. After several minutes, Todd excused himself and went upstairs to bed. He was amazed because his bedroom remained unchanged from the day eight years ago when he left for Whitefish. Matilda had preserved the room as some sort of shrine, dusting and sweeping but not disturbing his awards on the wall or the personal items that lay on his dresser. Even a half-finished novel, the last page marked by an earmark, lay on the bedside table just as he had left it.

Todd slept fitfully that night, and awoke at first light with the remnants of a dream still fresh in his mind.

Unlike most dreams that are undirected and indistinct, this one was more like a vision than a dream, as real and vivid as if he were living it. He was a teenager sitting in the barn on a bale of hay with a child in his lap, and a string of children patiently waited for him to attend to them. The little girl on his lap softly cried as he sutured and bandaged a wound on her hand. Matilda looking radiant in her favorite white dress helped the girl down and then searched the line looking for the child most in need of immediate attention. She brought forward a boy of seven or eight suffering with a festering leg wound, which if left unattended would certainly cause the loss of his leg or possibly even his death.

"In Jesus' name heal this boy," Matilda prayed as she led the boy to Todd, who examined the boy's wound and noted that gangrene had already invaded his leg. He couldn't treat such a serious wound, one that would require the medical attention of a doctor. Unsure what he could do for the boy, he looked questioningly at Matilda and asked, "What do you want me to do for him?"

"Heal him," she said. Todd looked again at the wound and then at his mother, who smiled and repeated, "Heal him." Todd placed his hand over the oozing wound and prayed. His hand tingled and then grew hot. When after a few seconds he removed his hand, no sign of the wound remained.

Matilda smiled at him. "See, just like I said, Jesus healed this boy." At this point, he woke up. Soft light from the predawn sky already filled his window. He lay there for a while and reviewed the dream, committing the details to memory, and then he got up and dressed. His father and Paul were in the kitchen. Paul was fixing oatmeal and a pot of coffee on the woodstove. John looked up from the table and smiled.

"Did you spend a good night?" he asked.

"Yes, I slept well thank you," Todd said and decided to keep the dream to himself.

"We would normally have breakfast this morning," John was saying as he apologized to Paul. "But this morning Todd and I will fast so we can receive Eucharist at Mass."

Paul nodded his understanding, "However I hope you don't mind if Luke and I have breakfast."

"Of course not," John said.

The smell of fresh brewing coffee tantalized, yet Todd was used to fasting before Mass.

They arrived at St. John's at 7:20 and Todd met Father Taylor in the sacristy to prepare for Mass. By 8:00 a.m., the church had filled to overflowing. Matilda's family arrived, including her sister from Titusville and older brother from Steubenville and three younger brothers from surrounding farms. They took the reserved front pews next to John. Both priests met the funeral director at the back of the church and blessed the casket. Two altar boys led a procession up the aisle with Matilda's casket carried by her brothers, then followed the priests and finally the funeral director. They set the casket on a covered table just outside the altar rail that separated the sanctuary. John requested an open casket for viewing before Mass began. The congregation filed up and one by one paid their last respects. First in line, John laid her favorite flowers on her chest, pink roses from her garden, and placed a cross from their bedroom in her casket.

Todd waited until the entire congregation had filed past before he approached. Matilda lay in the casket looking as if she were asleep rather than deceased. Dressed in her best white gown, her long gray hair fell about her shoulders and a sweet smile graced her face. What most amazed Todd was that she looked exactly like she had appeared in his dream, wearing the same dress with her hair draped over her shoulders in the same casual way. He then knew that she had come to him in last night's surreal dream.

When Mass ended, her oldest brother from Steubenville gave a short eulogy, and then everyone filed out to the church graveyard, where a freshly dug grave surrounded by a mound of dirt had been prepared under a large oak tree. Father Taylor said the interment prayers as the pallbearers lowered her casket slowly into the ground. Todd and John each shoveled the first dirt onto the casket, and then each person filed past and did likewise until the casket was entirely covered by a layer of soil. Peggy Weston, Matilda's best friend from town, invited everyone to come to her house where a funeral breakfast had been prepared.

That afternoon, John, Paul, Luke, and Todd drove back to the house. John looked very tired and excused himself to take a nap. Todd took the opportunity to speak privately with Paul.

"How is Dad taking all this?" Todd asked.

Paul did not immediately answer, but after thinking for a minute said, "Very hard, very hard indeed. I have not seen him shed a tear, but I know he has done so privately. John is strong in body and spirit, and his grief will pass, but only time can heal him."

"I cannot stay here long enough to see Dad recover. I must return to Minnesota tomorrow. I presume you and Luke will continue to work here on the farm. Dad needs you now even more than before."

"Yes, that is our intention," Paul said. "John cannot run the farm by himself. He and Matilda have treated Luke and me like family. We feel very welcome here and have no intention of leaving. Luke is young and may soon want to wander off, but I will live out my life here if this is you and your dad's wish."

"Yes, that is indeed my wish and I am sure it is John's wish as well. Thank you for helping Dad."

Knowing that his father was in good hands, Todd prepared to return to Whitefish the next morning. John embraced him for the second time and Todd gave his father a special blessing, and then waved good-bye to Luke and Paul and drove the buggy down the road. He stopped by the church to say good-bye to Father Taylor before leaving town.

"You had a dream the night before last, didn't you?" the priest said.

Todd looked surprised. "Yes, I did. How do you know that?"

"I had a visit in my dreams the other night from Matilda as well. She told me to tell you that she was proud of you, but life in Minnesota will continue to test your faith. You should know that she would always be with you and will pray for you in those trying times."

Todd didn't know how to respond to this revelation. He had already experienced many difficult times in Whitefish and his faith was severely tested yet he remained strong. Now his mother was warning him that even harder times were ahead. He couldn't imagine what these trials might be. He thanked Father Taylor and returned to Pittsburg where he caught the train to Chicago. While in Chicago the next day he had a layover of almost twelve hours before the train to St. Paul was due to leave, so he decided to walk to the nearby cathedral, only six blocks from the train station. Once inside he knelt before a statue of the Blessed Virgin, lit a candle, and prayed. If hard times were about to test him, he needed Mary and Matilda to guide his way.

Chapter 15
Homeward Bound

Todd arrived back at the St. Paul train station late Friday, May 30. Determined to get home as soon as possible, he didn't stop at the chancery but caught a taxi to the waterfront. The twice-weekly riverboat *Natchez* was due to leave for Grand Rapids later that evening and stevedores were already loading the last cargo crates. Todd found Captain Richards in his cabin. He looked up from his desk piled with papers and warmly welcomed Todd aboard.

"I would like to book passage to Grand Rapids tonight. Is there room for me?"

"Unfortunately, the riverboat has few staterooms and I am fully booked with folks heading to Brainerd, and a family going to Grand Rapids. I have no stateroom to offer you."

"I'm eager to return home. I have been gone almost two weeks and don't want to wait another four days for your next trip upriver. Is there any way you can find room for me on this voyage?"

"If you would be willing to share a stateroom with the Lutheran pastor from Brainerd, I could make up the extra bunk in his room if he will agree to a roommate."

"Do you mean Deacon Everett, the pastor of St. Martin's?"

"Yes, he's the one and he is already on board. Do you know him?"

"Yes, I know him. Please ask him if he is willing to have me for his roommate."

Captain Richards went out on deck with Todd and knocked on the stateroom number 10 door.

Deacon Everett answered and with his mouth agape said, "Father Bose. What a pleasant surprise. I'm sure glad to see you again. Are you traveling to Brainerd with us?"

"Well, no … not unless you are willing to have a roommate. The boat is full and there are no more staterooms available."

"I would be honored to share my stateroom with you, Father. Please, come on in."

Captain Roberts cleared his throat. "Well then, it's settled. Father, I will have another bunk made up for you. Dinner is served at 7:00 p.m. and we leave for Brainerd at 9:00 p.m. "By the way, did you get the telegram I sent to Titusville, Pennsylvania for you?"

"No, I didn't. Why did you send me a telegram?"

"Last week when the *Natchez* docked at Grand Rapids, Mike Dunn asked me to send you a telegram when I returned to St. Paul. It was about Whitefish folks who are sick and desperately need you. Mike wanted you to come home as soon as possible."

"What is the sickness?" Todd asked with growing apprehension.

"I'm sorry but Mike didn't say, just that many folks up there were sick."

"Even more reason for me to get back home right away," Todd said.

Stateroom 10 was small, even smaller than the other six staterooms. There was only one bunk and a desk, hardly big enough to set up a second bunk, but Deacon Everett assured Todd that there was room for a cot. Todd told him about his mother's death in Pennsylvania and his quick trip to make it in time to preside at her funeral.

"I'm so sorry to hear about your mother's death and your hurried trip home. It is good that you are returning to Whitefish, the folks up there will be sure glad to see you again," Deacon Everett said.

"Have you heard anything about the sickness in Whitefish?"

"Sorry, but I have no specific information to share with you, only rumors of a quarantine in Whitefish."

All the way to Brainerd Todd fretted over the telegram that he never received. He had only been gone for two weeks and everything was fine when he left. What disease could possibly have come on so quickly and be so serious that Mike felt compelled to have Captain Roberts send a telegram to Spartansburg? What could this sickness be?

At dinner that night, Todd met the family traveling to Grand Rapids. The Trapp family, Brian, Marilyn, and their three children, Albert, ten, Karen, seven, and Laura, two, were moving from New Orleans upriver to Grand Rapids.

"From one end of the Mississippi to the other," Brian mused.

He said that on his previous trip to Grand Rapids for an interview, the lumber mill at Grand Rapids hired him as their new supervisor and he had purchased a house just outside town. Now he was bringing his family with him to begin their new life in Grand Rapids. The family was Catholic and had heard of St. Patrick's in Whitefish.

"There is no Catholic Church in Grand Rapids," Brian commented. "It will be a long wagon trip to Whitefish, but you can expect to see us at Mass at least once a month."

Father Todd smiled. "Now that the road is improved with grading, culverts, and six new bridges, the 40-mile journey shouldn't take longer than five or six hours in good weather. I will look forward to seeing your family at Mass."

They arrived in Brainerd Saturday evening. Captain Pinot would tie up for the night before continuing up river the next morning. However, Captain Richards said that they would push off in just two hours for Grand Rapids and could expect to be at Grand Rapids by late morning. This was both good news and bad news for Todd. While he was glad that he would be home earlier than expected, he still worried about running the river at night. Captain Pinot would never dare run the river at night, especially upriver from Brainerd. "Damn logs or a rock will put a hole in the side of the *Itaska*, and we are apt to get stuck on a sandbar. No way will I run this part of the river at night," Captain Pinot would say.

Captain Richards on the other hand held a different opinion. While at dinner, he claimed the danger was exaggerated.

"By running the river at night, we can make two round trips each week rather than one. We have a powerful searchlight, an invention powered by acetylene, and I know the river and its ways like the back of my hand. There is only minimal danger, and I have run this part of the river at night many times before with no problems."

They cast off an hour before sunset and made headway up the river at full speed. Since the Brainerd passengers had disembarked, Todd and the Trapp family were the only passengers on board and Todd moved to another stateroom. He sat up on deck with Brian for a while and watched Captain Richards and his first mate Bill navigate the river, avoiding the flotsam and sandbars. As it grew dark Todd expected the *Natchez* to slow down, but Captain Richards continued up river at full speed. Todd thought that running this part of the river at full speed seemed reckless. Yet Captain Richards knew the river and his boat, and the searchlight lit up the river ahead, so Todd said nothing. After Brian went to bed, Todd stayed with Captain Richards and Bill in the wheelhouse. The captain shined the spotlight on the river ahead and on the riverbank to judge his distance from shore. He kept the boat in the main channel and maneuvered to avoid any floating logs or other debris in the river.

"See that dead skeleton tree leaning out over the river?" he said as he focused the spotlight on it. "That tree is 23 miles upriver from Brainerd. Dead ahead is Big Bend, a horseshoe curve in the river plagued with swift currents and shifting sandbars. He slowed down and maneuvered the *Natchez* to port where the current wasn't so strong.

The night was moonless and the river inky black. The firmament framed by sparkling stars and streaked with the Milky Way reflected on the still water but did nothing to light their way upstream.

"Watch the stars reflected on the water," Captain Richards suggested as he switched off the spotlight. "If you watch carefully, the river's refection distorts the stars and reveals shallows, currents and eddies."

Without the powerful gas spotlight to pierce the darkness and light up the river, running the river at night would have been pure foolishness. However, the spotlight lit the river yards ahead revealing floating debris. Captain Richards skillfully wove their way upriver with surprising ease, staying close to the western riverbank utilizing the western channel to avoid sandbars. He maneuvered around obstacles called out by Bill who sat on the bow watching for logs that drifted down the river this time of year. Bill would shout out the path of the channel and directed the boat away from the ever-changing sandbars and shallows. When he spotted a log or sandbar, he shouted directions to Captain Richards: "The channel runs portside, a sandbar to your starboard!" or "Log dead ahead!" After a bit, Todd decided to retire to his stateroom where the thump, thump, thump of the paddle wheel and chug, chug of the piston steam engine soon lulled him to sleep.

In the middle of the night he awoke to a thump strong enough to rock the *Natchez,* and soon afterwards the engines came to a full stop. Sensing something was wrong, Todd dressed and went up to the wheelhouse. The *Natchez* floated downriver leaning slightly to port. Neither Captain Richards nor Bill was on deck. He found them in the engine room trying to patch a hole in the port side. An 8-inch thick log protruded into the engine room through a hole in the side of the boat. Water gushed in around the log from the hole it had created. Already a foot of water flooded the engine room and was rising every second.

Todd climbed into the water to see if he could help. Bill and the other deckhand, Rob, were stuffing rags into cracks around the log but they could only slow the leaks. Captain Richards was shoveling coal into the firebox to keep the steam up so the bilge pumps and electric generator would continue to run, but the water was threatening to splash into the firebox and if it did, they would be without power. Water continued to rise in the engine room as Rob took over shoveling coal into the boiler.

"Without steam we will be at the mercy of the river, and without power we will have no lights or bilge pumps. I'm going back to the wheelhouse while the paddle wheel still going so I can navigate closer to shore. Without steam I'm afraid the *Natchez* is going down," Captain Richards announced without emotion, as if he were announcing dinner.

Todd stared at him. "Then shouldn't we prepare to abandon ship?"

"Yes. Go wake up the Trapp family and have them dress and get into their life jackets. After I get us closer to shore, Bill and I will prepare the lifeboat."

Todd climbed back up on deck that by now listed to port by several degrees. As he arrived at the Trapp cabin door, the ship's lights all went out and the paddle wheel stopped turning. He rapped on the Trapp's stateroom door. At first, no one answered, so he banged even harder until a sleepy Marilyn answered the door.

"Get the children ready to abandon ship. We've hit a log and the boat is sinking. Get dressed and put on the life jackets that are under each bunk. Meet us on the foredeck where Captain Richards and Bill are preparing the lifeboat."

Perhaps it was because she was still half-asleep or maybe she did didn't understand Todd, but Marilyn stood there dazed, not grasping Todd's instructions. He pushed his way into the room and aroused Brian.

"We hit a log and the boat is sinking. Get your family dressed and into the life jackets that are under the bunks and meet us on the foredeck."

Marilyn came to her senses, lit a lamp, got Albert out of bed, and told him to get dressed. Brian stood by watching yet doing nothing. Marilyn then got seven-year-old Karen out of bed, dressed her, and fit her into a life jacket. There was no life jacket small enough to fit two-year-old Laura, but Todd dressed her. Brian stood around looking lost. Todd grabbed him by the shoulders and shook him.

"Brian, the boat is sinking. Get dressed and into a life jacket," he ordered. Brian stared back with blank eyes.

"I'm going to take the children to the lifeboat," Todd finally said. "Get yourself and your wife dressed and into life jackets, and then meet us on the foredeck."

Todd looked over at Marilyn who nodded her understanding.

Todd carried Laura in his arms and herded the other two children to the foredeck where Captain Richards and Bill were struggling with the lifeboat by the light of a single lantern. The last latch that fastened the lifeboat to the deck was rusted. Bill hit it with a hammer, but it wouldn't budge. Captain Roberts opened a hatch and called down to the engine room where Rob was still trying to stuff rags into the hole. He told him to give it up and bring himself, the emergency waterproof bag, and a hacksaw up on deck.

The *Natchez* began to list dangerously to port, and without power she floated sideways, now at the mercy of river currents.

"Hold on to the children very tight," Captain Richards warned Todd, "if the *Natchez* lists another few degrees to port she will roll over."

Bill grabbed the hacksaw from Rob and started to cut through the bolt on the remaining clamp that fastened the lifeboat to the deck. The lifeboat was small, only 14 feet long with a 4-foot beam. Four rough-hewn seats provided seating for six people. Between the Trapp family, Todd, and the crew the lifeboat would have to carry nine.

"Isn't there another lifeboat?" Todd asked Rob.

"No, this is the only one," he replied as he threw the waterproof emergency bag into the lifeboat.

With a metallic clank, Bill finally sawed through the remaining bolt and the lifeboat broke free. At that moment, the *Natchez* hit a sandbar and the bow catered around in a sweeping arc and then hung up on another sandbar, almost throwing Karen into the water. Water now crept swiftly up the deck as the *Natchez* struggled to free herself from the sandbar. The foredeck was now shipping water into the open hatch.

"When she comes off the sandbar she's going down. Everyone into the lifeboat!" Captain Richards shouted. Todd got the children in as Rob and Bill pushed the lifeboat into the river and climbed in. Brian and Marilyn waded across the foredeck now knee-high in water, and Captain Roberts helped them climb aboard the lifeboat and then hopped in himself and pushed it away from the *Natchez*. The small overloaded rowboat had only four inches of freeboard remaining. Todd sat on the bow seat facing the stern and holding Laura to his chest in a bear hug and Karen to his right Brian and Marilyn with Albert sat facing him on the seat immediately in front of Todd. Bill and Rob took the middle seat and set the oars into their oarlocks. Captain Roberts sat on the stern carrying their only working lantern.

The *Natchez* groaned, broke free of the sandbar, and rolled over.

"Keep clear of the *Natchez*!" Captain Roberts shouted to Bill and Rob.

"Which way should we row?" Bill asked.

The Mississippi, almost a mile wide at this point, flowed from northeast to southwest. The moonless night was pitch-black and other than the weak light provided by the lantern, no one could see their hand in front of their face. Before the boat ran out of steam, Captain Roberts judged that he had maneuvered the *Natchez* within 100 yards of the lee side of the river, but after they lost power, the river current forced the riverboat to float downstream sideways and now disoriented, he wasn't sure which way to row. The captain looked up at the stars and finding Polaris knew that the shortest distance to land was to row against the current and let the river ferry the boat toward the shore. He told Rob and Bill to row upriver to their right at a 30-degree angle. This so-called crosscurrent ferry maneuver would allow the river to take them toward the south-western bank. Bill and Rob rowed with all their strength and after ten minutes Captain Roberts noted by where the stars merged onto the horizon that the shoreline lay about 25 yards ahead.

"We're almost to shore," he announced.

As they came closer, Todd felt the rowboat shudder as it slid over rocks.

"There are rapids up ahead!" Todd shouted.

"Come about and row upriver directly toward shore," Captain Richards ordered, trusting that they could avoid the rapids, yet the strong current forced the boat further downriver. Seconds later the boat bounced against a large boulder and floundered. Taking on water as the boat swung around the rock, they careened sideways downstream hitting other rocks along the way. Todd held Laura against his chest and grasped Karen's little hand as disaster struck. The rowboat climbed up onto a partially submerged rock and flipped over, throwing everyone into the cold, dark water. Todd spit out a mouthful of water and tightened his grasp on Laura with his left arm as his right hand held onto Karen. Once in the water he lost track of Albert and his parents. The river tossed him and the two children about like loose fronds in a stream, and then thrusting them over a submerged boulder pulled them into a hole that sucked all three under water. For what seemed like minutes yet was only a few seconds, Todd struggled toward the surface. He was so disoriented that he didn't know which way was up. With his lungs bursting he finally bobbed to the surface and filled his lungs with precious air. Laura coughed and took a deep breath, yet Todd's other hand that held her sister was empty. He shouted Karen's name repeatedly yet all he could hear was the noise of the river surging over the rocks. He thrust his free arm into the water, groped around in the dark, turbulent water, until he felt something soft brush against his leg. Was it a fish? No, it wasn't a fish. He reached down and felt a cloth dress. With his free hand, he lifted the little girl to the surface and held her head above the water. She didn't gasp for breadth as he expected, rather her whole little body remained limp against his. Even though he knew the riverbank must be close by, he didn't know in which direction to swim, but then he heard a man yelling, "Over here, over here!" With both children still in his arms, Todd kicked his feet and swam toward the shouting making sure to keep the children's heads above water. After a dozen kicks, his foot felt the sandy bottom and he dragged himself and the children onto the beach.

He couldn't see anything in the dark, but he saw a match light and then the welcomed light of a lantern. Someone had found the waterproof emergency bag and had rescued matches and a small miner's lantern from it.

"Bill, is that you?" Todd called out.

"Yes, Rob and I are over here," he answered.

Bill held the lantern high as he and Rob watched Todd come toward them with Laura in hand and Karen in his arms. He sat Laura down on the beach and laid Karen's limp body gently on the sand, turned her head sideways so ingested water could flow out, and gently shook her.

"Karen, can you hear me?" Todd desperately cried as he gently shook her. The child made no sound or movement whatsoever. "Bill, I need help with Karen."

Bill held the lantern over Karen's prone body as Todd clasped her nose shut and began breathing into her mouth. Her little chest lifted ever so slightly as Todd forced air into her lungs. After a few breaths, Todd placed both hands one on top of the other on the child's chest and pumped. Bill handed the lantern to Rob, knelt, and began massaging the child's arms and legs to bring life back into her little body.

"She's cold," he commented as he rubbed her. "Did you see the boy or his parents? Or Captain Roberts?"

"No," Todd replied between measured breaths and chest pumping.

Laura sat on the sand next to Karen and began to cry.

After a couple of minutes, Bill stopped rubbing Karen's arms and gently grabbed Todd's shoulder. "The child is dead," he said softly. "Her body is cold and lifeless."

Todd ignored Bill and continued giving Karen CPR that he learned while treating soldiers in the Baltimore hospital. Most times the procedure didn't work, especially if the patient had not breathed for some time, but it was always worth a try, especially with a small child who had drowned only minutes before.

A voice drifted over the sand that sounded like Brian's. "We're over here!" Rob shouted back.

Following the light, Brian and Marilyn stumbled onto the group. Seeing her daughter prone on the sand with Todd leaning over her and breathing into the child's mouth, Marilyn clasped her hand over her own mouth and cried out.

"Oh my God!"

Brian picked Laura up and hugged her to his chest as they all stood beside Karen praying for some sign of life from the child. A minute passed with no response from the child.

"Has anyone seen Albert?" Brian asked as he gave Laura to Marilyn. No one answered him.

Todd kept working on Karen as Bill again placed his hand on Todd's shoulder. "Give it up, Father," he said. "The child is dead."

Marilyn screamed and collapsed into Brian's arms. Todd stopped CPR for a moment, made the sign of the cross over Karen, and then resumed CPR blowing into Karen's mouth and stopping every few seconds to press firmly with both hands on her chest to squeeze blood from her unresponsive heart.

He stopped to rest for a few seconds before resuming CPR and prayed. "Jesus, you said that if we asked anything in your name, it would be granted. Please in your name restore life to this child."

He felt that familiar warmth again in his shoulder, the same warmth he had felt many times before in similar dire circumstances. It traveled down his arm to his hand and then into Karen's body as he pressed down on her chest. About to resume blowing into Karen's mouth, he felt her chest heave. Todd backed off and watched as she coughed and frothy water flowed from her nose and mouth. Todd turned her head sideways as she coughed again and water spurted from her mouth onto the dry sand. Then she took in a big breadth and began to moan.

Marilyn knelt and grasped the child in her arms, brushed the sand off her cheeks and hair, and hugged her as she cried. "It's all right, sweetpea, you're all right now." She looked at Todd still kneeling beside the child. "Thank you, Father," she whispered, "Thank you."

"Don't thank me, thank Jesus," Todd said.

Bill stared at the child in Marilyn's arms and then looked at Todd. "The child was dead. There was no heartbeat or breathing for several minutes. I felt her; she was stone-cold."

"Her little body was still alive and now thanks to God she lives," Todd said in response.

"It is a miracle," Brian said.

"No, it wasn't a miracle," Rob argued. "The child may have been cold, not breathing, and her heart may have seemed to have stopped, but she wasn't dead. Father Todd's efforts got her heart and breathing going again."

"I don't believe that for a minute," Marilyn argued. "Something wonderful and miraculous took place on this beach tonight."

Bill sighed. "Rob, you can say what you want, but the child was lifeless. I know death when faced with it. I have always considered myself an agnostic, not sure if there was a God or not, and if there was a God, he couldn't care two cents about me. Yet after witnessing this event, I must admit there is a God who deeply cares about us."

Todd smiled. "And it took a dying child to reveal this to you?"

He then asked those standing around, "Has anyone seen or heard from Captain Roberts or Albert?" No one had.

"We will search for the captain and the boy as soon as it is light," Bill said. "The river probably swept them downstream, but we will have to wait until dawn to go searching for them."

"I'm not going to wait for dawn, we have to find Albert now," Brian said.

"Please wait; you will only fall and get hurt. Wait for dawn," Rob urged

"There's no sense stumbling around in the dark," Bill added. "Wait until we can see where we are going,"

Brian brushed past him and disappeared into the night. Everyone was soaking wet and the night air had chilled all to the bone. Still in her mother's arms, Karen began to shiver.

Bill went over to his bag and retrieved the box of matches. "We are all wet and cold. We need a fire," he said. "Let's gather some driftwood and get a fire going."

Rob and Bill gathered armfuls of driftwood and soon a large bonfire thrust flames and embers into the sky. The bonfire lit up the small beach that was empty except for some logs and a few scrub bushes. The fire lifted everyone's spirits, and as their bodies warmed and clothes dried, their thoughts returned to the missing members, Albert and Captain Richards, and now Brian.

An hour later the sky began to glow with soft light that washed out the stars and promised dawn was near. As soon as it became light enough to make out the beach and rocks, Bill organized a search party.

"Todd and I will search downriver, and Rob can search upriver," Bill suggested. "Shout out if you find anything. Marilyn can stay here with Karen and Laura."

As the early light of dawn strengthened, Todd and Bill made their way around the rocks that blocked the beach downstream. They hiked less than a few hundred yards when they came upon Brian sitting on the sand. Todd asked him if he was all right. Brian blinked and tried to stand up, but his legs were wobbly.

"I must have stumbled over a rock and hit my head, but I'm okay now," Brian claimed.

Bill suggested that he wait there for them.

"No way. I'm going with you," Brian said.

Together they walked downstream for another hundred yards until they saw the outline of their lifeboat overturned on the sand. Beside the boat was a body, and as they approached they knew that it was Captain Roberts. Todd turned him over and a small land crab crawled out of his mouth. Todd made the sign of the cross over him and said a short prayer. When he said "Amen," they heard a small voice coming from under the boat. Turning the boat on its side, they found Albert sitting scrunched up underneath the overturned boat. When the boy saw Brian, he stirred and whispered, "Dad." Brian picked his son up and hugged him. Albert saw the captain lying in the sand. "Is he dead?"

"Yes, son, the captain is dead."

Albert sobbed, "He was only trying to save me and save the lifeboat, but the river got him."

"I know, Albert, but I thank God that you are safe."

"How about Mom, and Karen and Laura?"

"They are all safe, just downriver warming by a fire," Brian explained. "Come along, Father Todd and I will take you to them."

Everyone hurried back to Marilyn and the children. When Marilyn saw Albert with Brian, she burst into tears and threw her arms around Albert.

Finding nothing upriver, Rob returned to the fire's warmth.

"We found Albert and Captain Roberts," Todd said as Rob approached. "Albert is safe but Captain Roberts is dead. The lifeboat is on the beach about two hundred yards downriver. It appears he died trying to save Albert and the lifeboat. Fortunately, the boat seems mostly undamaged."

"Captain Robert's death is a tragedy, but finding the boat intact is a blessing," Bill said. "As far as I can tell, we are in the middle of nowhere, perhaps 60 miles upriver from Brainerd and 80 miles downriver from Grand Rapids. The only human habitation between our present position and Brainerd is at the junction of Willow River and the Mississippi. There's a small farming community there called Willows, about 45 miles downriver from here. Upriver, the nearest community is Jacobson, only 25 miles away, but rowing upriver is all but impossible. There are no roads or even trails on this western shoreline for us to travel. The thick woods would make our journey back to civilization by land impossible. We would have to blaze a trail through this thick forest, cross over dozens of creeks and rivers, and slosh through leech-infested swamps. No, our only hope is to travel downstream to Willows in the rowboat."

Brian spoke up. "I agree. The river is our best way out. Yet the river rapids almost killed us, and we may not be so lucky the next time. What's to say that there aren't even more and bigger rapids downstream?"

Bill argued that travel downstream by river was their only hope. "I know the river and there are only about a half-dozen rapids between here and Willows and none of them are as big or as dangerous as the one that upended us last night. If it wasn't so confounded dark last night, we could have safely navigated through those rapids, but in the dark we couldn't see the rocks. We can portage around or line the boat through the worst of the rapids, but I doubt we will have to. The river is really our only choice."

Rob and Todd agreed and hiked downriver to the boat and Captain Robert's body. Todd gave the captain the last rites as Rob examined the boat. Their news when they returned to the others was not good.

"We found the oars, but the boat is not in as good a shape as Bill first thought," Rob reported. "The collision with the rock has split some of the sidewall planks and opened cracks between them. The boat will leak like a sieve."

"Can we fix it?" Marilyn asked.

"Perhaps," Rob surmised. "We will need to find some caulking material to plug the cracks."

They all hiked downriver to the boat and Rob and Bill searched the woods for caulking material. Yellow-green mosses covered the forest spruce trees. The moss was dense and spongy, but Bill thought that moss wouldn't do the trick. Todd discovered a deposit of white soft clay sandwiched between layers of limestone along the bluff. Experimenting with clay as caulking, Bill found that it didn't dissolve in water and worked well as caulking. They spent the morning caulking the boat and by early afternoon they were ready to push off.

Before leaving, they buried Captain Roberts on a bluff above the beach in a shallow grave that Bill dug with one of the oars. Father Todd conducted a burial service reading from his pocket Bible damp from his swim, yet because it was covered with a chamois, it was still serviceable. Bill took some willow branches and fashioned a cross. Rob etched the captain's given name, Joshua Allen Roberts, and the date, R.I.P. June 2, 1880 on a flat piece of wood and stuck it into the ground to serve as a headstone. No one knew Joshua's birth date or birthplace.

After their swim in the Mississippi, no one was eager to get back in the rowboat. One by one they reluctantly climbed aboard and found a seat. Marilyn was especially nervous and took a forward seat while keeping her three children close to her. Bill, as first mate of the *Natchez*, had plied this river many times before and knew every bend, island, and landing along the way. The captain's sudden death demanded a new leader, so Bill assumed command of the party and navigated the river from the boat's backseat. He asked Rob and Brian to row the boat, and for Todd to sit on the bow seat and call out obstructions. They ran the small rapids downriver with no problem and they had put ten miles of river behind them when Bill said they would stop for the evening on a beach dead ahead.

"It will take us some time to set up camp and cook dinner, and there are few beaches along this part of the river, so row toward that beach ahead."

Bill was thankful for the emergency bag he had the foresight to stow on the lifeboat as the *Natchez* sank. The bag contained not only matches and the lantern, but also a pot, a small grate, four mess kits, fishhooks and line, a hatchet, and a bowie knife. Rob dug a few large river mussels from the river and using them for bait caught three good-sized perch and a catfish. Brian and Marilyn foraged in the forest and returned with a pot full of blackberries.

No one went hungry that night, but everyone would have to sleep on the sand under the stars. The night chill brought with it a promise of an early fall, and although the sand was warm at dusk, it didn't stay that way through the cold night. Those who couldn't sleep sat around the fire taking turns keeping watch and feeding driftwood to the flames. Todd took the midnight to 2:00 a.m. watch, and as he sat warming himself and throwing wood into the fire, he stared into the red-hot embers and reminisced over the events of the last two days. He prayed for the soul of Captain Roberts, a young man with a young man's lack of sagacity. It was risky, even foolish to tempt the Mississippi by running at night, and now his imprudence had cost him his life, and almost cost the life of an innocent young child.

His thoughts turned to Karen. Had he brought the child back to life by administering CPR, or was this, as Marilyn insisted, truly a miracle? Bill insisted this was so because for several minutes Karen had no discernible heartbeat or breathing. He was sure she had died. Todd reasoned the absence of life signs and her cold, ashen skin could have misled them. Children are resilient and given a spark of life, they can be brought back just as Jesus did with the girl in the New Testament who folks thought was dead. Jesus claimed that the child was only sleeping, and this was probably the case. Karen's life force had ebbed to a degree that she seemed dead, but an ember of life persisted. Todd reasoned that his CPR efforts to revive her had rekindled that ember and because of his persistence, she lived. Yet as he prayed over Karen, rhythmically pressing down on her chest to force blood from her heart, and blowing into her lungs, the familiar soothing warmth that traveled down his arm to his hand and then flowed into the child's chest. Was this evidence of a miracle and intervention by God through his minister? The memory of the rugby field so many years ago overwhelmed him. In his mind's eye, Jimmy Taylor again lay prone on the ground where Todd had viciously tackled him, unresponsive to the efforts to revive him. He lay there with an ashen look on his face and eyes that stared unseeing into the sky. The coach looked at Todd and without recrimination pronounced the boy dead. Todd initially backed away from the crowd, but then he returned and knelt beside Jimmy, place his hand on the boy's forehead, and say a short prayer. Unexpectedly, warmth traveled down his arm to his hand and then flowed into the boy's head. Jimmy suddenly woke up unaware of what had just happened to him. The circumstance surrounding Karen's revival was deja vu.

"No," he argued with himself, "I am a doctor trained to rescue life from the clutches of death. It was not a miracle but the CPR." Yet his argument was uncomfortably unconvincing, flawed at best. Whether by his doctoring or a miracle, God had answered his prayer and the child now lived. That was all that mattered.

He looked away from the fire and peered up at the myriad pinpoints of light that filled the sky from horizon to horizon. Each one was a distant sun just like our own sun and in numbers so copious that no one could count them. A couple of the brightest stars on the western horizon shone unwinking, like distant city lights. He surmised that they were not stars but were the planets Venus and Jupiter. The Milky Way shone as a chalky white highway spread across the sky, and as astronomers had recently discovered, consisted of millions of other suns in our vast galaxy. He concluded that a God who could create such a display could certainly use a human to cure a little child.

No one slept well that night on the cold sand and several took turns sitting beside the fire to warm up. The rising sun was a welcomed sight and welcomed by this group of weary travelers. Bill arose at dawn and went searching for food. He robbed dozens of killdeer nests of their small blue eggs, and gathered a hatful of blueberries. Scrambled with a hunk of lard from the emergency kit and served with the blueberries, the eggs made a small but warming breakfast. Afterwards they broke camp and floated down the river toward Willows.

The Mississippi river slowed to a crawl in this section of the river and a stiff upriver wind slowed their progress downstream. At this rate, they wouldn't make it to Willows by nightfall, so Bill ordered Rob and Brian to row against the wind. Toward midmorning, Bill's passengers were begging for a rest stop. The woods along this portion of the Mississippi grew side-by-side right down to the river's edge, affording few beaches or other landing opportunities. After rounding a horseshoe bend, the river split into two channels that flowed around a large island. A small sand beach dominated the point of the island, so Bill directed Rob and Brian to row toward it. Prone to spring flooding, the low island offered sparse vegetation with only grass, a few willow trees, and an occasional bush or patch of brambles stubborn enough to eke out life in this meager environment.

After landing, everyone needed to find a bush.

"Men to the leeward side of the island and women to windward side," Bill barked. Everyone went off to find a place to relieve themselves, yet the sparsely covered island offered few opportunities for privacy. Marilyn, Laura, and Karen walked about 100 yards downriver. Marilyn kept Laura with her and found a bush that allowed a bit of cover as Karen walked further inland through the knee-high grass. When Marilyn and Laura finished they assumed Karen had gone back and joined those gathered at the boat. Expecting Karen would return with Marilyn and Laura, Brian asked, "Where is Karen?"

"I thought she returned to the boat," Marilyn said as panic set in.

Bill did not seem to share Marilyn's growing concern. "The island is small and there's no place where she could go missing. If she doesn't show up in the next few minutes, we'll organize a search party and find her," he promised.

Neither Brian nor Marilyn were satisfied with Bill's lack of concern, and took off searching the beach toward where Marilyn last saw her daughter.

The island was indeed small, perhaps less than 100 acres of soil, sand, and grass, with a few trees and bushes scattered about. Only ½ mile long by a couple of hundred yards wide, one could walk all the way around the shoreline in much less than an hour. After Brian and Marilyn left, Bill said he would walk down the center of the island and asked Todd and Rob to circle the island in opposite directions. Laura and Albert were to stay with the boat in case Karen should return. When the shoreline searchers met at the downriver point of the island, neither Bill and Marilyn nor Todd and Rob had seen any sign of the child.

"This makes no sense," Rob said. "How can a little girl get lost on such a small island?"

"The grass is knee-high in places," Todd suggested. "Perhaps she fell down and the grass is covering her."

"Let's spread apart and hike down the center of the island all the way back to the boat calling out for Karen as we go," Todd suggested.

About mid-island, Todd met Bill, who on his initial trek across the island had also seen no sign of the child. On his way, Bill noticed a group of willow trees gathered in a circle and suggested that he and Todd investigate. They discovered that the trees hid a deep, wide sandpit, perhaps 20 feet wide. Todd thought he heard a cry coming from inside the pit and looking over the edge, he saw Karen standing on the bottom in knee-deep water. The pit was perhaps 10 to 12 feet deep.

"Karen, are you all right?" Todd called out.

"Yes, but I can't get out," the child responded. "Every time I try to climb out, the loose sand just drags me back down."

Little Church in the Wilderness

Todd yelled to the other searchers that he and Bill had found Karen and soon all five adults were standing around the edge of the pit staring at the child below.

"I'll crawl down and get her," Brian said.

"No, wait," Rob cautioned. "The pit is full of loose sand, and if you try to climb down into it, it may collapse onto the child. Bill, cut off a long willow branch and we will reach it down to Karen."

Bill cut off a long branch and leveraged it down into the pit. Karen grabbed the end and Bill and Brian hauled her out of the pit and into Marilyn's waiting arms.

"How did you end up in that pit?" Brian asked.

"I was taking a shortcut back to the boat when I saw this ring of willows and grew curious about what was inside the circle, but inside was nothing but this large pit. I walked to the edge of the hole to see what was inside and the soft sand collapsed under me. Then when I tried to climb out, the sand just kept falling in on me and I couldn't get a foothold."

When the search party returned to the boat, Albert was glad to see them because according to his figuring, they were long overdue and Laura was becoming difficult to control.

Bill said they should resume the trip. "The wind has died down, and the river runs faster along this part. We're halfway back to Willows, and if we press on we may see the town before nightfall."

As Bill promised, before the sun set they rounded a bend and the little community of Willows appeared immediately ahead. The village consisted of a half-dozen log cabins and a pier with a small steamboat tied to it. When Bill shouted a greeting, two men ran out from one of the cabins and onto the pier to greet the survivors. The two men tied the rowboat to the dock and helped the passengers disembark. One of the men introduced himself as Lars, and the other man said his name was Lester. The survivors each introduced themselves, and when Todd did so, Lars was surprised.

"So, you are that priest and doctor from Whitefish. Your reputation precedes you. How did you folks end up in a rowboat in this part of the Mississippi?" Lars asked.

Bill explained that the *Natchez* sank and that the rapids upended their rowboat dumping everyone into the river, including Captain Roberts who drowned.

"You mean to tell me that Captain Roberts was running the river at night?" Lars asked.

"Yes, and the *Natchez* hit a floating log and sank in the middle of the night," Rob said.

"That's terrible news about Captain Roberts and the *Natchez*. Captain Pinot would never run the *Itaska* at night for this very reason. This is also bad news for the folks up and down this part of the Mississippi who depended on that riverboat for their goods and transport," Lars said.

Bill sympathized with Lars. "We don't expect the *Itaska* to resume service for several weeks, and the *Natchez* was the only passenger and freight boat available to operate between St. Paul and Grand Rapids while the *Itaska* is being refurbished. Can you help us get upriver to Grand Rapids on your steamboat?"

"We don't want to wait for the *Itaska* to return to service," Todd added. "There is rumor of an infection in Whitefish and I must get back home as soon as possible to help those folks."

"Lester and I can take you to Grand Rapids on the *Little Fall*s, our miniature steam-powered riverboat. We were planning a trip up there anyway this week."

Bill looked over to the little boat tied to the dock. It was indeed small, perhaps 26 feet long with a 6-foot beam. A wood burning boiler with a black smokestack sat in the middle of the boat connected to a side-mounted paddle wheel positioned on the port side.

"Do you think this little boat can carry all of us over 100 miles upriver?" Bill asked.

"Sure, she can do this. It will be a bit crowded for a two-day trip, but while she may be small, she is powerful and dependable. She has taken us to Grand Rapids many times with no problem. We can push off tomorrow morning. For tonight, you folks can stay with the families in Willows."

Lars split the *Natchez* survivors into two groups: Todd, Bill, and Rob stayed with Lester and the Trapp family went with Lars to his cabin. The Willows families welcomed the survivors, feeding them well and giving each person a comfortable place to sleep. After two days on the river, the survivors appreciated the gracious hospitality these folks offered. The following morning, they all met on the pier to prepare the boat. Bill, Rob, and Lester loaded split wood onto the *Little Falls* while Todd, Marilyn, and Lars loaded enough supplies for the two-day trip. There was only enough room for less than a half-cord of wood, so Lars commented that they would have to land a time or two to take on more wood.

They said good-bye to the Willows families and pushed off at 8:00 a.m. The *Little Falls* huffed and puffed up the river making 3 or 4 knots against the Mississippi current. By nightfall, they had covered 60 miles and camped on an island beach.

"I don't care to camp on the mainland," Lars commented. "Too many wolves, wolverines, cougars, and bears in those woods."

Marilyn said a prayer of thanks that those varmints didn't visit them when they camped the first night on a beach not far from this island.

As the sun set on the second day of their journey, they docked at the Grand Rapids wharf. The first Grand Rapids citizen to greet them was Jacob Yearling, the proprietor of the livery stables. He was especially glad to see Father Todd.

"Father Todd, I suppose you are anxious to get your horse and buggy and head up to Whitefish, but you'd best wait until morning. You probably know that half the community up there is sick, and rumor has it that two folks have died. I suspended my coach service to Whitefish last week and no one has traveled there since Mike Dunn came into town and warned us about the quarantine and asked if we had heard anything about you", Jacob said. "We trusted that you might arrive on the *Natchez* four days ago, but when the riverboat didn't arrive on scheduled, we all became quite concerned about you and the *Natchez*.

"The *Natchez* sank and Captain Richards is dead," Todd explained. "It's a long story best told tonight at the hotel. I'll fetch Molly and my buggy from the stables first thing tomorrow morning and head up to Whitefish."

Eager to hear about the fate of Captain Roberts and the *Natchez*, Mr. Yearling led the *Little Falls* passengers down to the hotel for dinner and a night's lodging. The Trapp family said good-bye and prepared to walk down the street to their new home. Karen came over to Father Todd and gave him a big hug. She said nothing but her cheeks were wet. Bill and Marilyn took turns shaking his hand, and Marilyn put her lips to Todd's ear and whispered,

"I know Jesus performed a miracle though your hands. I will keep you in my prayers, and we will see you at Mass."

Bill, Rob, and Todd met with the townsfolk in the saloon. Everyone wanted to know what had happened to the *Natchez* and why it hadn't shown up when due several days ago. Bill and Rob told them about running at night, and how they escaped the sinking ship and made their way to Willows. No one seemed surprised that the *Natchez* now rested at the bottom of the Mississippi.

"A foolish stunt for Roberts to pull," Jacob said. "Captain Pinot would have never run the *Itaska* on the river at night. I tried to warn Roberts about the danger of his plan, but he remained determined to increase his revenues with two round trips each week. Now without riverboat service, we will be isolated for weeks"

Worried about the fate of the folks in Whitefish, Father Todd couldn't sleep that night. At first light he got up, dressed, and went over to the stables. Jacob had Molly and the buggy hitched up and ready to go.

"Godspeed, Father, and give our best to the folks in Whitefish," Jacob said. "Let us know as soon as the stagecoach service can resume."

Chapter 16
The Epidemic

June 1880

Todd wasted no time driving the rocky and rutted road to Whitefish. Molly, also sensing urgency, didn't object to Todd's urging her on. When he arrived at the top of Mesabi Pass, he looked at the familiar valley below and his heart leapt at the sight of Whitefish Lake and the little town hugging its western end. Molly seemed eager to return home but he held her back, keeping one hand on the brake as they descended the steep and rocky road.

"Whoa there, Molly, no need to run us off the road," Todd cautioned.

At the bottom of the pass the buggy arrived at Mike Dunn's farm, the geese loudly announcing him. Alerted by the geese, Mike and Mary ran out of the house followed by Ann, Tom, and Frank and greeted Todd.

"Father, you are sure a sight for sore eyes. We've been praying for your return every day," Mike said breathlessly.

Mary gave him a big hug as he climbed down from the carriage.

"Father Todd, we are so glad to see you. Please come inside and rest for a while."

"Well, only for a minute. I understand the town has been quarantined by some unknown sickness, and I am eager to get to the clinic."

Once inside, Todd sat down in a wicker chair with a cup of coffee and explained how his return had been delayed five days when the *Natchez* hit a log and sank.

"Sadly, Captain Roberts drowned in that accident," Todd said.

Before Mike could ask questions about the accident, Todd wanted to know about the disease that gripped the community.

"The sickness started the week after you left and has been getting progressively worse each day," Mike reported.

"How many folks are suffering from it?"

"About twenty or twenty-five folks that I know about, but more are showing up at the clinic each day and there's not much we can do for them. Some people are deathly sick while others are just beginning to show signs of the disease and a few are recovering."

"Mr. Nagel and the Callahan boys are the sickest," Mary added. "Sue and Theresa have been out visiting those who are sick and treating others who come into the clinic."

"What are the symptoms of the illness?" Todd asked.

Mary thought for a few seconds and then responded. "I've been helping out at the clinic for the past week. On their first visit folks complain about a low-grade fever, headache and cough. Then in a few days this progresses to red spots on the chest and abdomen and pea soup-colored diarrhea, followed by the third week with cramps and yellow or sometimes bloody stool."

Todd pondered Mary's report and then said, "I have seen these symptoms many times before. While at the Baltimore hospital, I treated hundreds of soldiers suffering from this disease. It sounds a lot like typhoid fever."

Mike gasped. "Typhoid? That's a deadly sickness. Folks die from it all the time. In 1858 my aunt and uncle died from typhoid."

"The good news is that I know how to treat and prevent it. The bad news is there isn't a cure that I know about. In a healthy person, it will run its course in about three weeks, but two out of ten soldiers eventually died of the disease despite my treatment at the hospital."

"Now that you're here we have renewed hope," Mike said. "I went into Grand Rapids early last week and gave Captain Roberts a message to send by telegraph from St. Paul to you in Pennsylvania."

"I'm sorry, but I never received your telegram. I probably had already left for home when it arrived. While on the river Captain Roberts told what he knew about the sickness in Whitefish, but he didn't know much."

"No matter, you're back with us now," Mary said.

Mike took a deep breadth. "You said Captain Roberts is dead and the *Natchez* sank. Tell me about it."

Todd explained how the *Natchez* sank while running the river at night, about their ordeal on the river, and escape on a rowboat to Willows, and finally the passage to Grand Rapids on the *Little Falls*."

"With the *Natchez* out of service, the folks up and down the river and in Grand Rapids will be cut off from St. Paul," Mike lamented. "I understand the *Itaska* will not return to service for another three or four months."

Todd placed his hand on Mike's shoulder. "That is my understanding as well."

"Without the *Natchez* or the *Itaska* Grand Rapids will be isolated, perhaps even until the end of summer," Mike lamented.

"I know that this isolation will devastate the economy in Grand Rapids and Whitefish," Todd said. "But right now, my concern is for this community. I must get to the clinic immediately."

Father Todd said good-bye to the Dunns and hurried Molly down the road to Whitefish. Molly seemed eager to get home and without urging trotted down the familiar road through town and to the clinic. June Brevick and Sue Gottwald greeted him as he tied Molly to the hitching post.

"Father, are we ever glad to see you," June said. "We have been praying for your return every day. We don't know what is causing this sickness or the best way to treat and prevent it. The clinic has been overwhelmed with sick people and all we can do is tell them to stay hydrated and send them home with some medication."

"June, I think I know what the sickness is and how to treat it. Please unhitch Molly and take her to the stable. Give her some water and hay, and then join Sue and myself in the exam room."

Todd followed Sue inside where he found a woman stretched out on the examination table with her distraught mother holding her hand. Todd recognized Clara Stein, the little girl he once cured of pneumonia. She had grown into a lovely young woman in her late teens. Alice Stein dropped her daughter's hand and greeted Todd warmly with a hug when he entered the exam room.

Todd placed his hand on Clara's forehead. She was burning up. Gently lifting her nightshirt, he examined her abdomen and chest. They were covered with red, dime-size spots.

"How long has Clara been sick like this?" he asked Alice.

"About a week."

"Has she had diarrhea?"

"Yes, kind of yellow-greenish in color."

"I'm afraid Clara has typhoid. Take her home and put her to bed. Keep her hydrated and force her to drink plenty of liquids." He handed Alice a package of salicylic acid. "Give her this powder dissolved in water every four hours. The medication will help bring her fever down. I will come out to see her in a couple of days. Is anyone else in your family sick?"

"No, Marty and Jason are fine."

"Now this is extremely important. How far away from the outhouse is your well?"

Alice looked at Father Todd as if he had asked a strange question.

"It's on the other side of the house, I guess about 100 feet or so."

"Good." He handed Alice a bar of astringent green soap. "Now this is critical. Make sure you wash your hands with green soap often and boil all Clara's bedclothes in water after washing them. Then throw all the wash water out far away from the house and well. Wash your hands thoroughly after you attend to Clara and especially before preparing food."

Alice nodded and then helped Todd and Sue get Clara into the wagon and covered her with a blanket.

Todd had read about Dr. Carl Eberth's recent work on the cause of typhoid fever. He explained to Sue that the doctor had discovered a bacillus that he believed responsible for typhoid. The bacterium, Eberth Bacillus, is found in the stools of infected people. Poor sanitation practices spread it to others through food and drinking water.

"Has anyone in town contracted this sickness?" he asked Sue.

"Not that I am aware of."

"Good, then it has not yet spread to town and their well water is safe," Todd said.

No sooner had Alice left when another wagon drove up with Tom Kelly holding the reins.

"Father … thank God you're back," Tom shouted as he climbed down from the buckboard. He went around to the back of the wagon and opened the gate. Theresa Kelly and her little six-year-old son Patrick both lay in the wagon wrapped in blankets. Todd felt their foreheads and each had a slight fever.

"Patrick got sick three days ago and then yesterday Theresa complained of a headache and diarrhea. Up till then she had been helping Sue at the clinic," Tom explained.

Todd examined them, but neither showed signs of a rash. "Leave them in the wagon. There's not much I can do for them inside the clinic." Then he asked Tom the same questions he asked Alice about how far apart from each other were the outhouse and their well and the distance of both to the house.

"Oh, I'd say they are about a dozen feet or so apart and two dozen feet from the house."

"Has anyone visited your farm recently?"

"Well, there was old Mr. Nagle. He had dinner with us last week and complained of feeling sick. I went over to his cabin two days ago and he was bedridden, barely able to move."

"Tom, I want you to fill some jugs with water from the town well and do not drink from or use your own well on the farm unless you boil it first. I assume Mr. Nagle used your outhouse when he visited. Typhoid fever spreads through contaminated water or food and I'm afraid Theresa and Patrick have contracted it from your well. Your outhouse and well are too close together. Do not drink or wash dishes with water from your well. Get your wash water out of the creek." He gave Tom some salicylic acid powder and coached him on how important hydration and personal sanitation and laundry procedures were, and then sent him and his family home.

"I'll come out to see how you all are doing in a couple of days," he promised as they departed.

Over the next two days, Todd treated a dozen more patients at the clinic, each suffering with varying degrees of the illness. Most victims like Theresa and Patrick had mild fevers, diarrhea and headaches, but others were much worse off, especially if they had had the illness for over a week. He worried about the elderly and children who were less able to fight typhoid. There was little he could do for his patients except ensure they remained hydrated and warm and to boil all their drinking water. For those who were suffering from typhoid fever, each person would have to let it run its course over the usual two or three weeks. The only medication that he could give them was salicylic acid, and all that would do was reduce their fevers and headaches. He stressed proper hydration and sanitation and warned them about contaminated well water and food, but he had no cure to offer them.

He called a town meeting at the hall to explain how proper sanitation would lessen the spread of the disease. He instructed the townsfolk about how well water could become contaminated if it was close to the outhouse and if so they should boil all drinking water. Proper washing of clothes and dishes, and the use of astringent soap when caring for the sick or preparing food was essential. Everyone must boil his or her well water before drinking it if it was less than 50 feet from the outhouse or where they disposed of wash water. Fortunately, he had a good supply of green soap and an extra supply of salicylic acid powder that he brought back with him from Pennsylvania.

Todd was in the exam room treating Albert and Connie Reilly when Sue burst in. "There are three Indians outside wanting to see you."

Tecumseh, Sekota, and Tamara were patiently waiting on their horses for Todd. He greeted his Indian friends and invited them to dismount and come inside.

"We hear from white hunter that Whitefish people sick with yellow crap," Tecumseh said as his companions took seats in the exam room. *A good description of typhoid*, Todd thought

"We bring good medicine for this sickness." Tamara laid a large burlap sack on the table, took out a handful of dried leaves, and showed them to Todd.

"This magic medicine. Tribe use to cure fever and yellow crap sickness. You make tea from leaves, boil good and make sick people drink it."

"Thank you, Tecumseh, Sekota, and Tamara. I will try it."

Tecumseh looked a bit offended and looked at Albert. "Not try, you give to this sick boy and other sick people. Without this medicine, many people die. You make some now and give to this woman and boy."

Todd nodded that he understood. Tecumseh watched as he set a pot of water boiling on the stove, and then crushed a handful of the leaves and dumped them into the boiling water. The leaves made a yellowish-brown tea that smelled acrid. After it cooled down, Todd poured some of the liquid into a cup and took a sip. The tea was bitter and made his lips and tongue tingle. Todd made a face.

Tecumseh pursed his lips. "No taste good, but make disease go away. You give to sick people. Make them drink whole cup every day."

Todd thanked the Indians who had made such a long journey to deliver this medicine.

"You come help our tribe. Now we come help your people," Tamara explained.

"We go back home now," Sekota grunted and motioned toward the west. "Time to hunt elk."

Todd waved good-bye as the Indians mounted their ponies and rode off behind a cloud of dust.

Sue took a sip of the tea. "This stuff tastes and smells simply awful. You aren't going to make your patients drink this poison, are you?"

Todd admonished her. "Yes, I am. Tecumseh would not have come all the way from his village to give me something that did not work. I trust him and these Indians know more about medicines than all our learned doctors do."

He took a cup of tea and gave it to Albert to drink, who after a small sip said, "I'm not going to drink this stuff. It's simply awful."

"You will drink it," Todd said in his most commanding voice. "It will make you well."

Todd forced Albert to drink the entire cup of tea. The boy had a difficult time keeping the bitter brew down. Then Todd also made Connie drink a cup and gave the remainder of the brewed tea to her in a jar along with a small bag of the leaves. He told her to make a pot of the tea with the leaves and make sure that she and Albert drank at least one cup each day.

"If anyone else in your household comes down with the same symptoms, then you also make them drink the tea. I will look in on you in a few days." Then he explained about sanitation and contaminated water.

The Reillys thanked Todd and returned home.

Two days later Todd traveled in the early morning from farm to farm, treating those who were sick and teaching folks about proper sanitation. He gave each family a package of crushed Indian tea leaves and told them to brew the tea and give it to each sick person twice each day. By his count, about thirty people outside of town had come down with typhoid. Half of these folks were suffering the symptoms indicative of the second week of their illness. He was most concerned about Mr. Nagel, who approached his seventy-fourth birthday and lived alone in his cabin about five miles outside town. The poor man couldn't even get out of bed to greet him when Todd walked through the front door. His bed smelled of feces and urine. No one had visited to attend to him since Tom's visit two days earlier. Todd changed and boiled Nagel's soiled bedclothes and made him as comfortable as possible. He brewed several cups of the medicinal tea for him and told him to drink this cup and all that remained. He went outside and examined the well that was very close to the outhouse. He filled a jar with creek water for Mr. Nagel to drink and promised that he would have Sue visit him in the morning.

The two children in the O'Neil household were also suffering through a second week of their typhoid illness. Dylan, the youngest boy, was listless and Andy, his older brother, hardly had the strength to sit up when Todd tried to make him drink a cup of the tea. It was difficult to get the boys to drink an entire cup, but he persisted until they each had done so. Then he gave the sanitation lecture and strictly ordered Gus and Beth to brew tea from a sack full of leaves that he left with them and force both boys to drink it each day. After visiting ten more farms, his last visit of the day was to Tom and Theresa Kelly's farm. Theresa and Patrick were both worse off than when they visited the clinic two days earlier. He made sure Tom was giving both patients the tea he prescribed, then gave Tom another sack of leaves, and again coached him on proper sanitation procedures. When he arrived at the Reilly farm, he was surprised to find Connie dressed and sitting in her kitchen eating a plate of scrambled eggs and Patrick finishing a bowl of mush.

"That tea tastes terrible, but I forced a cup down last night and made Patrick drink a cup. We each drank another cup this morning, and after our third cup, we're both feeling much better this afternoon," Connie said. "We no longer have diarrhea and our appetite is coming back." He examined her and the red spots that formerly covered her belly and chest on her last visit were almost gone. Patrick seemed normal.

"Keep taking the tea for two more days," Todd prescribed. "If Tom should come down with the disease, make him drink the tea as well, a full cup each day. In addition, don't drink the water from your well unless you boil it first. Use creek water for washing and drinking until this sickness is entirely gone."

The next day he made his rounds again and visited Mr. Nagel. Sue sat next to his bed with tears streaming down her face. "Mr. Nagel is dead," she cried. "He was dead when I arrived this morning." The cups of tea that Todd had left on the night table remained untouched. Father Todd gave the man the last rites, anointing him with sacred oils.

"Sue, there is nothing more we can do for old Mr. Nagel other than arrange for a funeral and burial. Please go back to the clinic."

Next, he stopped at the O'Neil farm to see the children. Andy was near death, his breathing labored and his pulse weak. He remained unresponsive to Todd's probing. Dylan hardly moved when Todd examined him. Todd noticed the two packets of tea leaves that he had prescribed sat unopened on the table, and the tea he had brewed the previous afternoon was still in the pot.

"Beth, why didn't you give the boys the tea as I prescribed?"

"I tasted it. It was bitter and the boys refused to drink it so I didn't force them," she said.

Andy was too far gone for the tea to help, but he made Dylan drink a cup. There was nothing more Todd could do other than administer the last rites (aka the Sacrament of the Sick) to the boys. Andy died that night and Dylan died the next afternoon.

The remainder of his rounds that day was more encouraging. Clara Stein was much better and everyone who had followed his prescription to brew and drink the tea was improving. No one else had died. Because of Todd's sanitation instructions, no one else had come down with typhoid fever. It appeared the epidemic had been contained.

That Saturday Todd celebrated funeral Mass for the O'Neil children and Mr. Nagel. Overcome with grief, Gus and Beth openly wept. The church was only half-full, for most of the parishioners were still too ill to attend Mass and many were afraid to mix with other folks.

They buried the bodies in the church cemetery down by the lake.

Chapter 17
Reassignment

July, 1902

Todd's skills as a doctor, renowned throughout northern Minnesota, encouraged folks from Grand Rapids and other towns downriver to travel to Whitefish to see Dr. Todd. The clinic thrived and another doctor eventually moved to Whitefish to assist Todd. Yet nothing lasts forever.

Over the intervening years since Todd's arrival, the town continued to grow and thrive, at least until the late nineteenth century. For the first ten years after Fr. Todd arrived, Whitefish grew from a few dozen farming families to a town and surrounding area of almost two hundred citizens. Most newcomers came to claim their 160 acres of bottomland, and soon dozens of farms filled the valley. Local lumbering brought dozens of lumberjacks to town and Jack Sprier hired a dozen workers for his lumberyard. As more folks settled in the area, the town of Whitefish expanded. The Grand Hotel & Saloon opened, new stores opened on Main Street, and the three newly built boardinghouses were always full. Folks filled St. Patrick's to overflowing every Sunday morning. In the late seventies, workers continued to arrive to mine or lumber the surrounding mountains, but after initial success, the mining played out and by the end of the eighties many newcomers had drifted away. After a few years of farming in the poor soil and suffering through the long, bitterly cold winters, some pioneers moved on to ply their farming or ranching skills in warmer and more productive lands. Eventually even a few of the original pioneers, now older and less able to cope with the cold winters and subsistent farming, had also moved away. The decline that began in the early 1880s continued throughout the next decade and by 1899, many stores and businesses in town had closed. The Whitefish Saloon and Hotel needed repairs, and all but one of the half-dozen boardinghouses closed. Half-empty pews greeted Todd at Sunday Mass.

Every year Bishop Byrne visited St. Patrick's to administer Confirmation to the teenagers thoroughly prepared by Father Todd in their faith, but each year the bishop noted a smaller congregation and took note of all the closed businesses in town. After one such visit in 1901, he wrote a letter to Todd's bishop in Baltimore suggesting that it was perhaps time to end the missionary work in Whitefish. A priest stationed in Grand Rapids, where a new parish had been recently dedicated, could now serve St. Patrick's parish. One hot July day in 1902 Todd received a letter from the new Bishop of Baltimore Diocese, Bishop Marcel, calling him home and outlining the changes the local bishop may have in mind for St. Patrick's parish.

The letter took Todd by surprise. Reassignment was always a possibility, but after thirty years as a missionary in Whitefish he assumed his assignment was permanent and thought he would live out his life as pastor of St. Patrick's. When reassignment inevitably comes, it is often the most difficult order for a priest to accept, but true to his vow of obedience, Todd went into the church and as tears wet his cheeks, he prayed for his parishioners and the good people of Whitefish who now might not have a resident priest. While he knew that his reassignment was part of God's plan, he struggled to accept this change. "Why now, after so many years of service in Whitefish?" he prayed out loud.

The reassignment order was immediate, and he was asked to return to Baltimore as soon as possible. Todd began packing his few possessions and then drove out to Mike's farm, to tell him and Mary of the reassignment. Mike and Mary were devastated. "How will we tell Ann, Frank, Tom, and their children, and what will we all do without Father Todd," Mary cried.

The news spread fast around town. At the next town meeting, Todd said good-bye to the people of Whitefish. After the meeting ended, everyone in town came up to shake his hand or give him a hug. Shaken by the knowledge that he would most likely never return, he gave Pickles and Molly to the Dunn family, and sold his buggy to the livery stable.

On August 5, 1902, Father Todd celebrated his last Sunday Mass at St. Patrick's, and so ended his thirty years as pastor of St. Patrick's. Saying good-bye to his parishioners was the hardest thing he had ever done. There wasn't a dry eye in the pews.

Early the next day Mike drove Todd by buggy to Grand Rapids and then on to Duluth. Ten years ago, the state had completed the road between Grand Rapids and Duluth. Grand Rapids folks no longer depended on the *Itaska* as the only way to travel to and from St. Paul. The grand old riverboat no longer provided regular passenger service and only transported lumber and freight on its once-a-week journey to and from St. Paul. They arrived in Duluth that evening and Todd purchased a train ticket to St. Paul. They rented a hotel room and checked out early the next morning to go to the train station. The next train to St. Paul was scheduled to depart at 9:00 a.m.

Mike gave Todd a hug on the train platform as he prepared to get on the train, saying, "Father Todd, we will meet again."

Todd doubted that they would ever see one another again, at least not in this life. He boarded the train to St. Paul and Mike stood on the train platform waving as the train pulled out of the station. Todd waved back and tried to hold back his tears. On the long train ride to St. Paul, then to Chicago and back to Baltimore, his thoughts lingered on those thirty years in Whitefish. It seemed like only yesterday that Mike Dunn paused at the top of Mesabi Pass and pointed out Whitefish Lake and the little town in the valley far below. Had it really been thirty years? It didn't seem like more than a handful of months.

After arriving in Baltimore, Todd hailed a gas-powered cab outside the Baltimore train station and experienced his first ride in an automobile. As they drove toward the newly built cathedral and chancery of St. Francis on the north side of town, he marveled at how the city had changed since he left thirty years ago. Newly constructed three- and four-story brick buildings fronted both sides of the paved main street now lined with telephone poles strung with a jumble of wires that reached out to various businesses and homes. Noisy automobiles honked to clear horses, wagons, and pedestrians from their path and chugged along the streets leaving clouds of choking smoke in their wake.

He arrived at Bishop Marcel's office not knowing what the bishop had in mind for him, but he hoped for an assignment to a small parish outside of Baltimore. The bishop graciously received him and thanked him for his many years of missionary service in Minnesota. Todd related how much he had enjoyed those years as pastor of St. Patrick's and shared how difficult it was for him to leave the good folks of Whitefish and his medical practice. He told the bishop how disappointed his parishioners felt when he told them that he had been recalled, and that St. Patrick's would no longer have a resident parish priest.

"Nevertheless, this is part of God's plan and I willingly accept whatever assignment you have in mind for me," he concluded.

"Father Bose, the reason I recalled you to Baltimore is that St. Michael's Hospital has requested me to assign a chaplin and is also in desperate need of another doctor. You can uniquely fill both requests."

Todd hid his disappointment. *After thirty-some years, I've come full circle, back to the hospital where I learned my trade as a medic*, he mused. *God certainly has a sense of humor.*

Bishop Marcel went on to say, "I received a letter from Bishop Byrne about your years of service at St. Patrick's. He praised your service to the folks of Whitefish and marveled that you not only served their spiritual needs, but also doctored those who needed medical attention. His letter admired how you built the church and then eventually built a clinic to provide medical care and received a medical degree from Kings College in St. Paul. His letter closed with a quite amazing story. He claims you are a healer, not just as a doctor, but a healing instrument of God's miraculous power. He listed several documented cases of miraculous cures attributed to you."

Bishop Marcel took off his reading glasses and stared at Todd. "Have you performed miraculous healings like people claim?"

Father Todd averted the bishop's gaze and looked down at the ornate Chinese rug.

"Some folks have claimed miracles, but I am simply the means for God to work his wonders. Most of those so-called miraculous cures were just a result of natural healing and good doctoring on my part."

Bishop Marcel shook his head in disagreement.

"Bishop Byrne sent me the written journal of your unusual healings in Whitefish. Most of these cases do have natural explanations but all cannot be dismissed as just good doctoring and normal healing. Several of them are extraordinary and preternatural. It seems that God wishes to use you to heal others, and who am I to argue with His wisdom. I am going to give you an assignment where you can practice both your medical and spiritual healing vocation."

Bishop Marcel handed Todd a letter of introduction and instructed him to give it to Dr. James Bennett, the administrator of St. Michael's Hospital. He then gave Todd a copy of the newly published Catholic edition of the English Bible, recently translated from the Latin Vulgate, shook his hand, and bade him God's speed.

"Keep me informed on how things go at St. Michael's," he concluded. "I want you to continue to journal each patient you attend, and if any of them experience unusual cures." He handed Todd's journal back to him. "I want you to thoroughly document each of those cases." Then he asked his secretary to show Todd to the rectory where he would spend the night before he reported tomorrow to St. Michael's.

Todd arrived by a Stanly Steamer taxi at St. Michael's Hospital early the next morning and found the administrator's office located on the first floor. Todd introduced himself to the outer office secretary, who poked her head inside the inner office, and then ushered Todd inside.

Dr. James Bennett sat behind a large mahogany desk in his well-appointed office, the windows decorated with fancy drapes, the floor covered with a lush Iranian carpet, and the room furnished with a comfortable ottoman, a maple conference table with matching high-back chairs, and an ornate cadenza. Several framed degrees, one from Harvard, another from Princeton, and a third from Boston College hung from the teak-covered walls alongside a large painting of the Harvard University commons. To Todd the office decor seemed rather luxurious and ornate for a Catholic hospital. Dr. Bennett, a short, thickset, balding man dressed in a white smock, didn't bother to get up to greet Todd. Without looking up from the papers he was signing, he made a hand gesture that Todd should take his seat at a chair in front of the desk. After a minute or so, he looked up at Todd and without even a hint of a smile or welcoming introduction, he asked for Todd's papers. The abruptness of this request and lack of a friendly handshake struck Todd as rude, but he handed the administrator his letter of introduction and other papers. Dr. Bennett frowned as he peered through square-cut glasses at Todd's MD license, university degrees, and letter of introduction from Bishop Marcel. After a few seconds, he took off his glasses and handed the documents back to Todd.

"Your license is only good in Minnesota, not in Maryland," Dr. Bennett said with a trace of a smirk. "We do not recognize degrees conferred by King's College, and I see that you earned your degree as a part-time student enrolled in that institution. You also skipped the four years of full-time study in a medical college for a legitimate degree and two years of hospital residency required for a MD license in this state. The license you hold is invalid in Maryland and we cannot allow you practice in our hospital as a doctor, at least not until you are fully degreed and licensed by the State of Maryland Medical Board."

"I was told that you desperately need doctors, and I am a licensed physician and have many years of practice."

"I cannot allow you practice in my hospital," Dr. Bennett said. "You must first be licensed by the Medical Board."

Dumbfounded by Dr. Bennett's unfriendly and condescending attitude, Todd asked, "What will that take?"

"The State Medical Board is responsible for licensing and that will take further education and residency on your part, and then with a successful appeal to that Board, and with recommendations, they may license you. However, I am pleased that Bishop Marcel has sent us a chaplin."

Stunned, Todd held his temper. "I guess I should be thankful that the state does not license priests. Nevertheless, I am honored to be your hospital chaplain, but I have no intention of going back to school for a piece of paper or doing a residency. As you can see, I am fully licensed and certified as a physician. I have been a licensed doctor in Minnesota for twenty years and I worked in this hospital as a medic

Little Church in the Wilderness

during the war. I understand the hospital needs a good doctor, and with my years of experience, they can have one with me."

Dr. Bennett opened a brown folder on his desk. "I am aware of your service here as a medic. This hospital file listed your work here as an orderly and medic thirty years ago during the war. The evaluations by two doctors who supervised you are positive, and in fact glowing. They claim you have a natural talent as a medic, and a note says that some of your patients experienced healing that was nothing less than miraculous."

He frowned and looked up at Todd, then in a condescending tone he asked, "Do you consider yourself a miracle worker?"

It was becoming increasingly hard for Todd to hide his irritation with this administrator's confrontational and smug mannerism.

"No, I do not claim that for myself. My job as a priest and doctor is to heal souls and cure bodies. I am skilled at both professions but I am not a miracle worker. I came to your hospital to offer my services as a doctor and chaplin, but if appears that your need for doctors does not transcend your requirement for paperwork. You have found my offer to serve at this hospital unacceptable, so I will go back to the bishop and ask for a different assignment."

Dr. Bennett closed the file and stared at Fr. Bose for a full minute before answering.

"I'm sure Bishop Marcel would not be pleased with that outcome. After all, he is on our hospital board and he sent you to me with good intentions. It would be inappropriate to send you back to the bishop and equally difficult for me to place you on our resident's staff without a recognized medical license. I don't believe in miracles, just good doctoring, and with all your experience you seem to be a competent medic. If you would be willing to appear before the Maryland Medical Board and answer their questions, perhaps they will make an exception and agree to certify your credentials and issue you a license to practice medicine in Maryland."

Confused by the sudden change in the man's attitude, Todd asked, "So, what about the required four years of medical college and two of residency you claim are necessary to earn a license to practice in this state?"

"That can be waived."

"Waived? Just like that?"

"Yes, they will most likely do so if Bishop Marcel and I appeal to them on your behalf. However, until that time, you will be our chaplain and orderly here at St. Michael's. I will arrange with the Medial Board to meet with you as soon as possible. Meanwhile, please report to Dr. James Mitchell, the head of our surgical staff on the second floor. He will show you around and introduce you to his staff." With that statement and no "welcome and good luck," Dr. Bennett returned to his stack of paperwork.

Todd left Dr. Bennett's office mystified about the administrator's attitude toward him. For unknown reasons, he acted unfriendly and even hostile. Perhaps the man had a bad night's sleep or just didn't know how to deal with someone who was both a doctor and a priest. Anyway, it was not an auspicious beginning for Todd and his misgivings about this new assignment grew deeper.

Todd's reception at Dr, James Mitchell's office was completely different from that with Dr. Bennett. Dr. Mitchell warmly greeted him with a big smile and shook his hand. "We are honored to have you on our staff, Dr. Bose, and even more honored to have a resident chaplain. Your reputation precedes you and your skills as a priest and doctor with years of medical experience are sorely needed in this hospital."

Dr. Mitchell's warm welcome so contrasted with the hostile interrogation he received from Dr. Bennett that he felt the need to say something about it.

"My meeting with Dr. Bennett did not go well. He did not receive me warmly, and in fact he was quite rude. He claimed that my assignment as a doctor at his hospital is contingent on the Maryland Medical Board accepting my credentials, so please do not introduce me as Dr. Bose but as Father Todd. Dr. Bennett claimed my Minnesota credentials are unacceptable in Maryland and until the Maryland Medical Board certifies me, I cannot practice here. For now, I am only your chaplain and orderly."

Dr. Mitchell's jaw dropped. "But I don't understand. The administrator just last week told me that you were joining our staff, as both hospital chaplain and physician. I must admit that someone who is both a priest and a doctor is a bit unusual, but the Maryland Medical Board should have no problem accepting your medical credentials from Minnesota. We desperately need both your priestly and medical skills at St. Michael's."

Todd smiled. "I have to confess that my interview with Dr. Bennett baffled me. I do not understand why he was so hostile toward me. You must have visiting doctors who are allowed practice here, and they do not each require Board Certification. I suggest that you speak with him. Meanwhile, consider me your new orderly and chaplain."

Dr. Mitchell took Todd on a tour of the second floor and introduced him to the resident doctors, nurses, and orderlies. Dr. Langley, the resident doctor, was especially gracious. Almost everyone greeted him warmly, all but one nurse who seemed aloof. When introduced to Nurse Jane Daugherty, a matronly, rotund woman probably in her sixties, she looked Todd in the eye and asked in a skeptical tone,

"What is it to be then, Father Bose or Dr. Bose?"

Todd smiled and answered, "For the time being simply address me as Father Todd."

Dr. Mitchell took Todd to visit the hospital chapel. A sign on the heavy oak chapel doors with yellow lead-glass windows read, "Mass Sunday at noon."

Dr. Mitchell noticed Todd examining the sign and explained, "Our previous resident chaplain, Father Xavier, was reassigned over a year ago and since he left we have only had Mass on Sunday. Father Boniface from Sacred Heart parish comes here each Sunday afternoon to say Mass for us. I asked our maintenance man to put the old sign back up as soon as I heard you were coming and it will announce Mass Daily at 7:00 a.m. I trust that 7:00 a.m. is the proper time for you?" Todd nodded his agreement and Dr. Mitchell led him inside.

Solemn and peaceful, the small chapel contained only a dozen six-foot long wood pews each spaced on either side of a wide center aisle designed to accommodate wheelchairs. The chapel impressed Todd as a tasteful and fitting place for worship or quiet prayer and contemplation. A life-size crucifix hung over the altar, a beautiful white marble table with a white linen cloth draped over it. A gilded tabernacle on a niche on the back wall, a single high-pack armchair, a credence table, and an oak ambo completed the sanctuary furnishings separated from the naïve by a low wood railing. A red sanctuary lamp flickering from a chain positioned to the left of the altar announced that the Blessed Sacrament was in repose in the tabernacle. On the back wall above the tabernacle a large round stained-glass window depicting a dove with its wings spread bathed the entire sanctuary with a rainbow of colorful light. Outside the sanctuary and on either side stood life-size statues of the Virgin Mary and St. Joseph who carried the baby Jesus in his arms. Alongside St. Joseph was a pole with an American flag and next to that was a papal flag. Another small table and two wooden chairs completed the furnishings immediately outside the sanctuary.

"I will be comfortable saying Mass here," Todd commented.

A one-kneeler box confessional was on the right side of the chapel, and a door on the left side led to the sacristy and to the chaplin's office, which on inspection looked more like a library than an office. Two white albs along with several chasubles and stoles of various liturgical colors hung in an open closet in the sacristy. Three rows of bookshelves lined the office wall behind a small desk and along each sidewall. Other than a desk chair, two visitor chairs, and a coat rack, the office contained no other furniture. A beautiful oval wool rug covered the floor; a wood crucifix and a painting of the Blessed Virgin graced the back wall. Todd studied the bookshelves. They contained various theological reference books, a copy of the *Lives of the Saints*, a Catholic encyclopedia, and the entire works of St. Augustine, St. Aquinas, and several recent papal encyclicals. A door in the office led to the chaplin's bedroom where his two valises rested on a low table. The second bedroom door opened into the main hallway.

"I will leave you alone for a while to unpack and make yourself at home. Please join us tonight at 8:00 p.m. for supper in the first-floor dining room. You can take all your meals in this dining room. We serve breakfast at 8:30 a.m., dinner at 1:00 p.m., and supper at 8:00 p.m.

At seven the next morning, Todd said his first Mass for St. Michael's Hospital staff and patients. A young boy dressed in a black cassock served Mass and spoke the responses to the prayers in Latin. After breakfast Todd reported to the resident, Dr. Langley, as the on-call orderly, and made the rounds with the other doctors.

One month after his arrival at St. Michael's, the Maryland State Medical Board summoned Todd to a hearing for his certification petition. Six doctors including Dr. Bennett sat in review. Their questions were friendly and straightforward, except those posed by Dr. Bennett, who read a twenty-year-old letter from the Minnesota Medical Board admonishing Father Todd for performing an appendectomy without a surgical license. Todd defended that action and explained the circumstances surrounding the emergency surgery. Except for Dr. Bennett, Todd's explanation satisfied the other board members. After additional questions and answers, the board chair asked Todd to step outside as they considered his petition. After a few minutes, they called him back in and the board chair said that his credentials were in order and handed him his certification to practice in the State of Maryland. Only Dr. Bennett avoided extending his congratulations.

An incident that occurred a month later gave Dr. Bennett cause to question Todd's judgment. A young boy with breathing problems showed up in the emergency room. The doctor on call sent for Todd to consult with him. Todd examined the boy whose breathing came in gasps as he struggled to get air in and out of his lungs. Todd asked the boy's mother what preceded this episode. She said a wasp had stung him. Todd determined the child was suffering an anaphylactic shock and his throat was closing. The boy was turning blue and death seemed imminent. Todd asked for a scalpel, made an incision in the boy's neck immediately below his Adam's apple, and inserted a surgical tube into the windpipe. The doctor on call was at first horrified for he had never witnessed this surgical procedure. The boy's color soon returned as he began to breathe through the inserted tube.

Although the boy recovered, the incident reached the desk of Dr. Bennett and he called Dr. Bose into his office and rebuked him for performing this "unauthorized" procedure. Todd replied that this procedure, recently described in medical journals, was considered an effective lifesaving operation, and he was familiar with the journal's recommendation and procedure. Without it the patient would certainly have died. The administrator's office contained shelves of medical books and journals, and Todd asked if he happened to have the quarterly Journal of Modern Medicine published two years earlier. Dr. Bennett found the journal in question and Todd showed him the article outlining the tracheotomy procedure. After that incident, he gave Todd no further trouble and six months later, Dr. Bennett accepted a job as administrator in a New York Hospital. Todd never understood the reason for Dr. Bennett's wrathful attitude toward him.

A second incident of note occurred six months after Dr. Bennett's departure. The hospital admitted Justin, a young boy with severe abdominal pain. Todd examined him and determined that Justin had appendicitis. Todd performed an emergency appendectomy, but the organ had burst and infection was in the boy's belly. Death was imminent. Todd removed the septic appendix, disinfected his abdomen, and closed the surgical wound. He prayed that the boy's immune system would take over, but with such an advanced infection, there was little else the medical team could do for him except make him comfortable The next day Todd visited Justin, whose mother, brother, and attending nurse Daugherty were at his bedside. Todd prayed with them, and then performed the last rites. As he administered the holy oils and laid his hand on the boy's forehead, that same familiar warmth traveled down Todd's arm to his hand. Todd kept his hand on Justin's forehead as they said the Apostles' Creed together. Afterwards, Justin smiled and fell asleep. Nurse Daugherty whispered to Todd that he probably would die in his sleep. The night on-call nurse woke Todd at 5:00 a.m. and led him to Justin's room. Todd fully expected to find Justin's mother and brother mourning the boy's death, yet when he entered the room the mother smothered him in a bear hug and cried, "It's a miracle."

Justin was sitting up in bed as Nurse Daugherty was taking his temperature and pulse. "Hi Father," he said cheerily while trying not to disturb the thermometer in his mouth.

"It's a miracle," Justin's mother repeated.

"Miracle indeed," Nurse Daugherty said sarcastically as she looked at the thermometer and then shook it down. "The boy just had a good night's sleep." She looked over at Father Bose and the look on her face highlighted her outspoken skepticism. Todd asked her what Justin's temperature was and Nurse Daugherty said, "Normal." He then examined Justin. His surgical scar looked as if it were two or three weeks old rather than only the few hours since his operation. Todd asked if he wanted to receive the Eucharist that Todd always carried with him in a small gold container called a Pix. Justin said he did and Todd prayed with him and gave him Holy Communion. Afterwards, Justin looked at Nurse Daugherty and asked, "Can I have something to eat?"

For the next ten years, Father Todd continued to serve St. Michael's Hospital as both chaplin and doctor. He saved many souls and lives while serving at St. Michael's and presided over several other "miraculous" incidents. As his bishop had asked, Todd documented each case under his care, writing down the details of a patient's admission to the hospital, his diagnosis, and details of the care and discharge. Most but not all of Dr. Todd's patients recovered from their illnesses, and most of his cures could be attributed to natural healing and good doctoring. Yet a handful of Todd's patients inexplicably recovered and those cures were so extraordinary that they were presented to the Maryland Board of Physicians for review. In at least five of these cases, such as a spontaneous remission of cancer and an unexplained disappearance of a brain tumor in a child, the Board could not attribute the patient's recovery to medical intervention. Bishop Marcel maintained the file of Todd's notes that he obediently submitted for each of his patients. The bishop knew that some of these incidents were truly miraculous and a day might come where he would be called on to present these documents to Church authorities.

Chapter 18
End Days

Baltimore, September 1913

Father Todd had just celebrated his seventy-second birthday when he collapsed while celebrating Mass. His doctor said he had had a coronary infraction and admitted him to the Baltimore General Hospital where the diagnosis was not good. The doctors weren't sure he would live to enjoy his seventy-third birthday celebration. Todd resigned himself to such depressing news, but it was difficult to accept the role of patient rather than doctor at this hospital. The room they stuck him in did nothing to improve his dark mood, but as always he tried to keep positive and trust in God's plan for him.

Todd's eyesight had grown weak over the past years and he put down the book that he had been trying to read and instead gazed out the single window in his room. The only view the window offered was that of an ancient brick wall, a plain, unattractive wall devoid of entertainment. He sighed and returned his attention to the book, but his diminished eyesight made reading so difficult that he again stared at the brick wall. Marked by age and decorated by mold and mildew, each brick had attained a distinctive patina that soon challenged his imagination. One brick pictured a windjammer tossed about by huge waves, another looked like an Indian teepee village, and still another a likeness of Teddy Roosevelt in profile. One brick uniquely caught his mind's eye, Whitefish Lake as viewed from Mesabi Pass. His mind flooded with memories of his mission to Minnesota and all those wonderful, rewarding years of service. Staring at the brick wall caused him to feel even more trapped in this depressing room, so when his doctor visited the next morning, he complained about the room and the hospital administrator agreed to move him to a cheerier room on the fourth floor.

He delighted in the picturesque view from the window in his new room. The City of Baltimore and Chesapeake Bay, three blocks to the east, filled the window with magnificent vistas. Across the street from the hospital, a scenic park shaded by hickory, ash, and elm trees and acres of grass decorated with bushes painted in yellows and reds in anticipation of an early autumn riveted Todd's attention. Dozens of people roamed the park, stopping here and there to enjoy the last flowers of summer or to watch a squirrel gather nuts for winter. A baseball field occupied one corner of the park and the other side contained a children's playground complete with swings, slides, sandboxes, and teeter-totters. A brook wandered through the park, cascaded over small boulders, and then worked its way to a pond filled with ducks and geese. At noontime, workers on their lunch break filled the picnic benches scattered throughout the park as gulls circled overhead to snatch a morsel of food. Hour after hour Todd watched the park drama unfold and after some time he assigned imaginary names to each frequent visitor.

There's Bill at sunrise walking his ugly bulldog, and Mark at the same bench every day eating his lunch from a paper bag. Here comes John and Mary holding hands and enjoying an evening stroll, and Peter jogging along the dirt path after work.

The window made life in this hospital bearable.

Bedridden and unable to read, he used the time away from the window to pray and reflect on his busy life. Despite his serious illness and the eventuality that it promised, he felt unafraid, satisfied, and fulfilled. He was ready for whatever God had in store for him and reminisced about his priestly life as pastor of St. Patrick's where he served the folks of Whitefish for thirty years with love and compassion, as both pastor and doctor. The eleven years since he said good-bye to his friends in Whitefish seemed like only a few months, and while his heart was weak, his mind and memories were sharp. He still loved each one of those Whitefish folks and he trusted that they still remembered him.

One day as he sat in a wheelchair by the window watching actions in the park, he received surprise visitors: Mike Dunn accompanied by a priest and two women. Mike warmly greeted Todd and the instant Todd recognized him, he threw aside the blanket that covered his legs, got up from the wheelchair, and embraced his longtime friend. Todd noticed how much older Mike looked than as he remembered him. Now the hair that remained of his former generous crop of black hair was gray and stringy. His face was wrinkled and paunchy, but his blue eyes still shone as Todd remembered. Todd didn't recognize either of the women or the priest who accompanied Mike. The older woman introduced herself as the bishop's assistant from the Baltimore Chancery and then introduced Father Jackson, the administrator from the same office. Mike then presented the younger woman who had traveled with Mike to Baltimore to see Father Todd. The woman looked vaguely familiar, but offhand Todd couldn't place her.

"Do you remember Clara Stein?" Mike asked. "The young girl whose life you saved?"

Todd took a second look, and then his faced blossomed in recognition. "My goodness, yes of course I recognize you, Clara." Clara stepped closer to Todd's chair and took his hand.

"I am Clara Reinhardt now, Father, and we have so missed you at St. Patrick's. I tell my four children about you, how you served the people of Whitefish and saved my life. Our oldest son was only a small child when you left and now he barely remembers you."

Todd squeezed Clara's hand and smiled at Mike. "It is so good to see the both of you, but what brings you to Baltimore?"

"You do, Father, you and Bishop Marcel to be exact."

Todd was befuddled. "What business do you have with Bishop Marcel?"

"It is complicated. Some time ago, a few of your former parishioners at St. Patrick's Church chronicled your service in Whitefish, especially the unusual healings you performed. Some folks even today consider those healings miraculous, and Bishop Byrne in St. Paul wanted Clara and me to testify to this as firsthand witness."

Father Todd's face dropped. "As I have said many times before, if those healings were really miracles, most were just due to good doctoring and natural healing. Those healings that folks may consider miraculous were God's power working through me and responding to my prayers. I have never considered myself a miracle worker, just a tool in God's hands. In addition, I am a good doctor."

Father Jackson approached Father Todd's chair and introduced himself. "Father Todd, I have been commissioned by Bishop Marcel to investigate the so-called miracles surrounding you. I have received written statements not only from the good folks of Whitefish, but from folks here in the Baltimore Hospital who testified to miraculous healings at your hands. Before Father Taylor of St. John's Parish in Spartansburg died some years ago, he wrote Bishop Allen about your power to heal. He said you showed this ability from early childhood and through your time in college. I also have testimony from a Deacon Everett in the town of Brainerd, Minnesota, and a letter from Frank Burns, the owner of a lumber mill in Brainerd. He claims that you revived his son Johnnie due to an accident in his lumberyard. However, he testified that those who witnessed the accident said Johnnie was not breathing and to all he was dead. That is not all. Another letter from a Mr. and Mrs. Trapp of Grand Rapids relates how you brought their daughter Karen back to life after she drowned in a boating accident on the Mississippi. There are several other testimonials about various healings at your hands; a few dozen in all."

Todd was silent for a moment and then he replied. "A miracle is a preternatural act that God performs in response to prayers. I brought Karen and Jonnie back to life by using CPR and prayer. A few bystanders thought they were dead, but as Christ said about the girl he raised from the dead, they were only sleeping. Some of these incidents may seem like miracles, yet my explanation is that they were due to good doctoring. If a miracle, they were in response to prayer and enacted through God's hand, not mine."

Father Jackson stepped back from Todd and said, "Miracles or natural occurrences, the bishop has asked me to investigate. We have testimony by various witnesses and letters that claim some of your cures are hard to attribute to natural healing. In addition to the letters we received from Bishop Byrne in Minnesota and from the Maryland Board of Physicians, some cannot be simply due to good medicine. If these instances are not miracles, then they are certainly unusual events for which I have no explanation."

Clara then chimed in. "Father, I don't know about miracles, but I had pneumonia and everyone expected me to die that night. Then you arrived and gave me the sacraments. I distinctly remember your warm hand on my forehead and the tingling sensation that seemed to flow from your hand and through my entire body. Then I fell asleep, and when I woke the following morning I had been cured. No signs of pneumonia or lung congestion remained. No one could explain my sudden improvement when everyone had expected me to die."

"I thought you would die as well," Todd admitted. "I was as amazed as everyone else was when you were alive the next morning and asking for food."

"My mother always thought it a miracle that Jesus performed through you. I still believe that to this day."

"Father Todd," Father Jackson interrupted, "sometimes God chooses good people like you to perform His works and answer our prayers. I appreciate your humility, but there is ample evidence that God has worked many cures through you. The bishop has assigned me to investigate and document these incidents, and this I have done. I conclude that you are truly a miracle worker."

Todd looked down. "If this is true, then I can only thank God for choosing me to do His work."

While Todd was glad to see Mike, Clara, and Father Jackson, their visit had tired him. This was obvious to the nurse who had entered the room to give Todd his daily sponge bath, so she ushered his visitors out.

After everyone had left, Todd again looked out this window and reminisced. Yes, he had lived a full life of service and accomplishment and he was at peace. He remembered the words written in 2Timothy 4:7

"I have fought the good fight, I have finished the race, and I have kept the faith."

Father Todd Bose died peacefully in his sleep on October 8, 1913. His body was transported to Whitefish where he was interred in St. Patrick's graveyard. His tombstone reads:

He unselfishly served both God and man as Priest and Physician

THE END.

www.ingramcontent.com/pod-product-compliance
Lightning Source LLC
Chambersburg PA
CBHW070052080526
44586CB00013B/1022